Managing *Difference* in Eastern-European Transnational Families

I0124982

Viorela Ducu / Áron Telegdi-Csetri (eds.)

Managing *Difference* in Eastern-European Transnational Families

PL ACADEMIC RESEARCH

Bibliographic Information published by the Deutsche Nationalbibliothek
The Deutsche Nationalbibliothek lists this publication in
the Deutsche Nationalbibliografie; detailed bibliographic
data is available in the internet at http://dnb.d-nb.de.

Cover Image: © 2015 Călin Ilea

This work was supported by a grant of the Romanian National Authority
for Scientific Research and Innovation, CNCS – UEFISCDI,
project number PN-II-RU-TE-2014-4-2087.

ISBN 978-3-631-70236-9 (Print)
E-ISBN 978-3-631-70237-6 (E-PDF)
E-ISBN 978-3-631-70238-3 (EPUB)
E-ISBN 978-3-631-70239-0 (MOBI)
DOI 10.3726/978-3-631-70237-6

© Peter Lang GmbH
Internationaler Verlag der Wissenschaften
Frankfurt am Main 2016
All rights reserved.
PL Academic Research is an of Peter Lang GmbH.

Peter Lang – Frankfurt am Main · Bern · Bruxelles · New York ·
Oxford · Warszawa · Wien

All parts of this publication are protected by copyright. Any
utilisation outside the strict limits of the copyright law, without
the permission of the publisher, is forbidden and liable to
prosecution. This applies in particular to reproductions,
translations, microfilming, and storage and processing in
electronic retrieval systems.

This publication has been peer reviewed.

www.peterlang.com

Contents

Acknowledgements 7

Notes on Contributors 9

Áron Telegdi-Csetri, Viorela Ducu
Transnational Difference – Cosmopolitan Meaning 13

Transnational Families in a Gendered Perspective

Alissa Tolstokorova
Partitioned Paternity: Models of Cross-Border Fathering in
Ukrainian Transnational Families 27

Rafaela Hilario Pascoal, Adina Nicoleta Erica Schwartz
How Family and Emotional Ties Are Used as Coercive
Instruments by the Exploiters on the Romanian Feminine
Migration. The Study Case of Italy 43

Anca Raluca Aştilean
The Issue of Emancipation in the Case of Romanian Migrant Women 63

Armela Xhaho, Erka Çaro
Gendered Work-Family Balance in Migration: Albanian Migrants in Greece 77

Couples within the Context of Migration

Magdalena Żadkowska, Tomasz Szlendak
Egalitarian Capital Gained in Norway or Brought from Poland?
Experiences of Migration and Gender Equality among Polish
Couples in Norway 97

Nóra Kovács
Global Migration and Intermarriage in Chinese-Hungarian Context 113

Viorela Ducu, Iulia Hossu
Bi-national Couples with a Romanian Partner in the European Context 131

6 Contents

Challenges of Transnationalism towards Childhood

Georgiana-Cristina Rentea, Laura-Elena Rotărescu
Yesterday's Children, Today's Youth: The Experiences of Children
Left behind by Romanian Migrant Parents.. 151

Bojan Perovic
Intercountry Adoption: a Human Rights Perspective....................................... 171

Index 187

Acknowledgements

This work was supported by a grant of the Romanian National Authority for Scientific Research and Innovation, CNCS – UEFISCDI, project number PN-II-RU-TE-2014-4-2087.

The articles published herein have been gathered on occasion of two events, Workshop "Managing "difference" in East-European TF at The 18th Nordic Migration Conference, Oslo, 11–12 August" and Panel: "New Families, Old Societies – New Challenges of Migration for Families in their Countries of Origin at The 4th International Conference of the Romanian Sociological Society – Sibiu, 29th of September – 1st of October 2016", organized by the research team members. The focal topic of these were Eastern-European transnational families. The calls were designed to refer to both EU and non-EU member countries.

Thanks of the editors go to authors for their prompt and esteemed contributions, and for team members for their support in creating this book.

The cover image has been taken by Călin Ilea, a team member, during fieldwork.

Not least, gratitude is owed to the Institute hosting this project, the Centre for Population Study by the Babeş-Bolyai University.

Notes on Contributors

Viorela Ducu has a strong research interest in alternative family types, such as ethnically/nationally mixed and transnational families. Her publications include: Romanian Migrant Women's Response to their Discrimination, in Migration, Familie und soziale Lage: Beiträge zu Bildung, Gender und Care, Eds. Thomas Geisen, Tobias Studer, Erol Yildiz, 2013 Springer VS and Strategies of Transnational Motherhood: the Case of Romanian Women, 2013, Argonaut, Cluj Napoca and Displaying Ethnically Mixed Families in Transylvania, in Supplement to the Transylvanian Review, 2016. At present, she is a post-doctoral researcher in the project "Intergenerational solidarity in the context of work migration abroad. The situation of elderly left at home" and principal investigator of the project *Confronting difference through the practices of transnational families* at the Centre for Population Studies, at the Babeş-Bolyai University, Cluj-Napoca.

Áron Telegdi-Csetri, PhD in Political Philosophy, has dealt with Kant's political philosophy in his thesis, reaching out towards contemporary cosmopolitanism in his post-doctoral projects. He has interests in models of cosmopolitanism and transnationalism, with an emphasis on cosmopolitan education and socialization. His publications include: Kant's Cosmopolitics, Contemporary Issues and Global Debates (co-editor with Garrett W. Brown), Edinburgh University Press; Kant's Cosmopolitanism. The Political Radicalization of the Kantian Idea of Philosophy in a Cosmopolitan Sense (author), Zeta Books, Bucureşti; Problematizing Cosmopolitanism (editor), Argonaut, Cluj Napoca. At present, he is Voluntary Researcher in the project *Confronting difference through the practices of transnational families* at the Center for Population Studies at the Babeş-Bolyai University, Cluj-Napoca.

Alissa Tolstokorova holds a PhD degree for a dissertation in Gender Studies. Currently is an independent scholar in women's, gender and family issues. Previously held positions of a head of research experts group at the International School for Equal Opportunities; Director of the Centre for Research on Family and Gender at the State Institute for Family and Youth at the Ministry of Ukraine on Family, Youth and Sports; senior researcher at the Gender Studies Centre at the State Institute for Family and Youth; a project coordinator in gender policy development at the Ukrainian Institute for Social Research in Kyiv, etc. Recipient of 6 international scholarships for research and teaching in social sciences. Made paper presentations at over 40 national and 40 international academic gatherings. Author of around 200 publications in 9 languages. Current research activities include studies about gendered aspects of labour migration from Ukraine, transnational family, care economy, academic migration, etc.

Rafaela Pascoal is a PhD student of Human Rights, at the University of Palermo with the thesis *The role of vulnerability of Nigerian and Romanian women leading to sexual exploitation. Motherhood as being a double vulnerability.* In 2012, she has concluded her Master in Human Rights, University of Bologna, with the thesis *The situation of the Nigerian human trafficking victims and their children in Italy. The study case of Palermo.* In the last 4 years she has collaborated with the CISS association on the subjects of Human Trafficking, migration and gender violence. In 2016 she has participated as a speaker in the conference "Traite des êtres humains et migrations dans le bassin méditerranéen" and in the "Conference Escapes". Currently, she is in her study visiting period in Romania for field research.

Adina Nicoleta Erica Schwartz is a researcher in the field of criminology, with focus on the victims' rights and victim assistance. She is a multidisciplinary, international PhD student at the West University of Timisoara – Doctoral School of Sociology and University of Palermo – Doctoral School of Law. The theme of the doctoral research is the assistance to the drug addicted, sexually exploited victims of human trafficking. Also, she is the head of the "Justice" department of Pro Prietenia Arad Foundation, involved in preventing human trafficking and assisting the victims of this crime.

Anca Aştilean is a second year PhD candidate in the sociology, anthropology field with the topic "Gender empowerment and the new wave of Islamic Feminism in Palestine". Furthermore, she has proficiency with the video field with an extensive video editing knowledge and a completed French documentary film in the portfolio. Her domains of interest include topics involving Muslim women, the Middle East, Islamic Feminism and Feminism as well as Media and Terrorism studies. At present, she is assistant researcher in the project *Confronting difference through the practices of transnational families* at the Center for Population Studies at the Babeş-Bolyai University, Cluj-Napoca.

Armela Xhabo is a PhD Research Fellow at the University of New York Tirana / RRPP working on the project "Industrial Citizenship and Migration from Western Balkans". She holds a MA on Gender Studies from Central European University, Budapest. Her interdisciplinary research activities include participation in many scientific social related research programs, more than 8 years expertise in project coordination and fundraising in civil society organizations, peer education/

trainings and gender consultancy. Her main research interests include Gender and Migration, Gender and labor regimes, Transnational families; Industrial Citizenship, Feminist and Masculinity Studies.

Dr. Erka Çaro is a Researcher and lecturer at the Department of Social Sciences and Philosophy, University of Jyväskylä, Finland. She completed her PhD in 2011 in Population Studies from the Faculty of Spatial Sciences at the University of Groningen, Netherlands. Actually she is the Principal Coordinator of the project "Industrial Citizenship and Migration from Western Balkans". Her research interests include migration and development; ethnography and anthropology; gender studies, labor migration, labor market regimes and welfare states; refugee studies; gender studies; social policy and inequalities, industrial relations and citizenship studies.

Magdalena Żadkowska PhD, is an assistant professor of the Faculty Social Sciences (University of Gdańsk). Magdalena is a researcher and coach dealing with couples and their work-life-balance in every-day life, partnership and domestic duties. Magdalena leads Work Package devoted to qualitative study on couples going to work in Norway in: *Par Migration Navigator Project*. She also takes part in the Polish project *So you are staying at home?*. An author of articles and chapters in books concerning: fatherhood, parenting, migration and gender roles.

Tomasz Szlendak, Professor of Sociology and Head of the Institute of Sociology at the Nicolaus Copernicus University in Toruń, Poland. Publications include: 'Supermarketization: Religion and Sexual Customs of Youth in Consumer Culture' (2004), The Sociology of Families: Evolution, History, Diversity' (2011), 'Heritage in Action: Re-enactment Movement as a Way of Participation in Culture' (2012) and 'The Neglected Playground' (2003).

Nóra Kovács is a sociocultural anthropologist working at the Minority Studies Institute of the Centre for Social Sciences of the Hungarian Academy of Sciences in Budapest. She studied extensively various aspects of the migratory processes between Argentina and Hungary. Her research interests include the anthropology of human movement. Her most recent research focuses on intimate relations between Chinese migrants and members of Hungarian society and on ideological aspects of ethnic return migration. She is the editor of Intersections: East European Journal of Society and Politics.

Iulia-Elena Hossu works as scientific researcher within ISPMN. She is a founding member of Triba Film, independent documentary film production company.

She has a focus on visual anthropology: she has worked as a camera operator and field researcher for the documentary film *Flori de mac* (Romania, 2013, 55 mins, director Enikő Magyari-Vincze) and is the co-director of the documentary *Valea Plângerii* (Romania, 2013, 58 mins, directors Mihai Andrei Leaha, Iulia Hossu, Andrei Crişan) multi-award winner at the international level. At present, she is post-doctoral researcher in the project *Confronting difference through the practices of transnational families* at the Center for Population Studies at the Babeş-Bolyai University, Cluj-Napoca.

Georgiana-Cristina Rentea is Lecturer at Faculty of Sociology and Social Work, Social Work Department, University of Bucharest. Her academic interests include migrants' integration, return migration, social policy and research methods. She is the author of several articles on migrants' integration issues and implications of return migration.

Laura-Elena Rotărescu is attending the master course of Counselling in Social Work at the Faculty of Sociology and Social Work, University of Bucharest. She graduated with a bachelor thesis focused on the issue of social consequences of migration process on children left behind. Her academic interests are migration research and intercultural studies.

Bojan Perovic is a PhD researcher at the University of Hamburg. He received his BA in Law from the University of Belgrade as well as his MA in International Humanitarian Law and Human Rights. Prior to joining University of Hamburg he spent two years as a research assistant at the Institute of Social Sciences in Belgrade. He participated in the last couple of years in the seminars and conferences presenting his work at some of the most prestigious universities including UCL, Royal Holloway, Lund University etc. His academic interests and research areas extend to international public law, especially human rights and international humanitarian law as well as transitional justice among others.

Călin Ilea is a photo-video expert and collaborates with Romanian and foreign press agencies, as Mediafax Foto or Columbia Missourian. In 2010 he completed an MA in photojournalism at the Missouri School of Journalism in Columbia, USA, with a project carried out within the Romanian community in Chicago and has participated 3 times at the Missouri Photo Workshop both as participant and as coordinator. At present, he is photo expert in the project *Confronting difference through the practices of transnational families* at the Center for Population Studies at the Babeş-Bolyai University, Cluj-Napoca.

Áron Telegdi-Csetri, Viorela Ducu

Transnational Difference – Cosmopolitan Meaning[1]

Abstract *The paper reviews the main issues and novelties of the book, focusing both on a thematically transnational and methodologically cosmopolitan approach. Practices of difference, strategies of coping and emancipation, new gender roles and social actors are identified, with a special emphasis on these as units of research – a feedback for academia.*

Social research in the age of globalization has increasingly come to cover territories of transnationality – in its most general sense of the term –, whence its natively *engagé* focus on „difference" as the space of domination as well as emancipation has undergone a turn we could denote as cosmopolitan (Beck and Sznaider, 2006) (in an ethically normative, not a cultural sense). However, this gesture of seemingly naive labeling has rightly been subjected to immediate cutting criticism (Glick Schiller, 2010) as it failed to bring to the fore just what the dimensions of power – hence of domination as well as possible empowerment – were in this allegedly unified global context. This is just what an insistence on difference intends to keep unblurred, namely the persistently shifting domains of power and empowerment, domination and subversion by choice, hegemonic discourses and displays of social existence, legal-political frameworks and practices of living and coping.

An Eastern-Europe-focused research on the transnational family receives its impetus, first of all, from the very demographic transformation it is inscribed in: the emergence of a mass of migrant worker population that has come in continuation of a long history of emigration (Poland, Hungary) or as a sudden change (Romania), altering Western demographic landscapes as well as leading to massive depopulation in the sending country (up to an estimated half of the working population, or a 20% total demographic decrease in the case of Romania). Concerning this state of affairs, one may hypothesize a numerically leading position among migrant populations within Western Europe, among sending country demographics, within local age groups and leading to historical lows in local demographic numbers. However, in contrast with transnational family research

---

1   This work was supported by a grant of the Romanian National Authority for Scientific Research and Innovation, CNCS – UEFISCDI, project number PN-II-RU-TE-2014-4-2087.

in other areas (or pairs) on the globe, this region is radically understudied (with the exception of Poland, perhaps).

Before a study on quantitative or qualitative specificities of the issue at hand (of which the latter is tentatively addressed by this book), one must also reflect on the specificity of research itself that has – or should have – been done upon it. With few exceptions (among them, some behind the studies below), research is financed by independent third parties, such as the Soros foundation, Norwegian or Swiss institutions, not by the incomparably more potent regular academia of the very same political landscape – the one that should make use of the results. In the labyrinth of academic curricula as well as of flows and fluctuations in financing, excellence may transpire, but mostly cannot maintain the constancy and predictability needed for encompassing projects and joined – transnational – research efforts. Hence the scarcity of research materials in the field is a vacuum that this book may barely hope to start covering.

Eastern Europe, as a *par excellence* geographical and mental frontier zone, comes as a hugely fertile terrain of difference in a plethora of senses. Not to mention its less recent political, cultural, religious and social histories, just since the end of the Cold War a number of historical events brought this fact into sight: the progressive EU enlargement (2004 Polish and Hungarian accession, 2007 Romanian accession, 2012 Serbian candidacy, 2014 Albanian candidacy) problematically bringing new identities into the bloodstream of an envisaged European society; the post-Yugoslav wars (up to the Kosovo crisis) creating flows of emigration and a neuralgic point in Europe's political texture; the global economic crisis altering trends of economic migration and emotionally charging the labor markets; austerity and financial rescue actions leading to political and social division between East-West and North-South; the Syrian war and the migration crisis raising fences and ending the presumably cosmopolitan politics of much of Europe; and finally, the deregulation of Western labor markets for Eastern-European workforce, significantly contributing to xenophobic sentiments, leading to a Brexit vote[2].

With this last observation, we may ask whether this accumulation of tensions even possibly has a limit, or is there some horizon upon which unity may be brought to diversity (while preserving it), or is there an identity to difference? What is the Eastern Europe that carries these questions and their possible answers?

---

2   „Thus the scene was set for a referendum in which the implications of EU membership for the economy and immigration became centre stage, with the question of 'sovereignty [...] also lurking not very far in the background." (Curtice, 2016, p. 5)

To be brief: we shall not descend into an analysis of historically loaded inter-pretations of (South) (Central-) Eastern Europe as a cultural and political unit, but merely designate it contextually as the territory that lies on the European edge of what we call the West. Even this is too much to say, since, as the present book shows, essential gradations and further frontiers are present within this schematically circumscribed space[3]: it is uneven in respect of political identity (consider Schengen EU (Hungary), non-Schengen EU (Romania), prospective EU (Serbia), and questionably adhering (Ukraine) countries); of majority reli-gion (Catholic (Poland), Orthodox (Romania), Muslim (Albania)); of economic prosperity (thriving (Poland) and poor (Albania)); historically (once part of a Western empire (Hungary) or of an Eastern one (Ukraine)); of script (using a Latin alphabet or Cyrillic) etc. More relevantly, these differences are translated into variations in the freedom of movement, residence, employment, access to welfare, inter-country adoption, granting of citizenship etc. – some of these issues do not follow the gradations in the closeness in ties to the West anymore.

As a consequence of the latter remark, it seems to be increasingly problematic to impose a top-down understanding upon the social phenomena that occurs massive-ly since the transnationalization of the societies inscribed in the Eastern-European space – some sort of a cosmopolitan endowment of actors (human rights) down to an analysis of empowerment following the logic of emancipation produced by trans-national acculturation. Rather – and this is the great import of a gendered family-focused approach – it is through fragmented life practices, here-and-now decisions, lived and done self-empowerment and networked solidarity that those new actors emerge, and they, by themselves, furnish the new – methodologically cosmopolitan – unit of research that transcends the top-down logic of the nation-state.

The refugee crisis and the Brexit vote are clear signs that Europe is confront-ing the unavoidable need to reevaluate its standards and their implementation – especially those concerning the presumed freedom of movement[4]. When speaking about the freedom of movement – an issue inherent in the very fact of the trans-national situation -, it is not just the above-mentioned gradations of this value that come into question. It is also not the freedom of movement of the individual – the subject of rights – that defines this freedom to begin with: through the fact of the individual's embeddedness in horizontal social structures – among which

---

3   „Even at its most cosmopolitan, then, Europe remains an imagined landscape of na-tional cities, national cultures, and national differences." (Favell, 2013, p. 32)

4   „The principle of free movement of persons, and the systematic breaking down of national barriers to economic migration and re-settlement across borders in Europe, remains one of the core achievements on paper of the European Union." (Favel, 2013, p. 34)

the family is exemplary and foundational – we witness a rearticulation of this freedom as such.

In the literature, the term "free movers" as against „migrants" (Favell 2003, Gaspar, 2009) is restricted to a certain „elite" category, a key element in defining it being the fact that they „do not define themselves as migrants". One might add that perhaps additional factors, such as the general public, the perceiving community as well as the social researcher are at play in imparting such categories, especially in such a permeable space like that of the EU member countries. Technically all EU citizens are at least theoretically „free movers" within the EU. None of the participants to the field research within the research project referred to in this book perceived themselves as „migrants"[5] – especially those who left Romania after its 2007 accession.

Through the above-mentioned non-individual logic of freedom, within which other factors, such as care practices and family duty come into play, further gradations and differences become manifest: the alleged „free-mover" proves to be a person who is either free of such horizontal embeddedness or financially capable to translate it into the consumption of services, and the „migrant" counterpart is a person who might „freely" move, but is still indebted – materially or socially – to the degree where her migration becomes limited and directed by more pragmatic and immediate considerations. Moreover, given these limitations, as well as the sentiments circumscribing the implementation of free-movement rights, it seems to be superfluous to talk more about this issue on the level of theory[6], – one needs to look at the degree it might be so in practice in practice.

---

5 Moreover, one of the experiences during field research might be relevant researchers understanding that labeling people as „migrants" or as „free movers" is just our conceptual framework rather then a reality in everyday perception. The researchers went out on a visit to a family, two of the members of which were known to be living in Spain. One of the researchers told a family members that we would like to talk to families with „migrant" members and that this family was pointed by people as being such. The respondent was very much surprised and said that some of their cousins have indeed moved to the US but that he hasn't been in contact with them, not knowing what to relate to the researchers on this. Learning that those in question were the family members in Spain, he very clearly expressed the fact that they are not migrants, they only work in Spain, and they will probably be back someday. Hence in the above logic, one would perhaps need to call them „free-movers".

6 „Our findings point to a tendency to think in binary oppositions – women versus men, adults versus children, staying put versus migrating, staying connected versus breaking family ties – when discussing transnational families." (Sørensen and Vammen, 2014, p. 100)

Also, since within the East-West divide (and not only), we need to confront more socially conservative – in short, patriarchal – societies, a gendered approach seems to be self-evident; moreover, it also brings the vantage point of a language that deals with difference and power in its very basics. Hence, the allegedly „freely" migrating subject – female or male – becomes a flesh-and-blood person with an overwhelming social luggage, one that she still needs to confront and translate into life practices once entering the transnational space, a sort of daily practice of difference that doesn't either escape or submit to conservatism (see a case for males in Tolstokorova, for females in Aştilean, Zadkowska and Szlendak). The result is not a new discourse against the hegemonic one, hence not a new model of behavior – it is rather a new set of practices that strikingly differs from the very language they are embedded in. Even though analysis may extract the meanings intended in them, it might not get as far as modeling new types of subjects, only new ways of „doing" – hence new actors. Social remittances by them – being done, practiced, active by definition – may nonetheless possess the impetus to alter conservative value systems in the long run, but they do produce factual emancipation in the present at home, too. Present-day samples of such frontier practices of coping are abundant in the book – a frontier on the frontier.

Hence the Eastern-European transnational family put in a gendered perspective shows a multitude of layers of difference and in-betweenness, but it also relies on strategies of cohesion, by „doing families" (Morgan 2011a, b), as well as image-creating social behaviour through „displaying families" (Finch, 2007, 2011, Dermott and Seymour, 2011), maintaining a connected existence up to the point of reciprocal „co-presence" (Ducu 2016, Nedelcu and Wyss 2016) through a common transnational household, transnational communication and mutual visits. By „doing families", one unfolds such care- and collective life-activities as to practically create and maintain what is presupposed in the idea of a family – but this is not so self-evident once in a transnational setup; also, a family itself does not exist anymore without „doing" it, which is a reversal of logic from action to existence. Displaying occurs as the performative element of the same practice, doing what families do, but now in the eyes of the beholder - now overturning the logic of action and perception: it is not action that is perceived, it is perception that informs action. Furthermore, the co-presence occurs as the transcendence of spatial separation through virtually practical presence – a dynamism that makes stayers into migrants and migrants into stayers. This is all made possible through transnational communication – especially electronic, but also objectual, through exchange of presents and money – that has increasingly become simultaneous.

Simultaneity as unified and permeable temporality has been a new development in migration. Through its rise – especially through its increasing accessibility and facility – life-worlds have come to be able to be effectively shared. Geographical, spatial distance has been bridged – up to its anthropological limits – unto a continuous network of human connections, a meta-space that is neither beyond nor within the physical one, but rather on the level of a new mental map that connects distant and different spaces, actively altering and mixing them in their very structure. Space itself has not become unified and permeable in the same way though – its composition and structural logic has been changed. And through this, its very territorial nature has transformed into something else; as migrants are present in foreign territories, foreign spaces are also present in domestic ones through migrant communication, giving birth to something that might resemble a new, though irregular, territory. The territory of whom? – one might ask.

Communication is revolutionized not only spatio-temporally, but linguistically as well. People with no common language, members of the same transnational family, communicate through Google Translate, people even date and form couples with the same method. Actors from within transnational families as gendered, embedded social agents manage to transcend local – geographical, political or mental – spaces through the transnational continuum, creating a practical and communicative environment that is pointing to a reversal of forces in the transnational social setup. To hint at what this could entail: it is not countries that choose quotas and identities of migrants anymore – it is people who choose countries, citizenships and entitlements, practically luring the state into the role of a juridical and political service provider – possibly quite a sensible development.

On the downside, of course, the scrambling of traditional territories of power and authority also makes for abuse, violence, structural and willed discrimination, deprivation of rights, various levels of vulnerability, exploitation and domination, new forms of – e.g. bodily – colonialism, and generally, various proofs of express cynicism, covert manipulation or plain misunderstanding. It is discouraging to see, for example, the fall in *de facto* protection for trafficked women once their country became an EU member – on grounds that together with their rise in political status, supposedly the consciousness of their right entitlements came too, as in a package (Pascoal and Schwartz). As of cynicism, it is not just the family-doing practices of transnational migrants, but also the constraining practices of transnational criminals that creatively make use of the elements of the frontier situation: using the children of trafficked women – even leaving them pregnant beforehand – as a tool in subduing them into prostitution; a practice made possible in the first place by the women's lack of, or impeded access to, rights, their spatial separation from their children, as well as their dependence on third parties for the transfer of childraising (Pascoal and Schwartz).

There is a new quality of difference that is at work here – and this is perhaps the main, although inexplicit, underlying issue of the present book. It is not just the political, juridical, economic, social, anthropological, cultural, religious differences – inherent in the transnational situation and the migrant herself – that beg the question; these could be regulated by a relatively simple global justice approach transposed into social analysis leading to policy recommendations to *Rechtsstaat* countries (at least). The truly cosmopolitan issue is at work regarding the very difference between the space of all these differences[7] and the space of no-difference, or the uprootedly non-allegiant, well-protected, superficially cosmopolitan worldspace of globalization. We could even say, there is an ethical divide between the „cosmopolitan" and the „transnational" – see the cosmopolitan Chinese not settling in Hungary (culturally or politically) and not practicing transnationalism (Kovács).

Hence when talking about the cosmopolitanism of transnationalism, one might renounce the presumptive gain from a greater openness towards cultural difference – or cultural cosmopolitanism – and focus instead on a world that puts freedom to work – a practical cosmopolitanism. We might commence seeing the recurrent difference between transnational reality and cosmopolitan normativity not as a by-product of globalization, but as its very symptom: it is not migrants' shortcomings in cosmopolitan attitudes that make difference an issue; it is being-different inherent in transnationalism that calls for a cosmopolitan empowerment of actors[8].

Such actors – some exemplified in the present volume – are of fundamentally fragmented, broken, equivocal, rhizomatic constitution. They do not necessarily conform the logic of much discussed nomadism, still they aren't graspable by *facile* identification either. However, a first step in approaching them as units of research is made by studies as those at hand. The senders of egalitarian social remittances mentioned above (as well as in Aștilean) are one example – as actors who do not renounce both their social embeddedness and their practical and symbolic empowerment. However, one needs to keep in mind that they do not seek for empowerment for its own sake, they are not politically conscious – at

---

7   A striking formulation of a similar idea: „We also detect a tendency to locate social concerns in a moral economy of emotions rather than in a political economy of human mobility. These tendencies are more pronounced in policy debates but also traceable in academic contributions." (Sørensen and Vammen, 2014, p. 100)

8   „…an acknowledgement of diversity in migrant experiences does not necessarily include attention to the structures that produce this diversity." (Sørensen and Vammen, 2014, p. 100)

least not relevantly so. They need and grip empowerment out of necessity – and they perform it within and in spite of the adverse social consciousness they live in. Emancipation comes as a by-product, and in some cases doesn't even get voiced. Yet, due to the generally higher level of egalitarianism in the receiving country (Żadkowska and Szlendak), or to the change in the gender balance of migration triggered by the economic crisis (Aștilean; Rentea and Rotărescu), even in a still somewhat patriarchal receiving milieu (Xhaho and Caro), women's emancipation does occur on the factual level: they become – often the main – breadwinners, reaching a strong negotiating position within the family, in its decisions and strategies, even redefining motherhood itself (Xhaho and Caro).

In other cases (Aștilean), by contrast, highly educated, egalitarian-minded, economically well-off and factually emancipated actors choose migration out of an existential necessity – as a means to be what they already are, namely, self-conscious, autonomous agents. Here it is the very propensity of Western-style, where free-moving, self-reliant people do not stop at the level of opportunities their country – and their position within it – can offer; hence it is not transnationalism *per se* that motivates them, it is just a constituent of their life vocation. However, it is not a cosmopolitan move either – choosing this country or another, depending on opportunities – that is at work here: it is „leaving" itself as a life-yet-unexplored possibility that adds to the existential endeavour.

Episodes of migration might even produce counter-migration mindsets in actors passively acted upon by it (Rentea and Rotărescu): children of migrant mothers might cope with the trauma of separation – a theme much exploited by anti-migrant media both at home and abroad (Ducu, 2014) – through the understanding of the greater sacrifice at the other end of the relationship. Through this understanding, children mirror the migration experience as the very condition of the possibility that they do not need to go through the same – sacrificial – experience again. It is important to note here that this understanding differs in value – it is positive – as well as in breadth – it includes the migration experience, although passively and from afar – from the mere opinion about migration a non-migrant may hold; it is the product of, not just a reaction to transnationalism.

Men – especially after the change in labor market trends due to the economic crisis – also undergo a practical and relational transformation in respect to their gendered family allegiance: fatherhood remittances (Tolstokorova) both overgrow patriarchal remittances and equivocally alter men's roles in migrant life stories. The analytic vantage point of the gendered perspective allows these men to be seen as en-gendered as against genderless, family-bound instead of autonomous, embedded and not ideally de-contextualized in their social practices; a masculine turn within a mostly feminine-minded field that is both welcome and productive.

Through this, we need to see how sociality is never the attribute of some modeled subject – such as the migrant –, but a quality of her relational as well as practical agency. Hence egalitarianism as a value does not come – at least not fully – through a mere mindset, it does not even pertain to a single agent as such. In a well-chosen definition of the unit of research, one might rather talk about such mindsets both in a multiple-person and a value-and-practice oriented conceptual tension.

The egalitarian capital couples possess (Żadkowska and Szlendak), although referring to values in principle, is something only validated through practice, that is, through common (couple) action, displaying the fundamental relationality of transnational concepts. On the one hand, acquisition of more egalitarian capital in an egalitarian country such as Norway seems obvious, on the other hand, it is less obvious whether such capital is genuinely acquired through so-called integration or acculturation – as in much of the public discourse on migrant administration – or it is always-already there, at least as a capacity, in the migrants themselves. It might be the case that the source of much of one's actual social practices is not the „culture" one carries, but the medium and relations one is embedded in.

Besides, by times even more speaking instances of relational social practices are constituted by inter-generation relations. From the family-enlarging and growth-optimizing mindset of endemic Chinese migrants (Kovács) that leads to a radical inter-generational divergence with the second generation – with a genuinely hybrid identity – being foreign-born, as well as the case of bi-national couples living in a third country (Ducu and Hossu) with potentially tri-national children, new and autocratic units of analysis emerge. Once the children can choose political and cultural identities furnished by their families, social milieu, state of birth or state of residence, it becomes clear that the abundance of choice has overflown the limits not just of traditional power relations, but also of the conceptual models that try to trace the afterlife of such territories of power.

It is also in this context of a voluntary disposal of allegiances that the very use of language – as a tool of communication which *par excellence* defines identities through collective practice – becomes relativised: beside the assimilating, dual and peripatetic uses of language in mixed couples, a fourth strategy in language usage emerges. Bi-national couples living in a third country (Ducu and Hossu) happen to use a strategy that is both origin-neutral and country-neutral: it might be a fourth language, in some cases the language of a former country of residence of the couple, the country where they met. Hence language use, as a social practice that escapes all power structures, has become a result of a focal moment in the couple's own subjective history. Needless to say that such a degree of difference is beyond encompassing into large-scale models, being foundationless in a theoreti-cal sense, however it does create a space within which further identity will flourish.

Bi-national marriages in third countries – hence without the interest of obtain-ing citizenship through marriage – are voluntarily – romantically? – instituted by simple migrants, having their own, converging or not, practical interests and limitations, not only by the hypothetical „free-movers" (Ducu and Hossu). Their very voluntary gesture is a point of departure for further foundationless trans-national practices, although still moving within limits set by their economical, juridical and cultural capacity.

Cultural identity does recreate its power field in the case of intercountry adop-tions (Perovic). After the fall of the Iron Curtain, following an initial deregulation, foreign adoption of Eastern-European children became increasingly difficult, even prohibited, due to ideas of a right to one's inborn cultural inheritance. This leads to international legislation reducing intercountry adoption allowance to cases where the country of origin cannot by itself ensure meeting the best interest of the child in question – a fact obviously difficult to establish, since no country would voluntarily put itself in such light. This actively goes against the ease in providing families with orphans, abandoned children or victims of war, in blatant need of – sometimes even the most basic – care. The unit of research here is the yet cultureless infant – if we don't want to descend into a cultural analysis of baby language – whose most basic rights are renounced for the sake of the self-interest of an alleged cultural community – a plain fetishism. A brief analysis of the child's social relations in more modest systems – immediate caretakers such as parents – could show that she is in need of a more basic insertion into the society, rather than the need for large concepts such as culture or a state.

Migrants – engendered, practically, relationally embedded actors – are dif-ferent both from hypothetical „free-movers" as well as from factually stateless persons such as refugees. Being together with non-migrant transnational family members, spouses, second-generation migrant descendants, or prospective in-tercountry adoptees, they form a unit of research that has an analytical potential for ethically (not culturally) cosmopolitan research that goes beyond the instru-ments of consecrated social science, practically creating domains of social life that radically exceed the transformation of scientific paradigms in the speed of their revolution. It seems that this overheating of the subject matter of analysis backfires on the scientific community, exposing presuppositions as prejudice and paralyzing reflection both temporally and perspectively. Similar to the imperative concerning policy – pointing to the limit of the freedom of movement that overturns the values behind the shared European territory – one might, in research, just as well confront the need to return to one's points of departure and perhaps encompass a higher degree of volatility and relativism into one's standpoint, or: being more different.

References

Beck, Ulrich / Sznaider, Natan: "Unpacking cosmopolitanism for the social sciences: a research agenda". *The British Journal of Sociology*, 57 (1), 2006, pp. 1–23.

Curtice, John: "Brexit: Behind the Referendum". *Political Insight*, september 2016, pp. 2–6.

Dermott, Esther, E. / Seymour, Julie: "Developing 'Displaying Families': A Possibility for the Future of the Sociology of Personal Life". In Seymour, Julie / Dermott, Esther, (eds.) *Displaying Families: A New Concept for the Sociology of Family Life*, London: Palgrave Macmillan, 2011, pp. 3–19.

Ducu, Viorela:" Transnational Mothers from Romania", *Romanian Journal of Population Studies*, 1/2014, pp. 117–142.

Ducu, Viorela:" Experiences from "Home" – Belonging to a Transnational Family". Romanian Journal of Population Studies. X, (1), pp. 91–104.

Favell, Adrian: "The Changing Face of 'Integration' in a Mobile Europe", 2013. Retrieved 01.09.2016 http://www.adrianfavell.com/CESweb.pdf

Finch, Janet: "Displaying Families". *Sociology* 41 (1), 2007, pp. 65–81.

Finch, Janet: "Exploring the Concept of Display in Family Relationships". In Seymour, Julie / Dermott, Esther, (eds.) *Displaying Families: A New Concept for the Sociology of Family Life*, London: Palgrave Macmillan, 2011, pp. 197–206.

Gaspar, Sofia: "Mixed marriages between European free movers". CIES e-Working Paper, 65, 2009. Retrieved 01.09.2016. http://cies.iscte-iul.pt/destaques/documents/CIES-WP65_Gaspar.pdf

Glick Schiller, Nina: "Old baggage and missing luggage: a commentary on Beck and Sznaider's 'Unpacking cosmopolitanism for the social sciences: a research agenda'". *The British Journal of Sociology*, 61 (1), 2010, pp. 413–420.

Morgan, David: "Locating 'Family Practices'". *Sociological Research Online*, 16 (4) 14, 2011a.

Morgan, David: Rethinking Family Practices, London: Palgrave Macmillan, 2011b.

Nedelcu, Mihaela / Malika, Wyss: "'Doing family' through ICT-mediated ordinary co-presence: transnational communication practices of Romanian migrants in Switzerland". *Global Networks* 16, 2, 2016, pp. 202–218.

Sørensen, Ninna Nyberg / Vammen, Ida Marie, Who Cares? Transnational Families in Debates on Migration and Development, New Diversities vol. 16, No. 2, 2014, pp. 89–107.

Transnational Families in a Gendered Perspective

Alissa Tolstokorova

Partitioned Paternity: Models of Cross-Border Fathering in Ukrainian Transnational Families

Abstract *The paper identifies the impact of migration and transnationalism on paternity practices of Ukrainian migrant men departing from the theory of "responsible fathering". A concept of "fatherhood dividends" is offered. 3 models of fathering are distinguished: "check-pay fathers" (high degree of paternal responsibility), "re-emerging fathers" (moderate degree of paternal responsibility) and "waning fathers" (low degree of paternal responsibility).*

Research problem, goal and analytical framework of the study

The restoration of the freedom of movement in post-socialist Ukraine entailed the emergence of a category of migrant men who sustain relationships with family and children in a cross-border regime. My goal in this article is to problematize the concepts of cross-border paternity and paternal care which are often neglected in migration scholarship, placing it within the context of migrancy and transnationalism and examining it within a gendered analytical framework. The institution of fatherhood is approached here as the most changeable, challenging and universal aspect of masculinity correlating both with the social institution of fatherhood, and with specific fathering practices and male identity, including self-identity, whereas the category of transnational paternity is conceived as "emergent fatherhood" associated with globalization (Inhorn et al. 2014). This article will thus consider the male perspective in the study of transnational family, which became a wide-spread phenomenon across Ukraine throughout the years of transition to free market economy.

Statistics show that despite the increasing feminization of labour migration flows from Ukraine (see Tolstokorova 2009), men still predominate over them. Thus, according to IOM data for 2013, males constitute 67% of all Ukrainians working abroad (IOM 2013, p. 5). Approximately two thirds of migrant men are married or in a common law relationship and 53% have dependent children (IOM 2008, pp. 22–23)[1]. Considering that according to the World Bank data Ukraine is the 3rd largest donor of migrant labour in the world (Mansoor / Quillin 2007),

---

1   This statistics refers to Ukrainian males who were victims o trafficking as a result of labour migration, but it reflects the overall demographic composition of Ukrainian male migration.

the issue of Ukrainian transnational paternity is gaining currency. Yet, notwith-standing the social relevance of this research problem, there was no study done to explore fathering practices of Ukrainian men working abroad and respective challenges they faced in their cross-border relations with family and children left behind. The failure to recognize the need to engage Ukrainian transnational fathers in research can entail their further marginalization from the benefits of policy development and decision-making.

I make the analytical sense here of Doherty's et al. (1998) stance on "responsible fathering", applying it to measure the extent of fathers' involvement with their chil-dren in the "age of migration" (Castles, Miller 2003). According to this approach, the major domains of "responsibility" in fathering include acknowledgement of one's paternity, willingness to be present in child's life, to be involved in upbringing and to provide economic support. Respectively, it is implied that some fathering that does not comply with these criteria could be judged as "irresponsible". I argue that this framework is useful in tracing the dynamics of the institution of paternity in transnational families of Ukrainian migrant men confronting chal-lenges of crossborderness.

Transnational family is conceptualized here as a *modernized model* of family relationship generated by transnational migration and global network society and vested in the transnational relationship of migrant workers with family members left behind by way of cross-border household management and the performance of family roles and parental obligations at distance (Tolstokorova 2013 a; b).

The challenges of transnational fatherhood were highlighted by Jason Pribilsky, who has given this phenomenon its impetus. In his seminal paper he posited that in many studies of the transnational family, only women's experiences of forging family ties in migration have been of paramount interest, whereas men's experi-ences as migrants have been explored in relation to transnational families mainly within contexts that emphasize their beliefs and behaviour as obstacles to forging strong family units rather than the joint efforts of men and women (Pribilsky 2004, p. 315). While not contesting this observation, it should be noted that over the last decade a body of literature emerged detailing the effect of migrancy on men, especially on their family roles (Osella /Osella 2000; Boehm 2004; Yeoh /Willis 2004; Charsley 2005; McIlwaine 2005; McKay 2007; Herbert 2008; Datta et al. 2009; Donaldson et al. 2009). Yet, the gendered effect of "transgressing norms of hegemonic masculinity" (Connel 1995) on self-identification of these men is heav-ily understudied. Fathering practices of this category of men are documented insuf-ficiently. Only a few works focused on these issues appeared lately (Cheng 2012; Busse 2012; Kilkey et al., 2014; Kilkey 2014; Lam / Yeoh, 2014; Arditti et al. 2015).

This defines the main goal of this paper, which is to study the effect of transnational family context on transformations of family and parental roles of Ukrainian migrant men, placing emphasis on gendered specificities of transnational paternity.

A useful analytical tool to study transformations of the institution of fatherhood in conditions of migrancy and transnationalism is the concept of "patriarchal dividends" (henceforward PD) (Greig et al. 2000, p. 7), collectively arising from men's higher labour force participation and incomes, unequal property ownership and greater access to institutional power (Connell 1995, p. 82–83). As a ramification of the notion of PD regarded in the familial setting, I offer the concept of "fatherhood (or paternity) dividends"[2] (Tolstokorova 2014, p. 96), which is understood as a variety of patriarchal dividends secured in the form of benefits to men's social status and emotional well-being due to paternity status vis-à-vis the "minimal investment required for parenting" (Thornhill 1980; Thornhill /Palmer 2000), conventional for men in a patriarchal society. Hence, a narrower objective of this paper is to identify PD of Ukrainian men working abroad as associated with their migratory status.

Research methodology

The findings herein draw on the results of a multi-staged field research, which encompassed non-participant observation, interviews and 2 focus group discussions with current and returnee migrants and members of their families, as well as interviews and 2 focus group discussions with experts.

Expert interviewing was conducted in 2008 in Kyiv and Lviv together with British and Italian scholars for the project "Care-work and welfare internationalization. Transnational scenarios and prospects for the future", carried out by CeSPI (Rome, Italy). It was implemented through in-depth interviewing and two focus group discussions covering 25 experts all in all, including NGO activists, journalists, researchers at research institutions and think-tanks, policy-makers at ministries, municipalities, employment centres, embassies, and representatives of international organizations, like IOM and Amnesty International.

Interviewing of the target group of informants covered 43 Ukrainian labour migrants working in low-cost labour, members of their families and extended migrants' networks mainly in urban communities (neighbors, relatives, co-workers). Among our responders were returnees and current migrants: both those who came home visiting from countries of work and circular migrants who temporarily

---

2   Henceforward FD.

stayed in Ukraine in-between voyages for employment abroad. Additionally, the group of responders included women involved in *au-pair* work in Austria and Germany. In Ukraine, interviews were taken in Kherson, Kirovograd, Kyiv and small towns of Kherson oblast. Others were interviewed in the countries of work (Italy, Germany, Austria, France) or on board of a plane, at the airports lounges and in the airport shuttle buses during the author's international travels for academic gatherings abroad. Interviews were made under the condition that real identities of the responders would not be disclosed in order to maintain their privacy. It was necessary because experience showed that many migrants were reluctant to discuss issues related to personal life of their own and their family members in the fair that the confidential information might be disclosed to outsiders. Therefore, in search of adequate methodology which is sensitive to confidentiality requirements of our responders, ICT was extensively employed as an innovative tool for field research, enabling respect to ethical considerations in information gathering. For instance field work was conducted via telephone interviewing, communication via SKYPE and e-mail messaging. These tools provided a greater freedom to respond-ers for expressing personal opinions and sharing intimate experiences, while at the same time enabling them to preserve relative anonymity. Additionally, two focus groups were organized with members of transnational families, including both migrants who came home visiting and their left-behind relatives at home. Inter-viewing was drawn on a semi-structured questionnaire with open-ended ques-tions, aimed to cover different stages of the migration cycle and to reflect on the gendered experiences of migrants. The interviewing process started with existing contacts with migrants and their families and in many cases followed by a snowball sampling method whereby new respondents were contacted through preceding respondents. Interviews with migrants, members of their families, members of migrants' informal social networks and most of Ukrainian experts were conducted in Ukrainian and Russian, but interviews with 5 international and local experts were conducted in English.

Results of non-participant observation represent a generalization of the au-thor's experience of socialization among the target groups of responders. The data of field research were supplemented by deskwork performed by way of the analysis of secondary theoretical sources and media overview.

As discussed earlier (Tolstokorova 2010), at the initial stage of this multi-staged research the study of transnational family *per se,* including challenges of males as fathers and family men, was not central to this project, which is aimed at the study of gendered aspects of Ukrainian labour migration with the empha-sis on migrant women. In the course of the field research, however, these issues emerged in interviews with both migrant men, members of their families and with Ukrainian experts. This prompted the necessity to pay closer attention to specific challenges of men, particularly those that they experience in their cross-border paternity practices.

Paternity at Distance: Models of fathering among Ukrainian migrant men

The field research showed that being assessed in terms of "responsible fathering" framework, paternity practices of Ukrainian non-residential migrant fathers fall into three scales defined by the degree of responsibility: highly responsible fathering represented by a "pay-check fathers" model, moderately responsible fathering embodied in a "re-emerging fathers" model and irresponsible fathering which may be identified as a "waning fathers" model.

High degree of paternal responsibility

"Pay-check fathering" model: busy bees

It has been argued that "one excellent way to raise the value of care is to involve fathers in it" (Hochschild 2003, p. 196). In conditions when family space is fragmented by borders, the maintenance of intimacy and care is challenged by geographic distance. The interviews confirm the observation that despite the relative normativity of the "father-away effect" in transnational families, the practices of cross-border parenting make a greater challenge for men than for women so far as it is harder for them to accommodate their fatherhood role in conditions of distant parenting (Parreñas 2008). Fathering at distance entails "emotional gaps" (ibidem), which may have a salient effect on men's psychological wellbeing and self-identity as fathers:

> *"What was important for me was to earn for the education of children and to cope with my "ego". <...>. It was hard to part with children, very hard. But what could I do? Don't I understand that children have to be with their mother? They need their Mom. They need their Dad too, but Mom is the most important. Children are children. I am a father and I have to comply with it."* (Dennis, a psychologist and a University lecturer, worked as a handyman in Moscow).

This interview aligns with Schmalzbauer's (2015) findings, challenging the view on emotional labour and sacrifice as exclusive domains of transnational mothers. It also confirms the argument that while the emotions of migrant fathers are not commonly broached, they suffer too, and are often even more self-destructive in their coping strategies than transnational mothers (Carlin et al. 2012, p. 195). This is exacerbated by the emotional effect of "double absence", when fathers are at the same time at distance from home and outsiders in hosting societies (Sayad 1999). This effect is offset mainly by financial investments into family and children left behind, that enables fathers to be "symbolically present" at home (Parreñas 2008). Even so, due to a stereotyped image of a strong man who is an agent in charge of his own destiny and that of his family, men refuse to admit their vulnerability and have to confront depressions, dependencies, conflicts, etc. Some struggle with severe loneliness and alienation by alcohol abuse and random unsafe sex as typical ways of dealing with the process of separation and the inability to live up to prescribed standards of masculinity (Worby/ Organista 2007; Schmalzbauer 2005). A Ukrainian psychologist observes a likewise trend: "Family problems are confronted by nearly all zarobitchany (labour migrants, A.T.) who referred to us for treatment. Strangely, it is men who are affected more, and especially those who have left. It may end up even in psychoses and depressions. With women the symptoms are more covert. Additionally, "those who stayed in marriage longer suffer more" (Mychko 2011).

Hence, migrancy may offset the advantages of PD as long as it entails respective responsibilities of transnational fathers to family and children that in turn may require the limitation of men's personal freedoms and needs and reprioritizing of individual interests. This is exemplified by an interview with the above Dennis, a college lecturer and a "solo living"[3] father of two, who worked as a handyman in Moscow to financially support his ex-wife and children in Ukraine. While working in Russia he met a woman who he lived with and intended to marry:

"I needed a formal consent for a divorce from my ex-wife. But she did not give it, she refused! She did not want me to marry again, although we've been living apart for many years and she has another man. Because what matters for her is only money, the payments for children she gets from me."

As follows from the data of my fieldwork, the devaluation of patriarchal authority in the family that accompanies the loss of a breadwinner status is detrimental for men's self-esteem and often serves as a push factor for international migration. An acute sense of his personal "masculinity crisis" resulting from the loss of financial agency served as a trigger to Oleg who in early 1990-s set off for his job search across Europe to be able to secure "the best possible future" for his small daughter:

---

3   The term "solo-living" was offered by a group of Scottish researchers (Smith/ Wasoff/ Jamieson 2005) to designate working adults living apart from their families.

"Look, you are asking: "Why did you leave? What was the trigger?" Well, what can the trigger be if you have no money even to buy a piece of sweet to your child? That was exactly the trigger. Ok, it was so... I went for a weekend walk with my daughter, just to have a stroll along Dneprovsky (avenue). And then there was such a shop-booth, with bananás[4]. Here you go, in a foreign language: ba-na-nás. In those years, bananás – Gosh, it was a big deal! A prodigy indeed! Well, and of course my daughter starts pleading for a banana! Gosh! What could I do? I had money only for a bus ticket, to go back home! What a shame! An adult man, a trained hostler, and I had no money even to buy a banana to my child! Then I told to myself: "Full stop. Never again! No more of this shame! I will do whatever I can, but I will never have this situation again. Cost what it may!".

The issue of *children's wellbeing* was underscored in men's narratives as a guiding factor for their foreign employment that gave them energy to overcome constraints and exigencies of their migratory cycle. Thus Serguey, a worker in the construction sector in Moscow and a single father of a 17-year old daughter, recalled how a group of immigrant workers, who have just received their wage, were caught in a men-hunt by police who confiscated all their earnings. In this risk-taking situation, the man dared arguing with the policeman, making a futile attempt to convince him of his paternal duties to his daughter:

"I tell him: "Look, bro, just leave me at least a few bucks. It is not for me, it's for my daughter. She is only 17, yet a schoolgirl and all alone at home. How can she survive without my money?". And he says: "Who's told you that I have no daughter myself? I have to take care of my own daughter too. Come on, where's your money?"

However, the sacrifices of men *for the best child's interests* are not always appreciated by their off-spring, given that labour migration of parents may entail *social parasitism* among their children, fostering a generation of young Ukrainians who are reluctant to work, but prefer to live on remittances sent to them by their parents. They do not see how hard their fathers work abroad for their wellbeing. They only see remittances arriving from afar which they often waste on whims. That is why they often regard their migrant parents as "paycheck fathers" (Mummert 2005) and *private cash machines* that produce banknotes for them. They associate international employment with easy money and *dolce vita*, and grow up with a belief that making money is worth only abroad. Being financially better-off than children from non-migrant families, they are perceived by their peers as a telling example of the validity of this belief. This is another argument testifying that the advantages of FD of migrant men may be offset by great geographic distances

---

4   This word-form is coined by the merging of two words: "banan" (banana) and "anan*ás*" (pine-apple).

which forge constrains to fathers' emotional connection and paternal authority in relationship with children and family left behind at home.

Although many men told scary stories about the challenges and deprivations that they confronted throughout their economic pilgrimage, most of them underscored that this experience was pivotal for their masculine self-identity. Thus, the above Oleg intimated that throughout his pilgrimage across Europe he had to starve and to pick up leavings from trash bins to eat, to stay overnight at park lawns, church-yards and even in a ward. But in his view, all the exigencies of migrancy served to temper his will-power and to secure new survival skills necessary to find his own place under the Sun which eventually enabled him to secure a high-income employment in Australia and to reunite with his family there. The wellbeing of his daughter was a key leitmotif of his narrative, whereas the opportunity to give her a University education in Sydney was voiced as a reward for his migratory hardships and a paternal dividend of economic migration. This story points to the fact that despite its challenges, migrancy serves to foster authentic masculinity of Ukrainian migrant men and to raise their self-esteem as fathers and males. Moreover, some members of transnational families in their interviews confirm the Nobles's (2011) finding that the temporary separation may strengthen men's ultimate involvement in family life and children's matters as returnee fathers may be commonly involved in their children's daily lives. This aligns with the argument that fatherhood and masculinity are experienced and practised in more diverse ways than stereotypes suggest (Gutmann 1996; Schmalzbauer 2015).

Moderate degree of paternal responsibility

"Re-emerging fathering" model: distance makes heart grow fonder

It is noteworthy that the feelings of loneliness and alienation pertaining to migration incited some pleasant surprises in the relationships between children and their migrant fathers. Thus, due to migrancy, some men began to value their fatherhood status more and set off to restore the connection with their children across borders, although before these international voyages they had had no paternal involvement with the off-spring. Such a story was intimated in an interview with Julya, an ex-wife of a migrant man working in Italy. Her marriage dissolved when her daughter was still a toddler. The girl's father never visited her after the divorce and did not maintain any connection with her. The daughter did not remember him and was only dimly aware of him through his photos. When the girl turned thirteen, her father emerged unexpectedly to offer her a modest financial support. By that time he had been working in Italy for two years, and was financially well off. He tried to reconnect with his daughter by giving her telephone calls, sending messages and presents from time to time, mainly for her birthdays. For the girls' mother it was a pleasant surprise to have her ex-husband offer modest care to their daughter. She could only guess at the reasons behind this surge of fatherly feelings. She assumed that the loneliness and emotional deficit of a single man living abroad in a foreign milieu without a family, coupled with the improvement of his social status and financial situation due to international earnings, incited the man to recall his paternal obligations. Labour migration caused the father to reunite with his daughter and meant that the girl received his attention which she needed a lot, but had been lacking for a long time.

Hence, the reinforcement of the traditional masculine role of a bread-winner and a family provider for the account of migratory earnings may serve as a mechanism that enables men to restore their paternity status by way of cross-border fathering. That is, migrancy and transnationalism may facilitate a reinforcement of the institution of paternity even in conditions of its actual decline and family dissolution that benefits both fathers and their children. This complies with Dreby's (2010) finding that in cases of divorce, transnational fathers were likely to use their change in status as an opportunity to strengthen their bonds with children. For them, it was "a welcomed part of otherwise unsatisfying lives" (Pribilsky 2004: 330) and an opportunity to reconsider the financial dividends of migration and make sense of their PD by exerting a closer emotional connection with their off-spring.

Low degree of paternal responsibility

"Waning fathering" model: "out of sight, out of mind"

As Carlin (2012) observes by pointing to an array of studies, migrant fathers are less likely than mothers to live up to gender expectations, and abandonment is not uncommon (Landolt / Da 2005; Schmalzbauer 2004; 2005). That is, although the wellbeing of children is generally a key incentive for economic migration abroad, upon their arrival at their destination, fathers focus on securing jobs which limits their time to communicate with their children and their wife, thus distancing them from their families not only physically but also emotionally (Busse 2012). This leads to the decline of kinship bonds and entails the dissolution of familial connections, giving way to the *waning fathering* model of paternity. Pribilsky (2004) argues that in male migration spousal abandonment, separation and divorce are inevitable results of any migration situation because geographical distance and separation from the family is a great challenge for these men, which they confront by seeking new intimate relations in hosting societies as a shelter against the emotional pressure of the foreign milieu. Thus, among migrant men working in Portugal, which is a key target country for male migration from Ukraine, it was found that "contrary to the picture of a family with a "breadwinner" father working in a European country to support his wife and children, there is a high proportion of transnational families in which the father has children both at home and in Portugal where he has a new family and is no longer in a relationship with the mother of the child at home" (Grassi/ Vivet 2014, p. 3). This complies with findings on labour migration from other post-soviet states, in particular from Tajikistan, evidencing that the longer men stay abroad, the more likely that they start new families there and stop sending remittances back home (ICGCA 2010). That is, some men refute their FD in families left behind in favour of new FD in countries of work.

Final remarks

Current research convincingly demonstrates that the issues of cross-border fatherhood practiced by men in Ukrainian transnational families are gaining ground. Despite that, available literature on families of Ukrainian migrants reflects a view on males as "non-gendered humans" (Hibbins/ Pease 2009, p. 5) and a "second sex" in social reproduction (Inhorn et al. 2009) who are not conceived as "reproductive in their own right" (Inhorn et al. 2014, p. 2). The challenges of "fathering from afar" (Parker 2008) by men who sustain their family relationships in a cross-border format and concurrent emotional, psychological, financial and matrimonial collisions they face in relationships with their financially independent *wives at distance,* remain a notable blank that requires immediate attention.

Meanwhile, the results of current study concur with the argument that "migration serves to reorient and question commonsensical and taken-for-granted gender roles and ideologies for both men and women, as they work to fit their daily routines into the new rules and priorities of maintaining a transnational livelihood" (Pribilsky 2004, p. 316). In these conditions, as Williams argues, "fatherhood is becoming increasingly individualized, as fathers are forced to confront change within the family and within society more broadly and as traditional models of fatherhood are progressively called into question by partners and by a range of social institutions including the media and government" (Williams 2008, p. 488). As this study showed, in these conditions the formation of a few cohorts of "new fathers" (Coltrane and Allan 1994) is being observed, performing their paternity roles across borders. In this article they are identified by the extent of responsibility in their relationships with family and children left behind at home. These may be highly responsible "pay-check fathers" who self-identify themselves as a "male bread-winner model" imperative in a patriarchal society. Requiring males to scarify their health, emotional and social wellbeing and sometimes even their lives for the sake of their dependents, it thus challenges both their PD and their FD. As shown in the results of the field research, not all men can withstand these exigencies, given that there are also not so responsible "re-emerging fathers" who first forfeit paternity status but then manage to restore it because of new economic possibilities enabled by migratory earnings. There are also failed "waning fathers" who lack skills of coping with family responsibilities spanning across great geographical distance and have their family ties gradually decline. These transformations in paternity roles make a tangible impact on FD of Ukrainian migrant men and are accompanied by paradigmatic changes in the institution of fatherhood *per se*.

At the same time it has been argued that the effect of "defamilization" (Lister 1997) resulted from dispersal in cross-border family relationships is even more deleterious for transnational fathers than for mothers. This challenges the construction of male migrants as independent and non-relational, but confirms the dominant framework of the gendered division of labour (Kilkey et al. 2014). The significance of FD for such men may diminish as a result of declining emotional connection with children left behind due to distance, but it can augment too due to the strengthening of paternal authority resulted from the growing economic status.

References

Anderson, Bridget: *Imagined Communities: Reflections on the Origin and Spread of Nationalism*. London: Verso, 1991.

Arditti, Joyce A./ Kennington, Mathis/ Grzywacz, Joseph G./ Jaramillo, Anna/ Isom, Scott/ Quandt, SaraA/ Arcury, Thomas A.: "Fathers in the Fields: Father Involvement Among Latino Migrant Farmworkers". *Journal of Comparative Family Studies*, 45 (4), 2015, pp. 537–557.

Boehm, Deborah A.: *Gender(ed) migrations: shifting gender subjectivities in a transnational Mexican community*. Working Paper 100. Comparative Immigration Studies, University of California, San Diego, 2004.

Busse, Erika: "The emotional costs of transnational fatherhood: Dilemmas of fathering from afar". Abstract of a paper for the Second ISA Forum of Sociology, August 1–4, 2012, Buenos Aires, Argentina, 2012. Retrieved 20.02.2016. https://isaconf.confex.com/isaconf/forum2012/webprogram/Paper20629.html.

Carlin, Jorgen/ Menjívar, Cecilia /Schmalzbauer, Leah: "Central Themes in the Study of Transnational Parenthood". *Journal of Ethnic and Migration Studies*, 38 (2), 2012, pp. 191–217.

Castles, Stephen/ Miller, Mark J.: *The Age of Migration*. 3-d edition. New York: Palgrave Macmillan, 2003.

Charsley, Katharine: "Unhappy husbands: masculinity and migration in transnational Pakistani. Marriages". *The Journal of the Royal Anthropological Institute*, 11, 2005, pp. 85–105.

Cheng, Yi: "Transnational Masculinities in Situ: Singaporean Husbands and their International Marriage Experiences". *Area*, 44 (1), 2012, pp. 76–82.

Connell, Raewyn W.: *Masculinities*. Berkeley: University of California Press, 1995.

Coltrane, Scott/ Allan, Kenneth: ""New" Fathers and Old Stereotypes: Representations of Masculinity in 1980s Television Advertising". *Masculinities*, 2 (4), 1994, pp. 43–66.

Datta, Kavita et al: "Men on the move: narratives of migration and work among low-paid migrant men in London". *Social & Cultural Geography*, 10 (8), 2009, pp. 853–873.

Doherty, William J./ Kouneski, Edward F. /Erickson, Marta F.: "Responsible fathering: An overview and conceptual framework". *Journal of Marriage & Family*, 60, 1998, pp. 277–292.

Donaldson, Mike/ Hibbins, Raymond/ Howson, Richard / Pease, Bob. (Eds.): *Migrant Men: Critical Studies of Masculinities and the Migration Experience*. New York, NY, Oxon, UK: Routledge, 2009.

Dreby, Joanna: *Divided by Borders: Mexican Migrants and Their Children*. Berkeley, CA: University of California Press, 2010.

Grassi, Marcia/ Vivet, Jeanne. *Fathering and Conjugality in Transnational Patchwork Families: the Angola/Portugal case*. Transnational Lives Network Working Paper Series, 5, 2014.

Greig, Alan/ Kimmel, Michael/ Lang, James: "Men, Masculinities & Development: Broadening our work towards gender equality". *Gender in Development Monograph Series*, 10, 2000.

Gutmann, Matthew: *The Meanings of Macho: Being a Man in Mexico City. Berkeley*: University of California Press, 1996.

Herbert, Joanna: "Masculinity and migration: Life stories of East African Asian men". In: Ryan Jouise /Webster Wenduy (eds.). *Gendering Migration: Masculinity, Femininity and Ethnicity in Post-War Britain*. Ashgate: Aldershot, 2008, pp. 189–203.

Hibbins, Raymond / Pease, Bob:"Men and Masculinities on the Move". In: Donaldson Mike/ Hibbins Raymond/ Howson Richard / Pease Bob (eds.): *Migrant Men. Critical Studies of Masculinities and the Migration Experience*. New York, NY, Oxon, UK: Routledge, 2009, pp. 1–20.

Hochschild, Arlie R.: *The Commercialization of Intimate Life: Notes from Home and Work*, Berkeley: University of California Press, 2003.

ICGCA. *International Crisis Group Central Asia: Migrants and the economic crisis*. Asia Report, 183, 2010.

Inhorn, Marcia C./ Tjørnhøj-Thomsen, Tine/ Goldberg, Helene / La Cour Mosegaard, Maruska: *Reconceiving the Second Sex: Men, Masculinity, and Reproduction*. New York, Oxford: Berghahn, 2009.

Inhorn, Marcia C./ Chavkin, Wendy/ Navarro, José-Alberto: "Introduction. Globalized Fatherhood. Emergent Forms and Possibilities in the New Millennium". In: Inhorn Marcia C./ Chavkin Wendy/ Navarro José-Alberto (eds.) *Globalized Fatherhood*. New York, Oxford: Berghahn, 2014, pp. 1–30.

IOM. *Migration in Ukraine. Facts and Figures*. Kyiv: International Organization for Migration, Mission in Ukraine, 2013.

Kilkey, Majella "Polish male migrants in London: The Circulation of Fatherly Care". In: Baldassar Loretta/ Merla Laura (eds.) *Transnational Families, migration and the circulation of care*. New York: Routledge, 2014, pp. 185–202.

Kilkey, Majella/ Plomien, Ania /Perrons, Diane: "Migrant Men's Fathering Narratives, Practices and Projects in National and Transnational Spaces: Recent Polish Male Migrants to London". *International Migration*, 52 (1), 2014, pp. 178–191.

Lam, Theodora/ Yeoh, Brenda S.A.: "Long-Distance Fathers, Left-Behind Fathers, and Returnee Fathers: Changing Fathering Practices in Indonesia and the Philippines". In: Inhorn Marcia C./ Chavkin Wendy/ Navarro José-Alberto (eds.) *Globalized Fatherhood*. New York, Oxford: Berghahn, 2014, pp. 12–128.

Landolt, Patricia/ Da, Wei W.: "The spatially ruptured practices of migrant families: a comparison of immigrants from El Salvador and the People's Republic of China". *Current Sociology*, 53(4), 2005, pp. 625–653.

Lister, Ruth: *Citizenship: Feminist Perspectives*, London: Macmillan, 1997.

Mansoor, Ali/ Quillin, Bryce (eds.) *Migration and Remittances: Eastern Europe and the Former Soviet Union*. Washington, DC: The World Bank, 2007.

Mummert, Gail: "Transnational Parenting in Mexican Migrants Communities: Redefining Fatherhood, Motherhood and Caregiving". *Paper presented at the conference "The Mexican International Family Strengths"*. Cuernavaca, Mexico, 2005. Retrieved 20.02.2016. www.ciesas.edu.mx/proyectos/mifs2005/.../03/gail_mummert.pdf

McIlwaine, Cathy J.: Coping practices among Colombian migrants in London. Department of Georgaphy, Queen Mary, University of London, 2005. Retrieved 20.02.2016. http://www.geog.qmul.ac.uk/staff/pdf/colombian.pdf

McKay, Steven C.: "Filipino sea men: constructing masculinities in an ethnic labour niche". *Journal of Ethnic and Migration Studies*", 33 (4), 2007, pp. 617–633.

Mychko, Svitlana: "U stani tymchasovoi smerti: Shukajuchy finansovogo poryatunku dlya svoih simej na zakordonnyh zarobitkah, ukrainci zdebil'shogo pryrikajut' jih na znyshecnnya" [In the state of temporal death: While looking for financial rescue for their families in the work abroad, Ukrainians most often doom them for destruction]. *Ukraina moloda [Young Ukraine]*, 88, 2011. Retrieved 20.02.2016. http://www.umoloda.kiev.ua/number/1886/188/67050/

Nobles, Jenna: "Parenting rom Abroad: Migration, Nonresident Father Involvement and Children's Education in Mexico". *Journal of Marriage and Family*, 73 (4), 2011, pp. 729–746.

Osella, Filippo /Osella, Carolina: "Migration, money and masculinity in Kerala". *The Journal of the Royal Anthropological Institute*, 6, 2000, pp. 117–133.

Parker, Dennis R.: *Fathering from Afar. Wisdom for men with children in multiple households*. Chapel Hill, NC: Amour of Light Publishing, 2008.

Parreñas, Rachel S.: "Long Distance Intimacy: Class, Gender and Intergenerational Relations Between Mothers and Children in Filipino Transnational Families". *Global Networks*, 5 (4), 2005, pp. 317–336.

Parreñas, Rachel S.: "Transnational Fathering: Gendered Conflicts, Distant Disciplining and Emotional Gaps". *Journal of Ethnic and Migration Studies*, 34 (7), 2008, pp. 1057–1072.

Pribilsky, Jason: "Aprendemos a convivir": conjugal relations, co-parenting, and family life among Ecuadorian transnational migrants in New York City and the Ecuadorian Andes". *Global Networks*, 4 (3), 2004, pp. 313–334.

Sayad, Abdelmalek: *La double absence. Des illusions de l'émigré aux souffrances de l'immigré*. Paris: Liber, 1999.

Schmalzbauer, Leah: "Searching for wages and mothering from afar: the case of Honduran transnational families". *Journal of Marriage and Family*, 66 (5), 2004, pp. 1317–31.

Schmalzbauer, Leah: *Striving and Surviving: A Daily Life Analysis of Honduran Transnational Families*. New York: Routledge, 2005.

Schmalzbauer, Leah: Temporary and transnational: gender and emotion in the lives of Mexican guest worker fathers. *Ethnic and Racial Studies*, 38 (2), 2015, pp. 211–226.

Smith, Adam/ Wasoff, Frann/ Jamieson, Lyn: *Solo Living Across the Adult Life Course,* CRFR Research Briefing 20, 2005. Retrieved 20.02.2016 from http://www.crfr.ac.uk/reports/rb20.pdf

Thornhill, Randy: "Rape in *Pinorfa* scorpionflies and a general rape hypothesis". *Animal behavior,* 28, 1980, pp. 52–59.

Thornhill, Randy/ Palmer, Craig T.: *A Natural History of Rape: A biological basis of sexual coercion.* Cambridge, MA: MIT Press, 2000.

Tolstokorova, Alissa: "Where Have All the Mothers Gone? The Gendered Effect of Labour Migration and Transnationalism on the Institution of Parenthood in Ukraine". *The Anthropology of East Europe Review,* 28 (1), 2010, pp. 184–214.

Tolstokorova, Alissa: "Ukrainian transnational family as a modernized model of family relationship: Panacea, poison of placebo?" *Sociology Journal,* 2, 2013a, pp. 40–62.

Tolstokorova, Alissa: "Transnational and Gender Paradigms in the Study of International Mobility". *Russian Sociologic Review,* 12 (2), 2013 b, pp. 98–121.

Tolstokorova, Alissa: "All the Daddies Are Welcome: Transformations of the institution of fatherhood in Ukrainian transnational family". *Journal of Sociology and Social Anthropology,* XVII, 3 (74), 2014, pp. 94–111.

Tolstokorova, Alissa: "Who Cares for Carers?: Feminization of Labor Migration from Ukraine and its Impact on Social Welfare". *International Issues & Slovak Foreign Policy Affairs,* XVIII (1), 2009, pp. 62–84.

Williams, Stephen: "What is Fatherhood?: Searching for a reflexive father". *Sociology,* 42 (3), 2008, pp. 487–502.

Worby, Paula A./ Organista, Kurt C.: "Alcohol use and problem drinking among Mexican and Central American im/migrant laborers: a review of the literature". *Hispanic Journal of Behavioral Sciences,* 29 (4), 2007, pp. 413–455.

Yeoh, Brenda/ Willis, Katie: "Constructing masculinities in transnational space: Singaporean men on the 'regional beat'". In: Phillip Crang / Dwyer Claire/ Jackson Peter (eds.) *Transnational Spaces.* London: Routledge, 2004, pp. 147–165.

Rafaela Hilario Pascoal, Adina Nicoleta Erica Schwartz

How Family and Emotional Ties Are Used as Coercive Instruments by the Exploiters on the Romanian Feminine Migration. The Study Case of Italy

Abstract *Romanian women are the second most victims of human trafficking in Italy. The present article intends to understand the 1) correlation between the phenomena: Children Left Behind and Human Trafficking; 2) The role of families in human trafficking; 3) Motherhood being used as a coercive instrument.*

Carrying a study on human trafficking is a very complex and difficult task, not only due to the privacy of the victims and ethical issues, but also due to the hidden nature of the crime. Therefore, the present article has combined three qualitative techniques: a) content analysis; b) participant observation; c) interviews. The content analysis technique has provided the author with new insights into the phenomenon through (I) literature analysis, (II) press analysis and (III) study cases. The participant methodology has been developed on the last two years in Italy. Finally the third technique was applied in Italy as well as in Romania in 2016 by the first author together with several associations: Dedalus; Intercultural mediator in Sicily; Save the children and the National Agency against Human Trafficking in Romania. Due to the nature of the phenomenon all interviews are anonymous and only pseudonyms are used.

General considerations about the Romanian migration to Italy

The Fall of Communism in 1989 was definitely the main emigration mark in Romania's history, pushing on the first year after the Fall an amount of 96,929 national citizens outside the national borders and up to 170,000 persons in the first three years. Despite that the first emigrants, around 75%, were mainly German, Hungarian and Jewish minorities, they were followed, on the following years, by Romanian nationals heading to Israel, Turkey, Italy, Hungary, Germany, US and Canada. However, with the lift of the Schengen Visa (2001–2006), the main destination country for Romanians started to be Italy, receiving 40% of all the labour migrants. According to a survey from the Centre for Urban and Regional Sociology, in 2005, 13 per cent of households had 1.5 members working abroad, which is approximately 1,400,000 labour migrants (CURS, 2008). Since then, it is estimated that the country has lost around 10 to 15% of its national population (IOM, 2008).

Despite the inexact statistics of the Romanian migrants in Italy, for example Caritas (2008) estimated a number of 555,997 Romanian migrants in 2007 (Caritas, 2007), while the Italian National Statistics Institute has reported a number of 342,200 Romanian migrants (ISTAT, 2016) in the same year. What is known is the fact that Italy in that year was on the 4th place of the countries that sent remittances back to Romania with an amount of 125,160 Dollars, after the UK, Spain and Hungary (Ratha & Shaw, 2007). The external financial support coming from migrants influences not only the Romanian families that have a relative abroad on an individual/family level, but sometimes also the entire community. For instance, according to Juverdeanu & Popescu (2008), the country lives an external inflation due to the remittances sent by the migrants, which raises the cost of life similar to many Italian cities, while the medium salary in Romania is 250/300 Euros.

One of the main job categories in which many Romanians are employed in Italy that the Italian sociologist Ambrosini (2011) has inserted in his four categories of migrant jobs, is the *badanti*. These people are employed in caring services, in the domestic sector, both in big urban areas and in rural areas. In fact, if we look into the statistics of main work sectors of migrants, we can identify the fact that working in private households is the third job category for Romanian migrants, accounting for 16.4 % of the total migrant community (CURS, 2008). The migration towards Italy is the main example of the massive female Romanian immigration that was originated from this work segmentation by the demand of emancipated Italian women who have entered into the labour market. In 2013, in Italy, the number of migrant women was higher than migrant men, being 52% of the migrant population (IDOS, 2014). Furthermore, despite the economic crisis which has affected Italy, recent data demonstrate that Italy is the OECD country with the highest concentration of migrant women, especially in the domestic sector (OECD, 2014). The Italian regions with the highest number of Romanian citizens are: Lazio (196.000), Rome (154.000), Torino (95.000) and Milan (39.000) (IDOS, 2013).

Despite the fact that, through the Romanian female migration, women have become the mainly or the only family's breadwinners, which is obviously a sign of roles redefinition and gender emancipation, this affirmation appears to be ambivalent, since discrimination and exclusion factors could also have been a cause to the feminine migration (Siurba, 2014). In addition, in order to maintain the role of women inside the domestic sphere, according to the patriarchal Italian society, the families started to request women with specific features. The women were requested to be alone, without any family ties or responsibilities in the destination country, in order to dedicate themselves to their occupation and be available seven days a week. This migration model, with no goal for integration of the immigrants, has led to precarious consequences both in the destination country, where the women were in a situation of invisibility and in the origin country, where many children were brought up without their mothers. In fact, through analysing the segregation context along with the migration policies before the lifting of the Schengen Visa, it is not difficult to understand how caring services were connected to domestic servitude and labour exploitation through human trafficking.

The exploitation in caring services and the domestic sector and deprivation of family

In 2005 a group of three Romanians and one Italian was accused of smuggling Romanian women into the Italian territory, in Palermo, and of committing violence against them. Allegedly, after the recruitment, the traffickers would have distributed the women to several Italian families. The group operated as a criminal network by transferring the women from Romania to Italy by bus, without any residence permit, with a fee of 500 Euros. While in the families, many of the women were subjected to working seven days a week with a salary of 400 to 500 Euros (Giornale di Sicilia, 2005). Furthermore, the members of the group have confiscated the women's passports which would only be given to them when the women paid their first salary to the group. In order to control their victims and avoid denouncing, the traffickers would also threaten their families back home, therefore the women would pay, without any complain.

Although Romanians are no longer in need of a residence permit in order to migrate to Italy, the domestic sector has certainly exposed many migrants to the private space exploitation. In fact, in order to understand the level of exploitation of migrant women in the domestic service, it is only needed to analyze the existing ads on different websites. It is visible that many ads ask for foreign women, which means no responsibilities attached, with a salary between 500 and 700 Euros, with food and accommodation included. The submission of living with the employers implies that the women have to obey the family's conditions, abdicating from their free hours after work. Furthermore, living at the employer's house deprives the women of their own personal space, where they can socialize and maintain relationships. Additionally, in the contract the employers usually define an amount of hours lower than the number of hours the women actually work, which is up to 16 hours a day, with a salary from 500 to 1000 Euros per month (Fondazione Leone Moressa 2011). Besides the intensive work and low salaries, some women live in total isolation in rural areas, as it has happened to P. that came to Italy, to a city close to where her mother was living, in order to work as a caregiver. Her only day off per week was Sunday, so when she requested the family of the elderly person she was assisting to be given a ride to the city, since the place she was living had difficult transportation to the city, she has received a negative answer. After one month and a half that she was not able to see her mother, she was able to go out of the house when her mother called the police to take her out (Sicily, 2015).

Beside the labour exploitation in terms of extensive working hours and low salary, some women working in the domestic service also suffer from sexual harassments and sexual exploitation. Despite the fact that these women are multiple exploited, the tendency of the local people is to stereotype them, by seeing them as the active agent in seduction, rather than the passive agent. Furthermore, according to the interviews led by Candia & Garreffa (2011) the women explicitly seduce the men in order to acquaint more money. During an interview with the association of Dedalus, a case of a 50-year-old Romanian woman was brought into the author's attention:

> *"I think that nowadays labour agencies, which are often represented by women who offer this work mediation services and pay to the agency (...) and in a way they choose the targeted persons, because they understand: "this one is easy to manipulate", and here in Italy they have a men or a person, which they sell the targeted persons to. So, I have seen a 50 years old woman, who has 5 children out of which the youngest one has an asthma problem. Her husband has contracted a debt and not being able to pay back for it, he had committed suicide. Therefore, her elder children were still in secondary school when she was the one who had to migrate. She went to such an agency which demanded from her, before the departure, an amount of 250 Euros and another amount of 250 Euros at her arrival. She was brought to here, in Naples, to a house of a woman in wheelchair. The men that received her at the station, during the night, came to her room and raped the woman all through the night and then closed her door with the keys. This woman, who did not speak Italian, was very afraid, as we can imagine, due to the violence that she was submitted to. When, on the next day, the person from the agency that was supposed to collect the other 250 Euros came she started to fight with the man that has raped the 50 years old victim. In this context, the victim has taken advantage of the situation in order to escape."*

This is the way in which the *"badante model"* perpetuates domestic exploitation, by raising the victims' vulnerability in a parallel economic vulnerability, by discriminating foreign women and by taking advantage of their "invisibility". Despite the privacy limitations and the lack of a line between work and personal life, for these women, living with their employers, is the best financial solution as they can save considerable amounts of money and send them back home to the families. From this perspective, Sen (1985) justifies the adaptation of limitation of freedom and violation of rights, due to the fact that women are used to the lack of fundamental rights, interiorizing that they are not worthy of such rights. As remarked by the researcher Sciurba (2013), the migration history of these women is marked by the "double absence", elaborated by Abdelmalek Sayad (1999), based on which, in the destination country they develop a survival mechanism, being submitted to a large deprivation of rights, keeping contact between them and their relatives in origin countries through technology while the employers are sleeping and by means of packages full of gifts (Sciurba, 2014). Furthermore, Sciurba in her book *La cura servile, la cura che serve* explains that the migration process of these women is based on the theory "The choice of Sophie" by Eva Kittay (2009), which can be attributed to the Directive 36/2011 which defines the concept of vulnerability as "no acceptable and adequate alternative", where the women have to decide between leaving their children, but being able to feed them and being able to raise them, but with no financial resources. Kittay (2009) affirms that the factors that push these women into this dilemma actually lie in the impossiblity of balancing economic and emotional values. In a way, we can say that these women live the migration project that they have designed for their lives, in order to achieve the goal of giving a better life to their children. Despite the fact that many women working in Italy in the domestic work live apart from their children, other women, in oder to maintain their children, have chosen to work in agriculture, exposing themselves to a higher violation of human rights.

Labour exploitation in agriculture and the use of children as coercive instruments

If the massive migration flow of Romanian migrants came to work in Italy on the domestic sector during the last decade, nowadays we can easily find Romanian women working in agriculture. The major concentration of agriculture camps are in the south of Italy and the most infamous place for labour and sexual exploitation is the one of Ragusa, in Sicily. The case was exposed in September 2014 by an article of Expresso (2015), even though it has emerged previously in an article written on the website Melting Pot (2016) by the researchers Palumbo and Sciurba (2014). According to the researchers, around 5000 women in Ragusa suffer from degrading and inhuman treatment while working in greenhouses, being exposed to chemical products and extreme temperatures during the summer and winter, with no safety working conditions. Besides the poor working conditions, the labourers are also hosted in decrepit buildings, isolated from the community, with no access to heating or toilets (Sciurba & Palumbo, 2015).

If in 2010 the Tunisian workers were paid 30 Euros a day, the Romanian women workforce now is paid only 18 to 19 Euros daily with up to 12 working hours a day, going up to 30 Euros for the sexual exploitation by the so-called "agriculture parties" (Galesi & Mangano, 2010). Western men look at migrant women who are exposed to an environment that is not her own, in an erotic way, in which their body becomes an object of new colonialism (Burgio, 2010). In fact, many migrant women, especially the ones that migrate alone are highly exposed to sexual harassment and have to live in a situation of multiple exploitation, not only in agriculture, but as we have seen before, also in the domestic service. For instance, in an interview in Galesi & Mangano (2010):

"This phenomenon is not only verified on the fields, but also for the caregivers that often are obliged to give themselves to the person that they serve."

The sexual exploitation of these women derives from a condition of vulnerability based on the total isolation from populated areas. Their employers profit from their isolation and dependence to have access to water or have their children taken to school. These woman and men live in a very vast and isolated area, where the greenhouses are distant from one another and the workers, in order to have access to the city, have to go hitch hiking on the highway. In order to avoid the profiting of the employers from the isolated women as well as of locals that establish a 15 Euros price to take the workers to populated areas, the NGO Proxima has arranged a free transportation which goes through the fields of Ragusa and gives access to mobility to the people living on the fields. However, as mentioned before, many of these women prefer to live in precarious conditions, so that they can have access to their family space, which would be impossible in the caring services (Sciurba, 2015).

If the persons living on the fields are at least able to live with their children, on the other side, the condition of being a migrant mother can increase the vulnerability of migrant women, since children can be used by the employers as a coercive instrument to maintain the women as sexual slaves (Beck & Beck-Gernsheim, 2011).

The reported story of Luana, a 40 years old Romanian woman, (Sciurba & Palumbo, 2014) who testimonies the coercion and violence submitted by these women in order to guarantee life conditions for their children. Luana has two children, whom the employer would take to school every day. The school is situated far from the farm that they are living. The employer's "favour" was in exchange of sexual services, which Luana was obliged to accept in order to maintain her job, accommodation and normal life for her children. Luana and her sister were the only women living on the farm. Even when Luana has submitted herself to be the subject of the sexual requests of her exploiter, she started to refuse these requests when he said that he wanted also to have sexual intercourses with her sister. Luana realized that this exploiter's coercion did not have any limit, when Luana refused to have sex with her exploiter, he stopped giving water to her and to her children. This was when Luana tried to seek external help. Luana was not aware of the labour exploitation she was a victim of (she has not seen herself as a victim of human trafficking), even when she would receive only 100 euros a week. She only felt abused because of the sexual exploitation she was subjected to. Thus, Luana only escaped from her exploiter, when she had realized that the life conditions of her children were not safe anymore.

If analyzing the existing data regarding abortions in Ragusa (with the mention of the fact that the data illustrate only the legal abortions the women have carried out by a qualified doctor – the real number of abortions and miscarriages is unknown), it is impossible not to link the high number of abortions to the sexual exploitation of women living on the farms. A number of eight abortions take place per week at the Vittoria Hospital, of which six are performed on Romanian women. Furthermore, these women tend to be accompanied by men, the majority of whom are Italians who are introduced by the women as friends (Sciurba & Palumbo, 2015). Despite that in this particular case the situation of abortions is evident, the general situation of sexual exploitation is characterized usually by a less visible phenomenon. However, the lack of traceable abortions carried out by the victims of sexual exploitation does not indicate the inexistence of it. Italian NGO workers who are active in assisting victims of human trafficking have reported, based on the statements of the victims, that when a woman realizes that she is pregnant, she tends to go to the hospital to have the abortion, but if the woman only realizes after the three-month period during which abortions can be performed legally, then there are cases in which she tends to return to Romania, where usually the network knows a doctor who performs abortions after the legal period. In Romania the issue of abortions is still a sensitive topic.

During the Communist period 1967–1989, abortions, at request, were prohibited in order to increase the level of nativity. In this time span, based on the Decree 770, only women older than 45, women who have already had four children, women who had critical medical conditions, women whose foetuses were malformed, or women who were pregnant due to rape or incest, were allowed to have abortions "by request". Also, for the purpose of increasing nativity contraceptives were no longer sold. By the end of the communist regime, all the women working in state institutions were obliged to undergo gynaecological exams in order to ensure the fact that they are not pregnant and that they have a healthy reproductive system. This situation has led to a very high number of unwanted children that were put into orphanages and to a high number of illegally produced abortions causing the death of thousands of women. The illegal abortions were performed by doctors, by persons who "know how to do it" or even by the women themselves. Women found different rudimental ways to produce abortions throughout these years. These "homemade" abortion methods still exist today and many of the victims who were sexually exploited in Italy or in other countries have performed or know how to perform abortions as the information was transmitted from one woman to another and from one generation to another. Today, the Romanian legislation allows abortions at request till the 14th week (two weeks more than the Italian legislation). This can be extended to 24 weeks for medical reasons and even more than that if necessary. The legislation in the field of abortions, however, is also very controversial and makes allowance for exploitation. The Romanian Criminal Code, in Art. 201 (7) states the fact that the abortion procedure undertaken by a pregnant women to herself in order to lead to the loss of the child is not punished by the criminal law. The same article, which does not state a time span in which such an abortion procedure can be conducted at home without legal consequences, leaves the stage open for such procedures.

Motherhood used as a coercive instrument in sexual exploitation

If, in the cases of labour exploitation, where the exploiters tend to be single individuals, the family members of the victims can be used as a coercive instrument; in the cases of sexual exploitation, this has become a common threat from the criminal organizations to control the victims. Furthermore, in sexual exploitation, the traffickers, who in the majority of the cases are the victims' co-nationals, are well known to the victims' family. As we can see on this case reported by a cultural mediator:

> "The case of two sisters, one of which was brought to Italy by the traffickers who abused her position of vulnerability. They were in deep poverty, adding to the fact that their mother had cancer. Furthermore, the recruiter was a female friend who has used her trust, as well as the trust of the woman's family to take the woman to Italy. The traffickers brought the older sister to Italy for sexual exploitation, while the other one remained in Romania with her niece who was 12 years old (the daughter of her sister, who was brought to Italy). In order to maintain the woman in sexual exploitation, the trafficker, who was considered by her family a nice man, menaced the woman that he would bring her sister and her daughter to Italy as well. Therefore, the woman tried to escape from her traffickers, but instead of asking help from the local authorities, she asked for help from her friends who were also connected to the traffickers. After the failed attempt to escape, the traffickers immediately brought her younger sister to Italy to work as a prostitute, too. The woman realized that the traffickers' threat were real

and became very worried, especially because she knew that her daughter who was 12 years old was probably the next one to be involved in the sexual exploitation ring. At this point, the woman decided to escape from the exploitation situation along with her sister and was able to denounce the exploiters to the police."

As we can see in the case, for traffickers that are the victims' co-national, which is real for 95% of the cases, it is really easy to use the family, especially the most vulnerable members such as a younger sister/brother, the victim's children or even the victim's parents in order to coerce the girls into sexual exploitation.

In Romania, according to a study conducted by the National Agency Against Trafficking in Human Beings, 757 victims were identified in 2014. 66% of them - 499 victims - were sexually exploited, registering a 14% increase in the number of sexually exploited victims in comparison with 2013. Out of these, 192 victims were exploited in private homes, 139 victims on the streets and 77 victims in clubs. Of the total number of identified victims, 74% were female and 26% were male, 62% of the victims were adults and 38% were children. The same study also shows that 55% of the victims were exploited in other countries, namely: Italy – 93 victims, Germany – 75 victims, Spain – 45 victims, Germany – 32 victims, Czech Republic – 29 victims, Ireland – 29 victims, Portugal – 22 victims, Greece – 19 victims, UK – 18 victims. With these numbers of identified victims, Romania is rated as the first source country in the European Union. As indicated by the study, the majority of the victims are sexually exploited in various destination countries, mostly in the Western - Europe.

Criminological studies show that one can identify the following categories of sexually exploited victims: victims who were deceived in the recruitment stage or were recruited by force (i.e. Kidnapping) and were then forced into prostitution; victims to whom, in the recruitment stage, were proposed erotic activities (ex. strip-tease) but not sexual acts; victims who received proposals of sexual acts but ended up in sexual exploitation. Among these three categories, the last one raises most controversies as it is still difficult both on the prosecution phase and in the court (especially in countries where prostitution is not legalized) to proof the fact that a person who had agreed to enter prostitution (and commit a criminal act or a con-travention) did not sign up for being a victim of exploitation – therefore it is not the case in which "business went bad" but it is a genuine case of human trafficking.

According to the statistics of the National Agency Against Human Trafficking for 2015, the above mentioned facts are even more evident than in 2014. Out of the 880 identified (not the real number) victims from Romania, 294 victims were aged between 18–25, 50 of them are from Timis county, situating Timis county on the first place as source counties of Romania, 117 of the victims being married, mostly coming from rural areas, with a low level of education – 129 have only completed elementary school, 393 have completed secondary school but there were also 9 identified victims who have completed university studies which shows the fact that not just the lack of education, the lack of information can also create a position of vulnerability. When analyzing the statistics with regards to the method of recruitment and the relationship with the recruiter, the Agency has identified the followings: 733 persons were recruited face to face and only 35 persons through internet, job agencies and other methods. In the case of 479 persons the recruiter was a friend, in the case of 51 persons the recruiter was a neighbour, in the case of 42 persons the recruiter was the boyfriend or husband, in 38 cases the recruiter was the former pimp and in 33 cases the recruiter was a relative. With regards to the method of exploitation, out of the identified victims, 498 were sexually exploited, 180 victims have suffered labour exploitation, 69 victims were forced into begging and the rest through other forms of exploitation. The main destination country was again Italy, with 111 identified victims. During the exploitation period, 305 victims have reported physical abuse, 276 emotional abuses, 43 sexual abuses, 37 stealing of travel documents and identification papers, 13 isolation, 8 lack of water and food. With regards to their free movement, 237 persons were allowed to go only in some places, 139 persons were allowed to go out only when accompanied by other members of the criminal group and 54 persons were absolutely not allowed to move out of the residence.

Based on the above mentioned statistics, it is evident that in most cases the trafficker has connections with the family members and that the threat made is imminent. Furthermore, even if the traffickers have not a direct connection to the victim's family, they often approach the families in order to gain their trust or to get to know their habits. This method was used by a group of traffickers that observed the victim's family with the aim of gathering as many information as possible about them, which could be used in order to threaten the victim and in order to demonstrate credibility. When the victim A.P. was kidnapped, she was asked to be obedient, otherwise they would harm her little brother, who in about 10 minutes time was about to cross the street for swimming lessons. When the girl saw that the traffickers knew so many details about her family, she did everything asked only to protect them. Even if during the trafficking period she had the chance to run away and ask for the support from the police, because of the psychological cage, she and so many others had, she never did so. Eventually she was rescued by the police based on police intelligence and investigations.

The trust usually gained by the victims' families is also usually connected to the lover boy method, which is used in most of the cases regarding involving

Romanians who are sexually exploited victims. When it regards to sexual exploitation in Italy, the majority of the victims are not aware of their own exploitation, since their "fake boyfriends" use an emotional manipulative method in order to maintain them on the streets in order to work for them. In Palermo, during the operation *Caffè Export* the Police have arrested six people for pimping and sexual exploitation and each of the traffickers was the boyfriend of the girls who were exploited. During the wiretappings of their cell-phones, it was possible to understand that their boyfriends have threatened not only the victims with frequent violence, but also their children in Romania and their family relatives. In order to maintain the girls in the emotional attachment, their boyfriends let the victims take a percentage of the money for themselves or for their families. The emotional manipulation that usually involves financial manipulation is not only regarding the girls, but also their families.

This is the case of a Romanian girl who was trapped into sexual exploitation in Italy by her boyfriend, who was from her hometown. During the wiretapping, the police understood that the boyfriend was sending money to his mother back in Romania, but during the telephone conversation, his mother referred that his girlfriend's mother had complained that she did not send any money. Thus, in order to maintain the figure of a good son-in-law, the boy told his mother to give 50 Euros to his girlfriend's mother. With this gesture, not only the exploiter is able to avoid further complaining of the mother-in-law about the financial aid of the daughter, but he also manages to pass the image that he is the perfect son-in-law, by granting her 50 Euros, from her daughter's exploitation.

The perfection of coercive instruments used by Romanian traffickers has increased, especially after the entrance of Romania into the European Union. Romanian women, who are now regarded as European Union citizens, hic est., are supposedly more aware of their rights. However, due to the lover boy method, some exploiters are able to use severe forms violence on their victims and still keep the victims there based on the manipulation characteristic to the Stockholm Syndrome. For instance, the case of F., a Romanian woman that had four children, two of them living in foster families and other two living with her family in Romania. She was all day long on the street, exerting prostitution. Despite the money that she earned on the streets, she would give all the money to her husband and was obliged to search for food in litter containers.

"*When she was pregnant, she was on the street until the last day of her pregnancy when her membranes ruptured. On that day she called her husband, who passed by and got angry with her, since she was not able to work and did not gain any money. Her husband went away and she was carried to the hospital, where she had her child born. When she got back home, which was an abandoned building near the train station, her husband took her child to another woman living in their community. The deprivation of her child has led the woman to ask for help. Therefore, we were able to put her and her child in a shelter, yet she was not able to leave her husband, so she abandoned the child at the shelter and went back to her abuser".*

Motherhood, as mentioned before in labour exploitation, can increase the level of the victim's vulnerability, especially when the children are exposed to the traffickers and they are an object of threat. This is the case of "Francesca", a 19 years old Romanian, mother of a child of a few months who was enslaved by a group of co-national. The group that brought the girl from Romania by bus and promised her a work in agriculture has obligated her into prostitution and has paid her an amount of 50 Euros a day. In order to control the girl, the group has drugged her and has also threatened her to kill her family and her son.

Despite the fact that the traffickers used the victims' children to maintain them sexually exploited, not always these menaces are perceived by the authorities and governmental institutions. There are also cases in which the authorities see sexual exploitation as a simple case of prostitution and the abandonment of their children as lack of interest and affection. In the case of M., she was recruited by a friend whom she knew from school. The recruiter informed her that being deaf she could go to Italy, where she could receive some disability funding. Since her husband had recently passed away and she had three children, the proposal seemed to be the best option. She decided to go to Italy with her young one-year-old boy, where she was received by an Italian family that arranged her to marry an Italian man, who was also deaf. After some months, M. was coerced into indoor prostitution by the family that has received her and her husband. Since the child was considered a problem to the traffickers, the family went to social services to report that M. had no more interest in being with her son. Practically, during a year, the social assistant that was taking care of the case did not grant access to M. to expose her truth regarding to her son. M. was deaf and only knew Romanian sign language, so she needed at least a person who was able to understand basic sign language or, since she was able to write in Romanian, she also could need the assistance of a Romanian culture mediator. However, after a year, a social assistant who was aware of human trafficking indicators has called a Romanian mediator in order to listen to M. After one session with M. the Romanian culture mediator perceived that M. was trafficked and that she was desperate to be with her child. At this point, the exploitation situation was proved and M. went to a shelter with her son.

As it can be seen from the case, M. was in a very vulnerable situation, not only regarding the vulnerability of being a mother, but also because of the total isolation she had when living in Sicily, since she was constrained to indoor prostitution and also to her deaf condition. However, despite the visible trafficking indicators, the lack of awareness on human trafficking can turn governmental institutions into raising the victim's condition of vulnerability. This was the case of M. who, in the destination country only knew her exploiters, the family and her husband who also used coercive instruments as well as menaces to not denounce her exploitative situation. However, despite that motherhood can be an increased vulnerability, in this case and it was also verified in other trafficking cases, especially regarding to Nigerian woman, being a mother it is sometimes the only strength that a victim finds way to escape from her exploiter.

This is the case of Marina, a twenty three years old Romanian in Italy, she worked in an apartment near the train station in Naples from 8 am until 10 pm. The owner of the apartment gained 1000 Euros per week, from which 50% was going to the recruiter of the girl that had seduced the girl in Romania. During a police check, her documents were seized, which led her into knowing a policeman that spoke to her about a shelter. When she went to the shelter, she discovered that she was pregnant. Despite the fact that she wanted to abort, the people from the shelter led her into embrace her pregnancy and this has given her the strength to exit from her exploiter.

Even though many women live submitted to their boyfriend- exploiters, some of the victims are able to see the exploitation and denounce their exploiters. This is the case of 21 years old, Romanian girl that has come to Italy to work as a waitress, yet her boyfriend has forced her into sexual exploitation. The submission to her trafficker's violence, as well as the obligation to live with 3 Euros a day with high lack of hygiene, has pushed the girl into denouncing her exploiter to the police.

Even though the families are often unaware of the traffickers' intentions and they present themselves as friends of their daughters, it also has been proved that some family members are also engaged in human trafficking cases for sexual exploitation. In some cases, the families are not directly involved, but as presented by volunteer workers in Palermo, many of the girls that are on the streets show the photos of the houses that they are building in Romania for all their families. Furthermore, even if the girls swear that their families don't know about what they do in Italy, it is impossible not to notice how the families depend on the money sent to their families. Cases in which the family was directly involved in sexual exploitation have also been reported in Italy. Recently, a case has been identified, in which an uncle promised to help a twenty years old Romanian girl with cognition disabilities in learning Italian and getting a job in Italy. However, her uncle's behaviour changed some days after her arrival, when he locked the girl in and began to sexually abuse her under the effect of drugs. His goal was to initiate the girl and force her into prostitution under threats of death. He also started to take photos of the girl in order to attract clients online. In this case, the exploiter has profited from the family ties and from the relationships with the girl's parents to receive their consent in taking their daughter who, despite of not being a minor, was in a strong position of vulnerability, due to her cognitive disability. The parents, being unaware of their daughter's exploitation, contacted the police since they could not make contact with their daughter.

Though in this case the family member was the uncle, other cases have been verified in which one or both of the parents were involved in their daughter's exploitation. This was a case that happened in Catania, where a group of Romanians held hostage a group of 6 girls with threats and violence, one of the traffickers is the father of one of the victims. The 20 years old victim was allured by her own father into coming to Italy to have a better life. Yet, the father along with the uncle and another couple of co-national had the group of victims for sexual exploitation. The girl during the day was locked in the apartment and had also her document confiscated in order not to leave the house.

The so called Children Left Behind or White Orphans

Despite that the phenomenon of Children Left Behind and Human Trafficking in Romania have been analysed separately, it is impossible for the authors to go through an article on the Romanian Human Trafficking and the role of the families without correlating both phenomena. Therefore, the present chapter will analyse the link between both phenomena regarding, in the first part, how the Children Left Behind can be more exposed to the risk of human trafficking and, in the second part, the Children Left Behind by the trafficked mothers.

Despite that attention has been given to the issue only recently, especially due to the number of children's suicides, around 40 from 2008 to 2014, the phenomenon has emerged along with the migration flow after the Fall of Communist. The increase of the number of suicides has put into surface an already existing problem, which has led to a high stigmatization of the women, usually perceived as the ones causing the rupture of the family and not the breadwinners. This stigmatization that according to the researcher Viorela Ducu (2011), is verified at a micro level, inside the community and at a macro level as a spread negative perception, especially regarding the information passed on the media. However, many of the women who migrated were already totally responsible for their children, since they were divorced, separated or with husbands who were totally irresponsible for their children (Bonizzoni, 2009).

In 2008, entities in Romania have perceived a high flow of immigration, due to the worldwide economic crisis, which again was pushing the parents to leave their children with relatives of friends. This emergent problem has led Associations and Private Entities into doing lobby in order that the government could take measures regarding this vulnerable category. In this sense, the government has come with the modification of the law 104–108 of Law 272/2004, in which the parents, when planning to go abroad, should report to the municipality a specific tutor for their children. In spite of the existent law, many of the parents are afraid of reporting a guardian for their children since the lack of information leads them into thinking that the state might take their child. In fact, the data regarding to the situation of the children Left Behind remarks a huge discrepancy between the child that were reported by their parents (85.194) and the identified children by the schools (212.352) in 2015. The implementation of such a law has permitted to also act on the impact of the parents' departure, such as early drop out from school, deviance behaviour and emotional problems. A study from Soros Foundation on the Children Left Behind (2007) has identified that children that have one of their parents abroad are more exposed to abuse alcohol and cigarettes and have a lower performance in the school. Furthermore, the children have a higher risk to feel depressed and abandoned. If these children have been identified as more exposed to higher risks, shouldn't human trafficking consider one of them? And if yes, is the government focusing on this?

Recent data from the National Romanian Agency Anti Trafficking has identi-fied that a percentage of human trafficking victims in Romania are minors that did not grow up with their parents. According to a functionary from the Agency, the lack of a parenting model, as well as of affection exposes the victims, girls, especially with the so-called lover boy method, where traffickers manipulate emo-tionally their victims into sexual exploitation. The reported last year victims, who were also boys, fall easily in love for the first person that shows them affection. In fact, when the victims' profiles are reviewed, the majority of the victims share the lack of family stability with families that are separated or parents that went abroad and absence of a parent model that can supply the defences to their children. However, looking into the phenomenon in a deeper way, we understand that the children's problems are not only regarding to the migration of their mothers, but also to other factors that were present even before the migration such as economic and emotional poverty, alcoholism and families with fragile bonds. For instance, according to a representative of the ANITP, most of the victims we were also children Left Behind, had also other problems in their families. Therefore, should we consider that the parent's migration is one of the causes to the increase of the children's vulnerability or the fact that the victims are Children Left Behind is just a result of a disruptive family background? In other cases, unstable families or families that are apart are some of the major causes pushing victims into the traffickers through the lover boy method. Furthermore, the lack of affection as well as the absence of a parent figure in the children's life, leads to a perpetration of disruptive motherhood into the next generation.

The phenomenon of Children Left Behind does not only expose these children to a higher risk of being trafficked, but it also affects how these children perceive motherhood. For instance, according to the last year victims' profile, some of the trafficked victims that fell into the lover boy method were minors that were already mothers. According to a representative of the ANITP, the victims perform motherhood according to their experience with their parents, which allow them to leave their children with other people in order to be with their trafficker. Furthermore, many of these premature mothers that come from broken families often cannot rely in any family to leave their children with, so they leave them directly to the social services. However, after the exploitation period the mothers try to get the children back from the social services, but due to their background, they don't understand that this requires some efforts, such as getting a job or arranging a proper house for the children. Furthermore, in some cases, the children went to foster families and the mothers, instead of understanding the social services' measures to regain the guardianship of the children, they tend to blame the foster families for taking the children from them. However, this situation is prejudicial for the children, since they cannot go back to their mothers, but they also cannot be adopted, since the mothers are against their adoption.

In some cases, victims also leave their children with their relatives, in this case we have two types of mothers that are able to communicate with their children and send money often, especially through Facebook and Skype, and the mothers who don't communicate with their children during the exploitation period. On the second case, which is usually connected with the mothers that deliver their children to social services before the departure, the mothers tend not to seek to contact their children or to send money. While on the first case, for the victims their children are the main motif that they are going abroad, even if while exploited by their boyfriends. According to a social operator in Sicily, many of the girls often show their children's photos to the street Unit, they tell how they miss them and that often the children complain about their mothers' absence. Their goal is to achieve a certain amount, buy the house for them and their family and then return to Romania. However, even if they can communicate everyday with their children and family, they know that they their freedom is limited and many are not able to go every year to see their children.

The absence of their mothers, which the children see once or twice a year, is usually substituted by the receiving of gifts that unleashes a sense of affection that is satisfied through the material consumerism (Sciurba, 2014). Recently one Romanian mother that is working in Sicily was able to take her son to Italy for a small period, so in order to compensate the child for the absence period, the mother was giving what he asked, which was mainly sweets, instead of what he needs for a nutritional balance. Consequently, the child had to go to the hospital, since he was suffering from ketonamia. This case remarks how damaging it can be to the children the self-guiltiness of these mothers that try to supplement the lack of presence and physical affection with material goods.

Conclusion

The unstable economy after the Fall of Communism in Romania has led many of its citizens into a situation of vulnerability, in which the only alternative was to migrate. However, Economists warn that the inflation of the economy of the origin country caused by the migrants' remittances in Romania can no longer absorb the return of migrants into their origin country. The high migration flows of Romanian citizens to Italy have permitted the flourishing of criminal networks, by their co-national, as well as by the employers who are Italians to exploit the vulnerable position of these women. The big link between Romania and Italy, especially due to established communities, allows traffickers to use the familiar bonds to coerce and control their victims and consequently avoid any kind of de-nounce. Furthermore, the segmentation of work and exploitation that is reserved to migrant women in Italy that frequently does not allow the reunification of the family has also increased their vulnerability by leading them into a more isolated situation. The migration process of these women have led three generations into the exposion to human trafficking 1) the mothers that have endured hard work and exploitative conditions in their destination countries 2) the second generation that has grown up with the absence of a parent figure and lack of affection 3) The children of the children left behind who are perpetuating an absent motherhood role with a major impact on the future generations.

References

Ambrosini, Maurizio: *La sociologia delle migrazioni*, Molino, 2011.

Beck, Ulrich/ Beck-Gernsheim, Elisabeth: *Lebensformen in globalen Zeitalter*, Berlin, Surkamp, 2011.

Bonizzoni, Paola: *Famiglie Globali. Le frontiere della maternità*, Torino, Utet, 2009.

Burgio, Giuseppe: "La commercializzazione dell'Intimità. Esperienze di genere nella migrazione delle donne". *Esilio/Asilio. Donne migrati e richiedenti asilo in Sicilia.* Studio e storie, 2012.

Candia, Giuliana/Gareffa, Franca: *Migrazioni, tratta e sfruttamento sessuale in Sicilia e Calabria,* FrancAngeli, 2011.

Ducu, Viorela: *Strategies of Transnational Motherhood: The Case of Romanian Women.* (Babes-Bolyai University - Cluj-Napoca,). (Doctoral thesis), 2011, Retrieved 09/07/2016

http://doctorat.ubbcluj.ro/sustinerea_publica/rezumate/2011/sociologie/FOamte_Ducu_Viorla_En.pdf

Fondazione Leone Moressa: *Quali badanti per quali famiglie, Studi e Ricerche sull'economia dell'immigrazione,* Venezia, Retrieved 09/07/2016

(WWW.fondazioneleonemoressa.org), 2014

Galesi, Laura/Mangano, Antonello: *Voi Li chiamate clandestini,* Manifestolibri, 2010.

Giaretta, Rita: *Slaves No More: Casa Ruth, the Courage of a Community 2009.*

Juverdeanu, Lacramiora / Popescu, Cristian: "Areremittances important for the Romanian economy?". *Annals of the University of Oradean Economic Sciences,* 2, pp. 392–396, 2008.

Kittay, Esther: (trad. it. Brunella Casalini), "Il danno morale del lavoro di cura migrante: per un diritto globale alla Cura". *Società Italiana di Filosofia Politica,* 2009.

Sayad, Abdelmalek: *La double absence. Des illusions de l'emigré aux souffrances de l'immigré,* Paris Seuil. 1999.

Sciurba, Alessandra: *Effetto serra. Le donne rumene nelle champagne del ragusano, in L'altro diritto. Centro di documentazione su carcere, devianza e marginalità,* 2013. (www.altrodiritto.unifi.it)

Sciurba, Alessandra: *La cura servile, La cura che serve,* Editore Pacini, Quaderni de L'altro Diritto, 2014.

Sciurba, Alessandra: "Storie di donne migranti in Sicilia. Razzismi, scelte confinate e inclusioni differenziali nel mercato del lavoro". In Marco Pirrone (Eds). *Mitologia dell'Integrazione in Sicilia. Questioni teoriche e casi empirici di Marco Pirrone,* Mimesis Edizione, 2015, pp. 153–186.

Sciurba, Alessandra / Palumbo, Letizia: *Vulnerability to Forced Labour and Trafficking: The case of Romanian women in the agricultural sector in Sicily,* DOI: 10.14197, 2015.

Sen, Amartya, "Gender Inequality and Theories of Justice". In Nussbaum Martha C. / Glover Jonathan (eds.) *Culture and Development,* Oxford: Oxford Clarendon Press, 1985.

Ratha, Dilip/Shaw, William: *Bilateral Estimates of Migrants Stocks Database, South-South Migration and Remittances*, World Bank, Washington, D.C. 2007.

Torre, Andreea: *"Migrazioni femminili verso l'Italia: tre collettività a confronto*, in the project" Lavoro di cura e internationalizzazione del welfare, CeSPI, 2008.

Newspaper articles

Adnkronos, 13/07/2016, Retrieved 09/07/2016

http://www.adnkronos.com/fatti/cronaca/2016/07/13/costretta-prostituirsi-ru-bava-all-aguzzino-per-poter-mangiare-arresto-torino_dxOz7wh2EwFpuYRb-SYrVAK.html?refresh_ce

Catania meridionews 13/06/2013, Retrieved 09/07/2016

http://catania.meridionews.it/articolo/9320/prostituzione-4-arresti-in-zona-stazione-non-ce-ununica-regia-dello-sfruttamento/

Giornale di Sicilia, 29th December 2005, Retrieved 09/07/2016

Il resto del Carlino 20/07/2016 http://www.ilrestodelcarlino.it/ancona/cronaca/arrestato-zio-orco-seviziata-1.2361513

Il tirreno 2011/ 06/26 http://iltirreno.gelocal.it/grosseto/cronaca/2011/06/26/news/riduzione-in-schiavitu-da-ieri-e-in-carcere-il-quarto-rumeno-1.2557352

Melting Pot, 16/04/2016, Retrieved 09/07/2016

http://www.meltingpot.org/Le-donne-delle-serre.html#.VzNY4Y9OJdg

New York Times 14/02/2016, Retrieved 09/07/2016

http://www.nytimes.com/2009/02/15/world/europe/15romania.html_r=0

Rai News 13/05/2014, Retrieved 09/07/2016

http://www.khalidchaouki.it/khalidchaouki/?p=12145

Espresso, Violentate nel silenzio dei campi a Ragusa. Il nuovo orrore delle schiave romene, 2014/09/15, Retrieved 09/07/2016.

http://espresso.repubblica.it/inchieste/2014/09/15/news/violentate-nel-silenzio-dei-campi-a-ragusa-il-nuovo-orrore-delle-schiave-rumene-1.180119

Reports

Caritas, *Dossier Caritas/Migrantes* 2007, Retrieved 09/07/2016.

http://www.dossierimmigrazione.it/schede/pres2007--scheda.pdf

Centro Studi e Ricerche IDOS, *L'integrazione dei romeni in Italia tra famiglia e lavoro, 2013*

Center for Urban and Regional *Sociology survey 2005, the assessment of the occupational status abroad is based on multiple-response questions in Lăzăroiu, Sebastian and Monica Alexandru Who is Coming after Who is Leaving? Labour Migration in the Context of Romania's Accession to the EU. Country Report. International Organization for Migration, Geneva, 2008*

Center for Urban and Regional Sociology survey 2005 in Lăzăroiu, Sebastian and Monica Alexandru, *Who is Coming after Who is Leaving? Labour Migration in the Context of Romania's Accession to the EU.* Country Report. International Organization for Migration, Geneva. (2008)

IOM: *Migration in Romania: A Country Profile*, 2008.

ISTAT: Annual Report 2016. Retrieved 09/07/2016 http://www.demo.istat.it/str2006/

OECD, *Is Migration really increasing?*, in Migration Policy Debates, 2014.

Anca Raluca Aștilean

The Issue of Emancipation in the Case of Romanian Migrant Women[1]

Abstract *Women's emancipation and gender empowerment are much discussed issues, but there is very little information on this dimension in the case of Romanian migrant women. This paper inquires on how a feministic approach can influence the lives of migrant women, how it changes their perspectives and how it helps or hinders their migration project.*

Theoretical context

The sociologist Pierrette Hondagneu-Sotelo (2000) has examined migration trends and the direct link women's emancipation has to them, the conclusion being that currently we may find ourselves in the third wave of feminist migration: the focus has shifted from the second stage where the women were drifting from countries not in conformity with their view of life, "trying to escape a traditional and backwards country" (Hondagneu - Sotelo, 2000). The third wave is breaking the barriers that focus only on women and adds the comparison between male and female. The reason why this shift is necessary is, in her opinion, not to put more emphasis on women, since this would distance them too much from the main research.

However, Rhacel Salazar Parrenas (2009) argues that there is no problem in discussing only the women in transnational migration studies, furthermore the comparison between men and women when studying migration from a feminist perspective needs to be stopped. "As a feminist, I believe that we can still study gender even by solely focusing on women. This is because when we speak about women's gendered experiences, we are always already referring to men [...] men if invisible are still omnipresent when we examine women's gendered experiences." (Rhacel Salazar Parrenas 2009, pp. 3–6)

Amidst the theories that are international and focused on the US, Asia or Europe, we must incorporate the viewpoint of Eastern-European women, who have had different experiences and who come from different backgrounds (Robila

---

1 This work was supported by a grant of the Romanian National Authority for Scientific Research and Innovation, CNCS – UEFISCDI, project number PN-II-RU-TE-2014-4-2087.

2010). In this particular case, the Romanian women who migrated after the fall of Communism in 1989 have a particular view on women's emancipation and they relate it differently to the migration process. Cezara Crisan (2012) reveals the interesting fact that before the Communist period, the majority of migrants were men, whereas after the fall of the dictatorship women started leaving the country, and she quotes Hughes (2000) for the main reason of the change: "Women began to emigrate as a strategy for survival because of increased unemployment in the new economy." (Donna Hughes 2002, p. 8)

There is also the question of the shifting of the gender roles in the very traditional Romanian society, especially when it comes to the children of the family that encompass a migrant (Robila, 2004). Therefore, after the first shift in roles within the transnational family (because of the high demand of care jobs – done mostly if not exclusively by women), the role of the mother had to be replaced by someone else, and in the majority of cases the function of motherhood was transferred to the grandmother; however, the father resisted the motherhood status (Crisan 2012). We can examine the shift in gender empowerment through the prism of the income and the person providing it (Zentgraf 2002).

As Crisan (2012) argues, the demand for caregivers from Romania opened up a new market, where women dominated. Hence they became the prime breadwinners, experiencing an economic empowerment, resulting also in greater gender equality. This renegotiation of gender roles within the household did not only have beneficial aspects, but as a side effect, women also found themselves alone, their husbands having abandoned them for another woman, or their relationship having ended in divorce (Keough 2016).

In some cases, the welfare system works for the liberation of women, in others against it, but either way, maternity leave plays an important role in migration (Rhacel Salazar Parrenas, 2009). In the case of Western countries, either maternity leave is generous, which is the case in Scandinavian countries where women are able to feel a double fulfillment by combining two major aspects in a woman's life (motherhood and work), or families are in the financial position to employ domestic workers – usually migrants – to take care of their children. The conclusion to be drawn from these examples is that women's migration and women's emancipation are intricately related, and that this is a dynamic field, where the role of the woman keeps changing depending not only on the type of migration (temporary or permanent), but also on the employers (Shamim and al, 2014). Employers (receiving mothers or families) find themselves in a gender switching role play with a new significant other – in ideal cases, they are equal, but in addition, they also provide money. The role of the mother is substituted rarely by the patriarchal figure of the family, but mostly by migrants – including Romanian women who take care of their child. The paradox arises when the migrant who takes care of someone else's child is leaving her own children at home, and all this for a more secure economical position in the Romanian society (Constable, 2014).

Of course there exists the reverse situation where the migrant woman abandons her family and starts a new life with another man abroad, leaving her life partner and her children in the country and substituting her presence by financial methods. (Misra 2004) This can also be considered a form of women's emancipation, who were once oppressed by a prude culture, now finding themselves in a different environment where the values are unlike anything they have ever lived, and where they meet someone who makes them feel like a woman and not only like a spouse or a mother, fulfilling the needs they never thought they had. They undergo a "sexual revolution" of some sort, which would have never happened without the migrant status. (Espin, 1999)

In May 2016, Eurostat provided a gender migration chart where the number of Romanian male migrant workers slightly surpassed the number of female workers, but what we can draw from this is that even though the number of men is slightly bigger, the number of women has grown since 1990 when the majority of migrant workers were men. This is a step towards equality, but as a form of gender empowerment, we also need discuss the level of pay (Barbera 2012). "Migrant women, in a sense, face a double battle; first to migrate and integrate as foreign-born people in their host country, and then to overcome the gender bias in the labor market" (Rubin 2008, p. 48)

Romanian migrant women usually work as caregivers, meaning that they don't always work under a stable contract with a fair pay, and that their salary is often unregulated, which deepens the gender wage gap. "This segregation of job opportunities into male and female areas also captures the roots of gendered disadvantage on the labor market [...]; the rewards are also quite different. Women's jobs, particularly those in caring professions [...] are consistently undervalued." (Brodolini 2011, p. 22)

In cases of the migration of more skilled Romanian workers, we can encounter a trend of equalizing the power levels and lowering the gender gap. Therefore we can speak about the higher level of education as a measure of raising the bar and empowering Romanian migrant women to a higher paycheck and a higher status in the society they live in, an issue to be dealt with in further research.

The problem of caring professions is the reverse of the medal; in this situation, even if the Romanian female migrant worker is skilled, she actually needs to downgrade in order to get the job. We can see this trend especially with Romanian migrant nurses who end up working as a caregiver in a clinic or a hospital in the foreign country.

Methodological aspects

The paper is based on the qualitative field research unfolded by the research team in three Romanian communes (Prundul Bârgăului, Dorna Arini, Jidoștița) three towns/cities (Cluj Napoca, Turda, Drobeta Turnu Severin) as well as a capital (London) and the city of Mons in Belgium. More than 40 Romanian women – migrant workers and members of transnational families – have been interviewed. The data were thematically analyzed. To ensure privacy, pseudonyms were employed.

Discussion

Breadwinners

As Crisan (2012) has argued, the concept of gender empowerment in the case of Eastern European women (this paper is solely focused on the Romanian women) is directly linked to the idea of providing for the family, being the primary provider for the family and obtaining a different status at home. In order to have a better grasp of this idea in power shifting – which is of course a trait of the gender empowerment in the workplace – we present the discussion with Corina and her husband, Laszlo.

They both live in London and she works as a kindergarten teacher now. When she first got to London, as the majority of Romanian migrant women, she worked in the caregiving domain, taking care of an old lady. Her husband worked in construction, but when the economic crisis hit, he found himself out of jobs and had a problem providing for his family. During the interview it was obvious that she was a powerful and independent woman. The interview was a couple interview with her and her husband, however, she was doing most of the talking. Furthermore, she was very proud that she was the one who brought her husband to London, supporting him financially in the beginning:

> „I was the one that brought him (her husband) here. I was living there for a couple of months already and he started growing restless, asking me – when am I coming. And I said, wait until I gather some more money (…) I spoke to everyone but it's very hard to find a job for a man, I couldn't find anything for him." (Corina)

As she put it, it was very difficult to find jobs for men, especially for ones who knew little of the language spoken in the country. However, jobs as caregivers for Romanian woman are abundant. This means that the power shifting is palpable at this level and even the common migrant could feel it. This can be registered as a negative trend in the market where the women have taken over the jobs while the men cannot do the caregiving jobs, even though it would not pose a problem. One could address here the issue of discrimination against migrant men at the workplace, where they are not considered to be able to do the work of a woman in a so called „women's field". (Mahler 2001)

Viorela Ducu (2013) discusses the issue of gender empowerment in Romanian migrants through constituting a level of professional equality as well as a financial one with their spouse, and this is exactly what Corina is doing with her husband. She was the one who found the job for him and she was the one that brought him to the UK. This emancipation of the migrant woman happened of course after years of migration by the men only, with very few women leaving the country for work. After the transition period of the '90s, the tables have turned in the favor of the women.

The question of money arose in the couple, and one can observe that Corina's husband not only was uncomfortable with the discussion about money, but also somewhat tried to save his manhood by proving his capability when we spoke about how he got to London.

„*I had a thousand pounds saved...not even that much*" (Corina)

„*It's not about the money, I also had money!*" (Laszlo)

„*No, it's not that, you had some but what I want to say is that... everything I've saved up I used, I found a rent where he could stay, I would still live with the old lady I was taking care of for a period of time, but something... I remember he found some sort of work to do through an agency... something like masonry.*" (Corina)

Throughout the interview, there was an emphasis on how much she was the one helping her husband succeed. She admitted he had a very good job before the crisis that allowed him to provide for the family even better than her, but then he found himself less and less employed, increasingly relying on his wife's salary. This is the switch in gender power that we spoke about earlier, where because of the economic crisis migrant men (mostly working in construction) found themselves without jobs, since suddenly no one was building anymore. (Kofman 1999)

"*We made some money*" (Laszlo)

"*Yeah the crisis had not struck yet and in 2010, 2011 you were still doing great, we've managed to buy an apartment [...] but after that your company didn't have a lot of work, and you barely got any jobs*" (Laszlo)

They needed to adapt, but Laszlo was unable to make the step towards a different profession, leaving Corina to be the one in charge of the family finances. This changed the way he was seeing himself and chipped his pride. Throughout the discussion on the matter of money during the economic crisis, he stayed very quiet. This means that his wife was now the main decision maker, although before, in Romania, it used to be him.

Diana is also living in London, married to Vlad. She is currently unemployed and fully supported by her husband. She is trying to take back her professional identity, after having worked for many years in a field not in accordance with her studies, first as a cleaner and then doing different administrative jobs. She has finished her PhD in anthropology, but does not work in the field. Her unemployment for several months pushed her towards an internship which she quit because of increasing financial problems. Her husband is a designer in a company and he is working in the field he graduated. Her frustrations about her workplace were affecting her daily life, so she quit in an effort to reclaim her identity, not as a spouse supported financially by her husband but as a self-established woman.

We could observe through the interview that her husband was the one making the decisions and, not being in a bargaining position, she followed his word. Their imminent move from the UK was viewed very differently by them: while Diana would rather come back to Romania, where she was professionally thriving, Vlad would rather move his family to a more northern country. The problem of the weather was also brought up, aggravating Diana's desire to return to her home country and not go to a country which had an even worse weather than London.

> "I'm starting to think of a move, together with her of course, to a more northern country, it would be our last move, for her it will be difficult because she's all about the sunshine, she likes it when the temperature is above 23 degrees Celsius, for me, this temperature is too much." (Vlad)

> "It's strictly in your favor! I suffer! (Referring to the move and the climate) (Diana)

The responsibility of childcare

Virginia has one of the most difficult but also beautiful stories a migrant woman can have: at first, she raised her two children alone in Ireland, then she moved to the UK, she was married in Romania but dreamed of something more and so she had pushed the border before the fall of communism and was supposed to go to jail for betraying the country and leaving to Serbia. She returned to Romania to take her son, a fierce mother looking for a different economic status and a better life for both of them. She met her husband Alex and they have been happily married for more than a decade. She recalled her journey without bitterness, but emphasizing how difficult it was for her to migrate, and to do this migration with a baby.

"Ever since he was little... after I came back after the Serbia experience (when she illegally crossed the border to work in a Serbian factory, this happened under the Communist regime), I asked my (now ex-) husband if he wanted to leave the country with me and our son. He said no, so I left. I left the country with my son. [...] I took my 1-year-and-8-monthold son and I left! I was all alone in raising him. At first we lived in Germany and then moved to the Netherlands, where we stayed for a long time and only after that we moved to Ireland and then to England. I had a good, well-paid job and I went to a lot of classes to deepen the knowledge that I already had and I managed, somehow with my son we managed, I had to educate myself." (Virginia)

In a patriarchal society like Romania, a man could traditionally leave his children at home with his wife without being condemned by the society, even for instilling the feeling of abandonment in the child. He is also not expected to take the child with him when he does the resettlement process. Things are quite different in the case of mothers: they are deemed unfit mothers if they leave the child with (in most cases) the grandmothers, or even with the father, even if their goal is the same as the men's – to provide for her family better and to give the child a better life. This is a gender bias that would rather downgrade the woman to the trivial label of a "bad mother", while praising "good father" for working hard to provide for the family (Pratt and Rosner 2012). The woman is judged regardless of the position she holds: either she is at home and her husband is working and providing for the family, in which case she will be called lazy for not working as much as he does; or judged as abandoning her child and being a bad mother for leaving that child in the country, even, and I cannot stress this enough, the child is left at home with his father (Keough 2016).

The separation for periods of time due to migration between mother and child can have different effects in different families. As said, society can judge the person, but on another level the mother-child relationship undergoes a shift of focus. If we take the example of Iulia and Adriana, we can clearly see that, through some abandonment issues that the girl had and a somewhat tough love and the image of a cynical mother, they managed to change their relationship. This comes as a response to the situation of being left at home with her father, raising the question how it would have been if he were the one to migrate. Even though this relationship is still changing, you can feel the grudge that Iulia feels for her mother leaving:

"At home remained Iulia with my husband, my mother, and my mother in law" (Adriana)

"Yes, everyone is living at home, in Cluj, except for my mother who lives here (London)" (Iulia)

"(Addressing her mother) And how did I react to your leaving? I don't remember." (Iulia)

"You were still at a very difficult age, a teenager [...] it was not like 'oh my mother is leaving me', I mean it was a bit but not so strong" (Adriana)

We cannot necessarily say that their relationship is better or worse now, just that interestingly enough, it underwent a change of roles, in which the mother became more like a friend and the mother figure were transferred to the grandmother.

> *"We speak on Skype at least once a week, and I have a special option on my card, meaning that I have 150 international minutes and I call her. But it's mostly WhatsApp that we use."* (Iulia)

WhatsApp is a text messaging platform which is online and free. The medium through which their relationship is developed (meaning less on Skype and the majority of the conversation on WhatsApp) is a sign that their relationship has shifted, usually on this platform you speak with your girlfriends and do not text your parents. To add to this particular case, the daughter was smoking in front of the mother, something that children are usually shy to do in front of their parents, as well as the habits how they interact with each other, going out for a coffee even when her mother comes back to Romania. They even discuss all of their relationship problems.

Professional emancipation

As Viorela Ducu (2013) states, there is more than one type of gender empowerment in the case of Romanian migrant women, and there is an increasing trend of which Adriana is an eloquent example of. Ducu (2013) speaks about the professional emancipation of women: they are already career-wise established at home, but through this move they expect a professional emancipation, either by perfecting themselves in their field or by studying for a new occupation.

Interestingly enough, Adriana did not leave the country to have an economically better life, given that her husband is quite stable financially: she wanted to prove herself she could be independent and empower herself through the career she was pursuing. The main reason that led her into living and working in the UK was her thirst to become more in life and in her career than she already was.

> *"My husband was very sympathetic when I first told him I was going to leave; it was not about money [...] It was all about my career, if I can call that, it's quite a big world, to try here (London) what I was doing back home, in Cluj. And I said maybe I could try, because working in the University Hospitals brought me into contact with different doctors, who already migrated and then returned, and I discussed with them and this is what gave me the strength to leave and try to do something."* (Adriana)

> *"I don't know how much longer I want to stay but I know I still have a lot of things I need to accomplish, for now I feel like I want to stay. I have many more things to do, now I like this and afterwards I want to move to something I've been thinking about, I truly hope it goes well for me."* (Adriana)

We can clearly see that her migration was about establishing herself even more in her career, her relationship with her husband or her child was moved to the second place after her work goals. Interestingly enough though, she only left the country when the child was more or less grownup, at an age when she had other preoccupations. Adriana challenged herself and succeeded, realizing that it was never too late: in some cases it is through the migration process that you have the chance to obtain the career you've dreamt of.

This is also the case of Adela, who moved to be with her boyfriend (now her husband) in Leuven, Belgium. She left a good job as a kindergarten teacher in a private kindergarten in Romania. Until she mastered the language – Flemish – she got hired as a baby-sitter, and she moved to Brussels with her husband to work as an English kindergarten teacher only after a while. Hers is a success story, being able to move from a good position that she liked to something different in another country, but managing to get an equal status as she previously had in Romania.

Somehow Adela knew all along she was not meant to live and work in Romania and that she wanted more.

"I don't think I've ever seen myself as getting older in Romania [...] having a career in Romania. And this is something that I've wanted ever since I was a child. I used to say constantly that I wanted to live in a country where they speak English." (Adela)

Love and home

We can say that there is a desire to thrive for some of the interviewed women, not only in the country but also in the diaspora. Nevertheless, in many cases the situation is that these women were also looking for love to feel fully satisfied. Although Adriana's story was different, since she felt like she did enough sacrifices for the family and that she deserved to build a career in London, this was just a particular case.

Violeta, for example, has a very powerful story: she got married, her husband lived in Mons, Belgium as a contractor and she had a job that she was not ready to leave in Braşov, Romania. What happened was, she got pregnant and decided while she was expecting that she would stay in Braşov, not moving to Belgium with her husband. It was a decision that she took when thinking about the future and about what could happen to her and she wanted to be cautious and get the maternity leave from the state. She spent her entire pregnancy alone, without her husband, but it was a period that, as she said, was not as difficult as one might think.

"I was pregnant and it was a bit complicated, my husband came over every three weeks, but, you know, I worked a lot so I didn't quite feel it (n.r. the distance) and he came two days before I gave birth." (Violeta)

When it comes to the issue of employment, she stands firmly and doesn't want to accept a different type of job, downgrading her work situation. She is thinking of getting a job in Belgium, and she doesn't want to go back to Romania even if there she can re-take her position in her firm. Violeta is currently on maternity leave from Romania and has another baby daughter born in Belgium.

> *"I would like to start working again, I am a design engineer in the auto domain for the agriculture industry, so not the regular automobiles you see daily on the streets. So I worked in this domain for a company in Brașov, where I was technically hired. [...] I still have one more year of maternity leave and afterwards I will see what I can do job-wise, if I can find something or if I cannot find anything. I don't want to stay at home! You limit yourself from what you can do! You only have one life, I want to work. It's something completely different!"* (Violeta)

Nonetheless, having a career is not necessarily important for every woman. We may find women who would rather focus on family life, and that is an aspect which we should take into consideration: that some women fight for the right to stay at home as mothers and that they have a different reference to success. For example, we have the case of Maria, married to a Belgian citizen and living in Belgium for more than 25 years, who doesn't know what she will do in the future but for now is very happy with her life.

> *"How do I see myself? I don't really know what is it that I want from life or where I want to get in life. Or even to say that in ten years I want to do this...no I really do not know! I've had this discussion even yesterday in the group I'm activating in, the young moms, and we've said that we didn't have time to sit and to make plans for our future [...] because I was already pregnant when I was nineteen years old. Me, personally, I didn't have time to think of the career. I had a child, a man, a house, I was fulfilled, I didn't think of having a career,"* (Maria)

Mihaela was another woman who chose to be home mom. Her husband was assigned to Belgium, she followed him, leaving Romania and getting pregnant after a month abroad. She doesn't have any regrets for not working because she takes care of her (now two) children. She had previously worked in Romania but she quitted her job to follow her husband. So again we find the recurrent theme of moving abroad for the partner: after the economic migration, this is a very widely encountered reason to move abroad.

> *"I said I would quit my job and I would go and live with him and I would eventually find some work [...] so I left Romania with the sense of what could happen, in the worst case I would go back home. [...] I got pregnant in the first month I got to Belgium to I didn't even want to look for a job. Why? Because I wanted my child to adapt to the new life (she migrated with the older son) and he was about to start the first grade and I wanted to teach him more things, I couldn't leave him alone, where could I leave him? I wanted to find him some extracurricular activities, something that would help him, but I couldn't find anything, because he was not registered in the system. In that period I didn't know much, how to do*

everything, I didn't know...so we both stayed wandering through Brussels. It was a beautiful period and I said to myself that I was only going to stay at home until September, but by that time I was pregnant it was already visible and I didn't look for a job. My daughter was born after a while and I stayed with her." (Mihaela)

Things got more complicated when the boy started school and Mihaela found herself without a job, with a husband working full time and with not much to do to make time pass.

"First of all, my status was completely different from what it was in Romania, I had never stayed at home without a work, so I took advantage of the new life.[...] I used to ride bikes with my son all day long, it was like an adventure, like vacation. [...] Afterwards, school started. It was different, very different. I used to ask myself what we were doing here, what I was doing here. I used to sit on top of the bed, I remember even now it was the first day we arrived, and we had just come from the airport. And this was at weekend and Friday was my last day at work and I was thinking: "Oh my God, what have I done?". Home was perfect; we didn't have any problems, so yeah I realized everything had changed. I cannot say the difference is good or bad, it is just different." (Mihaela)

The beauty of women's emancipation is to constantly advance, but in its own pace, so activists fight for equal pay and equal rights with men in the workplace, for example. But if one feels that the best job for one is at home taking care of one's family – provided the option to have a career, or a family, or both is there in the first place – one's actions are more empowered and autonomous.

Conclusions

We can start by saying that migration changes more than a woman's life, it changes her perspective, how she is viewing her status in the new society, what she had to go through to get there and most of all, to what extent they are fulfilled. Most of the women whose stories you read above feel accomplished, either through the nature of their work, either by following the loved ones (usually their husband) to a new place, either by having children.

The perfect example is that of Virginia, the one who has apparently struggled the most, since she had to bring her child along, much like Mihaela, and even though they have different life stories, they would have been judged by the community for leaving their children at home. Mihaela's husband was already in Mons when she was pregnant back at home, but this did not constitute a major issue, the fact that she was strong was left without recognition, and that is what you would expect in a patriarchal society like Romania.

Adriana left her family to be better at her job, she studied, she worked very hard and she managed to succeed and to become something more than when she was at home. She felt unsatisfied and unaccomplished and so she left the country; her child was already a teenager when she left. However this changed both her and her daughter's life completely, as well as the very nature of their relationship changed: the daughter did not recognize her authority as a mother figure; rather their new relationship was that of a friend.

Romania is still very much a patriarchal society, hence women are challenged not only to prove to themselves that they can have a better life, but also to prove everyone wrong. They go abroad, mostly as caregivers, and they succeed in their life, and all the perspective is changed, not only economically but also from their own vision of the world. Some migrant women have left the country at a rather advanced age, some of them have never really existed as autonomous individuals, but they have now expanded their lives and there would be no choice of going back to the previous situation – this is why some of the women divorce after many years of marriage and after leaving the country.

We are a very long way from reaching gender equality, and even though Romania has been a member of the European Union for some time and is supposed to be aligned with European norms and regulations, we can see that the situation is still stuck somewhere: in a culture of male control. The general level of social consciousness has not advanced enough to have a clear understanding of women's migration, which is still deeply misunderstood. (Piper 2006)

References

Barbera, Maria C.: "Intersectional-Gender and the Locationality of Women in Transit", Feminism and Migration, *International Perspectives on Migration* Vol. 1, 2012, pp. 17–31.

Constable, Nicole: *Born out of Place: Migrant Mothers and the Politics of International Labor*, University of California Press, California 2014.

European Women and Feminist Practices after 1989, Feminism and Migration. Cross cultural engagements, Springer, New York 2012.

Ducu, Viorela: "Transnational Mothers from Romania", *Romanian Journal of Population Studies*, 1/2014, pp. 117–142.

Ducu, Viorela: *Strategii ale maternității transnaționale: cazul femeilor din România*, Argonaut Publishing, Cluj-Napoca, 2013.

Espin, Olivia: *Women Crossing Boundaries: A Psychology of Immigration and Transformations of Sexuality*, Routledge, New York 1999.

Tazeen/ Naveeda Qaseem: "Labor Migration and Gender Empowerment: A Case Study of Housemaids", Canadian Center of Science and Education, Asian

Social Science; 10, (3), 2014, Retrieved 29.08.2016 http://dx.doi.org/10.5539/ass.v10n3p232.

Fondazione G. Brodolini: "Equal pay for equal work and work of equal value. Responding to unequal pay", paper presented in the conference *Equality between Women and Men*" European Commission, Brussels 19–20 September 2011.

Hondagneu-Sotelo, Pierrette: *Gendered Transitions: Mexican Experiences of Migration*, University of California Press, Berkeley 1994.

Hughes, Donna M.: "The Natasha Trade – The Transnational Shadow Market of Trafficking in Women", *Journal of International Affairs*, Spring 2000.

Keough, Leila J., *Gender and Migration between Moldova and Istanbul*, Indiana University Press, 2016.

Kofman, Eleonore: "Female 'Birds of Passage' a Decade Later: Gender and Immigration in the European Union", *International Migration Review 33*, no. 2 (1999), pp. 269–299.

Mahler, Sarah J/ Pessar, Patricia.: "Gendered Geographies of Power: Analyzing Gender Across Transnational Spaces", *Identities: Global Studies in Culture and Power*, 2001, pp. 441–459.

Misra, Joya, et al.: "The Globalization of Carework: Immigration, Economic Restructuring, and the World-System", *American Sociological Association*. San Francisco 2004.

Pratt, Geraldine ed. /Rosner, Victoria ed.: *The intimate Feminism in our time*, Columbia University Press, New York 2012.

Piper, Nicola: "Gendering the Politics of Migration." *International Migration Review 40*, no. 1 (2006), pp. 133–164.

Robila, Mihaela, et al.: *Families in Eastern Europe*, Elsevier, New York 2004.

Robila, Mihaela: *Eastern European Immigrant Families*, Routledge, New York 2010.

Rubin, Jennifer, et al: *Migrant Women in the European Labor Force, Current Situation and Future Prospects*, Rand Corporation, Cambridge 2008.

Salazar Parrenas, Rhacel: "Inserting Feminism in Transnational Migration Studies", Migrace Online, 22.05.2009, Retrieved 29.08.2016

http://migraceonline.cz/en/inserting-feminism-in-transnational-migration-studies

Zentgraf, Kristine M.: "Immigration and Women's Empowerment", Gender and Society 16 (5), October 2002, pp. 625–646.

Armela Xhaho, Erka Çaro

Gendered Work-Family Balance in Migration: Albanian Migrants in Greece[1]

Abstract *This paper explores how Albanian migrant working parents in Greece experience the pressure to balance their family life and work demands. Relying on 42 migrant biographies, we look particularly at the gendered negotiation of work and family conflicts, and how particularly our transnational mothers expand the concept of "hegemonic mothering".*

Introduction

A growing body of research indicates that combining work and family is a challenge, and more so for many migrant working parents. Often times the challenges arise from the demands imposed by assumptions regarding the traditional gender roles of men and women embedded into the traditional kinship structures (Xhaho, 2013). Migrating parents and to a greater extent, migrating mothers, experience more pressure, often due to their migrant status, ethnicity, and lack of support from social and family networks in the host society (Doyle and Timonen, 2010). Another important element that has made the balances shakier is the economic crisis, which has altered the gender roles at home as well as in the labor market (Caro and Lillie, 2016). The economic crisis, result of neoliberalism (Becker and Jäger, 2012) and trigger of austerity policies, has deregulated the dynamics of labour market (Castles et al. 2014). The austerity policies challenged the employment regimes and hit mostly the male (migrants) dominated sectors of economy, decreasing the demand for migrant male labour while migrant women, working mainly in the service sector such as cleaning and domestic were not affected (ibid). The new labour segregation based on gender became the trade mark of the new global division of labour (ibid: 257).

This paper focuses on Albanian migrants, working mainly in the domestic (women) and construction (men) sector in Greece. Our aim is to explore the gendered care-giving practices among Albanian migrant families working and living in Greece as being affected by structural changes such as the economic

---

1   This research is conducted part of Regional Research Promotion Programe Project Grant, "Industrial Citizenship and Migration from Western Balkans: Case studies of Albania and Kosovo migration towards Greece, Germany and Switzerland". Principle Investigator Erka Caro. Website of the project: www.icm-westernbalkans.com.

crisis. More specifically, we aim to understand the variety of ways in which individual behaviors are transformed and influenced to comply with changing labor markets and family relations and to understand how migrant's gender and ethnicity become the factor to keep/find the job, how work-life balance is sustained in times of austerity. This research will contribute to the ongoing discourse on gendered outcomes of austerity in the globalized labour market as being affected by the economic crises.

In the first part of this paper, we highlight the wide body of research on the work–life conflicts for working mothers and fathers in migration. Secondly, we thematically analyze our biographies based on the main assumptions: mapping out the differences in terms of sacrifices, negotiations and dilemmas of working parents in balancing work and family. Then, we explore the gendered parenthood care perpetuated by notions of masculine and feminine roles. Finally, we discuss how the Greek economic crises provided migrant mothers with additional burdens by making them even more vulnerable and ideas about transnational motherhood. At the end we draw our main conclusions on work life balance and care in migration.

Albanian migrants in the Greek labor market

Greece, as typical Southern European migration and gender regime show high presence of underground economy, lower occupational mobility for migrant workers and stronger segregation for women migrant (Fullin, 2015; Caro and Lillie, 2016). There are around half a million Albanians living and working in Greece, by far the biggest migrant group in the country. This migration flow is often in form of irregular labour migration, which is typically followed by participation in unregulated labour markets.

Albanian's migration strategies are focused around exploiting family relationships, and strategically moving for the good of the family unit. This is partly because they are not covered by the EU-rights of individual freedom of movement; families relationships help establish ground for residence permits and help migrants to find jobs, whether or not they have official status. Female migration from Albania is for this reason often discussed in terms of a family migration oriented discourses, with women regarded as followers and not as primary migrants (Caro et al., 2012), facts that might shape their experiences in the destination countries as much as does austerity (King et al, 2011).

Albanian migrants engaged in the Greek labor market are characterised by strong ethnic, territorial and gender segmentation (Karamessini, 2010). Moreover, the labour market in Greece shows strong traditional gender roles and family relations: full time working men, with women bearing the burden of domestic work and care (Lazaridis, 2000; Kamburi, 2013). Partly as a result of their over-representation in the underground economy, migrant workers experience low occupational mobility, with female migrants suffering particularly (Fullin, 2015). For migrant women the easiest to access opportunities are usually in the domestic sector while men are concentrated mainly in the construction industry.

Gendered impact of the crisis in South Europe and Greece

Crisis and austerity hit mostly the male (migrants) dominated sectors of economy, such as manufacturing and construction, decreasing the demand for male labor while migrant women did increasingly enter the labor force mainly in the (less impacted) service sector (Castles et al, 2014; Pearson and Sweetman, 2010). Labor market segmentation scholars have argued that social cleavages such as ethnic and gender divides are used to create labor hierarchies (Caro et al, 2015, Bonacich, 1972; Peck 1996). The economic crises promoted more flexible and cheap labour especially in the service sector that in countries such as Greece is often facilitated by undeclared labour and underground economy (Maroukis et al, 2011).

In South Europe, the combination of the economic crisis, austerity measures, immigration, neoliberalism and deregulation of the labor market is prompting radical change in the welfare system and traditional model of family care with increased needs for care provision with private means as the state delegates care provision at the family level (Maroukis et al, 2011). The region is at the receiving end of the flow of increasingly feminized migration and it has also increasingly involved women migrant in the labor market. The female migrants are cheap and flexible while the new immigrant-based care model is comparable to that of the USA, where immigrants have long been an alternative of services and care (Bettio et al, 2006). In particular, Mediterranean countries like Greece and Italy form a distinctive cluster where the management of domestic work and care is outsourced almost entirely to the family (Scrinzi, 2009). In Greece, as well as Italy, the recent patterns of the economic crises and of migration now alter the traditional organi-zation of the domestic and service sector (Bettio et al, 2006).

The welfare system in the southern Europe often at times includes (not officially) the gendered social relations and migration which both have facilitated caregiving and services (Bettio et al, 2006). According to Morreli (2004) the labor participation of migrants after the World War Two did allow native women to stay at home while nowadays the increased participation of migrants (especially women migrant) in the labor market is allowing native women to enter the labor market. Indeed the female migration has grown to be crucial to the redefinition of the welfare states through transforming the labor market (Scrinzi, 2009). Many European countries have implemented severe austerity measures offering less adequate services for children and elderly and have reduced allowances for families relaying mainly on a vulnerary system of care, unpaid work of women at home and underground labor market (Kofman et al, 2008).

According to several studies, the employment of women (although often in the informal economy under precarious conditions) produces elements of agency and possible empowerment (see Caro et al., 2012; Ghosh 2009; Athinas et al, 2013; Caro and Lillie, 2016). However the emerging pan European labour market context, is based on gender segregation and ethnic-based discrimination-structures which has become crucial and effective during the current crisis as a way to producing low-paid and precarious work-force putting working migrant (women and men) in more vulnerable conditions than before (Athinas et al, 2013).

In the context of austerity measures and labour market flexibilization with an increase of the so-called atypical forms of employment (fixed term employment), the benefits of migration vary depending on migrant's motivations, expectations, background characteristics, social and legal status and the presence or otherwise of their partner in the household.

Data, methods and limitations

The results discussed in this paper are drawn from 42 biographic interviews carried out between 2015–2016. The in-depth interviews were conducted using biographical-oriented interview method, following Adam Mrozowicki's (2011) three-phase interview structure. The majority of the biographic interviews, 31 were conducted in the destination country, Greece and 11 interviews in Albania with return migrants. The starting points for the recruitment of participants were several personal contacts, followed by the use of the snowball sampling technique through different points of entry.

Table 1: Migrant Information

Education	Years in Migration	Sector	Gender	Age groups	Return migrants
6 have primary school	18 have migrated from 91 to 94	14 domestic worker	19 men	20-30-5 migrants	3 returnees in the period 2000–2004
5 have secondary school	19 during 97–99 t	2 construction	23 females	31-40-12	4 in the period 2005–2009

Education	Years in Migration	Sector	Gender	Age groups	Return migrants
6 have university	5 during 2001–2004	3 hairdresser		41-50-11	4 other returnees in the period 2010–2014
24 have vocational educational training		2 work in agriculture		51-60-9	
1 have post-graduation		1 graphic designer		61-70-1	
		1 specialist in factory,			
		2 waiters			
		1 deliver,			
		2 entrepreneur			
		1 seller			
		1 cooker,			
		1 baby sitter			
		10 unemployed			

Duration of the interviews varied from 35 minutes to four hours after which they were transcribed and analysed through MAXQDA-data analysis program. The interviews were transcribed preserving the original language, then the transcriptions were analysed using the qualitative data software MAXQDA. The first cycle of coding involved identifying both inductive and deductive codes. In the second cycle, the codes were grouped together in code families. A thick description was made based on the code families and their relationships, which resulted in the identification of three overarching themes of the migration process outlined in the finding section.

Theoretical consideration: Work-family balance among migrant parents

While there is an overwhelming body of literature that confirms the pressure that working parents experience in trying to balance the demands of a family and work (Tammelin, 2009; Tézli & Gauthier, 2009; Poduval and Poduval, 2009; Craig and Sawrikar, 2009) research on family migration tend to emphasize the effect of migration in reconciliation of work and family conflicts (Masselot, 2011; Ackers and Stalford, 2007; Doyle and Timonen, 2010). According to Greenhaus and Beutell (1985) work-family conflict, occurs when demands in one domain are incompatible with expectations in the other domain. Working parents vary at different degrees in integrating work-family balance. Since they have limited amount of time and energy to divide among various roles that they have (Powell and Greenhaus, 2010), conflicts might emerge especially from triple role as a worker, parent (Tézli & Gauthier, 2009) and as a migrant (Wall & Jose 2004). Therefore migrating parents face the pressure to reconcile the family work balance to a higher degree, as they have sometimes to overcome the obstacles coming from the migrant status (stigmatization and discrimination). Separation from family members or descendants is done sometimes because of illegal status and difficulties to visit family members in the country of origin (COFACE, 2012). Many other difficulties and pressures arise for migrating parents considering the absence of personal, family and social networks to provide hands-on care and support for the migrants' descendants (Masselot, 2011); irregular working hours of multiple part-time jobs with sudden changes in workloads (COFACE, 2012). Such pressures are often felt more among mothers, given the gendering of caring responsibilities (COFACE, 2012) since women's participation in the workforce has increased the balance of family, and work has become a major concern especially for migrant women who are extensively employed in the low paid such as domestic and 'unproductive' jobs (Peterson, 2007; Craig and Sawrikar, 2009). Because work and family conflicts involves a perceived failure to meet the demands of work or family responsibility, crossing the boundaries between the two domains is a primary reason for feelings of guilt and anger (Judge at al. 2006), especially for working migrant mothers who often have to face the burden to fulfill the cultural expectations of femininity that is domesticity and child caring (Doyle and Timonen, 2010).

Migrant working parents merging work and family demands

Albanian migrant working mothers and fathers in migration continuously negotiate their personal arrangements, work load and free time in order to balance their work demands and family commitments. When it comes to social activities, many of our migrant parents admitted not having time at all for such activities, especially in their earliest settlement in the host country. They had to work for long hours, overtime and often even during weekends, which left almost no time to spend with their family and children, not to mention other social activities.

While it is widely accepted that both working parents feel pressure in consolidating work and family, working mothers face much more of such strains in comparison to their male counterparts (Tézli and Gauthier, 2009). For instance, Bona (60), who works as domestic worker, pointed out that when she first came in Greece, beside the atypical long working hours and shifts in multiple jobs, she was supposed to work in her words as a "slave", also during the evenings and weekends in order to meet her work demands. Hochschild (2003) describes how working mothers deprived themselves the need to rest and to fulfill their personal needs. Liza (41) chose to work in precarious job in order to stay more at home with her children: *"I choose to do the most difficult job, that of domestic worker [without social insurance], instead of working in pizzeria with social insurance, because I wanted to be in home with my daughter and serve the family during the evening".* At the same time, Tina a 52 year old domestic worker, the mother of three children chose to recompense the "no time" with the child by buying him fancy toys, however, regrets the time spent away from her child. Overall, the narratives of the migrant parents we interviewed reflect somehow Liza's history of trying to manage the workload with household care time.

Men showed similar experiences. When asked to describe his experiences in managing care work and work duties, Landi, a 29 old hairdresser and entrepreneur, married, with one child in Greece claimed: *"I miss my little daughter, when I leave she is sleeping and again when I return she is still sleeping. So, I see her once in two or three days".* Another migrant man, Gimi (59), the father of three children regrets not spending enough time with his children and family. He understands that what a family needs is not only money but also love and time, which was almost impossible to give while working as a seasonal worker in Greece for about 25 years *"Maybe I have been working here [in Greece] since the year 1991 and I have sent money back home, but I have lost my family, my children. The family needs not only money, it needs affection as well".* As the above cases show, work time spilled over family time and parents experienced a 'time-based conflict'- investing more time on working, while leaving behind parental roles (Tammelin, 2009).

Migrating parenthood between 'good parent' and 'good worker'

Considering that caring responsibilities are often seen as woman's 'naturally' given role, and man's position and especially the figure of migrant father is articulated in terms of the 'breadwinner role' (Hochschild, 2003) migrant mothers were more likely to talk in details about their "motherhood anxieties" when not meeting the demand of the "good mother". For instance, Klara, a 35 year old domestic worker in Greece and a mother of a child, shows clearly the importance of mother-child bond as she sees the mother as the primary caregiver: *"I see it as motherhood obligations, the duty to stay home and take care of children. I see the negative points of mothers who work all the time".*

Poduval and Poduval (2008) argue working mothers have to justify their employment in terms of family income, children benefit and sacrifice instead of personal independence and fulfillment. This is the case of Orjana, a 35 year old seasonal agriculture worker and a mother of three children, who said: *"I am never sure if I have fulfilled the role of the mother. I feel a sense of guilt: Why am I in this situation? Who brought me at this state...? But I could not step backward... I have to sacrifice".* Fearing the stereotype that working mothers are less dedicated to their family than non-working mothers (Cuddy at al. 2004, p. 701), many mothers in our study experienced feeling of guilt for not spending enough time with their children (Hochschild, 1997). In their narratives the feeling of regrets were most commonly experienced as a result of them negotiating their "motherhood role" for the "sake" of family survive/economy. For instance, Valbona, a 60 years old domestic worker and a mother of two children, said:

> When I think about it today, how I left my 5 year-old-boy alone in the house, I feel disappointed with myself. It was terrible that he did not want to stay with me but mainly with his father. I could not get enough of my children, I worked even Sundays".

While asked about her absence from the family Tina (52) replied *"I am never sure if I have done the duties as a mother...I had to sacrifice my son for the economy".* Following the logic, we see that the belief of not being a "good mother" becomes a source of anxiety for many migrant women. Working migrant mothers are often confronted with the assumption that their ambitions exceed the traditional gendered role of care in the domestic sphere (Caro et al. 2012; Dushi 2015).

In the accounts of many migrant fathers we notice the expectation to be the primary providers. When men became unable to support financially the family (in situation when they have been laid off), it was a source of anxiety for them. This was further illustrated by the story of Landi, (29) who spoke about the sacrifices he had to do in order to perform his 'fatherhood duties': *"I am trying to fulfill all the duties, but it is better this way (seeing his daughter once in 2 or 3 days) as I would prefer to miss my family and child instead of not being able to provide for them".*

The narratives of many of our informants were reinforced by the idea that it was the mother who had to take care of the children and the father who had to be the breadwinner.

Mothers' (re)productive work and double burdens in the time of economic austerity

Many Albanian migrant women in Greece entered labor market when the Greek economic crises emerged. Many others were obligated to work in multiple jobs, extra hours and under more precarious and vulnerable conditions when their husbands lost their jobs. Faced with hard times, migrant women had to negotiate and shift between the multiple roles she had to manage. Increasingly Albanian women have to stand up and assume the role of the primary, often the solo, provider of the family.

> I felt I was a woman and a man at the same time. My husband was not always working, so I had to take up the role of the breadwinner of the family. As a mother I was feeling bad because my children did not have the same conditions as the Greek children. As a woman I did not have time to take care of myself, drink a coffee as the Geek women. It was not only me but all the other Albanian women. Our aim was only work, home, children and nothing else (Mira, 42, cook)

Even though working and providing for the family might fuel some feelings of emancipation and empowerment, scholars that have examined the impact of economic crises into the gender division of labor within the household found that women employment outside home have led to an equal division of labor within the family and greater gender equality (Chesley, 2011). Many of our migrant women experienced a sense of liberation and economic independence by upgrading to the new breadwinner role assigned to them in time of crises. For example, Meri a 31 hairdresser women in Greece recalls "*A woman should stand on her own feet. It is only then she feels free. I want to move forward, to live alone, not being deepened by anyone... I don't turn my head back any more*". However, in our study the shift in the public sphere was not followed by a shift in the domestic sphere where women were expected to preserve the traditional roles of nurturance and domesticity. This was illustrated by the story of Klara, a 57 year-old domestic worker in Greece:

> I worked even Sundays as a robot. Working 10 hours per day are too much because it was not that kind of work where you could sit down. It was physically demanding, and when I came back home [after work] I still had to clean 3 rooms of my house, together with the kitchen. I had to wipe out, to clean, I had to do the ironing, to take care of my two small children, and in the morning I had to go again to work and start all over again. In the beginning, I worked more than 12 hours per day until I got seriously sick.

Fearing that her husband will not manage to support economically the family because of the crises, Tina (52) admits:

*I had to take the life into my own hands. I had 3 small children and the youngest was 40
days. I had two necessities: the first was to work and the second was to stay at home with my
children. I did not have that kind of reliance on my husband [who was often jobless] without
documents and paying the rent…but such sacrifices were worthwhile as I was earning money.
I took the life into my own hands.*

It seems that women's decision to enter labor market and provide for the family
was somehow a necessity emerged by the family's economic conditions. Even
though out of necessity, migrant women do experience feeling of empowerment
through actively navigating the labor market or, as Tina (52) articulated, by "taking the life into my own hands", they are confronted with double burden as she
had to equally fulfill the role of the main provider also in the domestic sphere
as demonstrated by the story of Klara (57). According to European Network of
Migrant Women and European Women's Lobby (2012, p. 20) though women
may be 'upgraded' to a breadwinner status as a result of the global financial crisis,
they have to take additional burdens. Women's multiple burden, maintaining her
domestic role and managing the "new breadwinner" role, affects her emotionally. Though men have decreased their economic contribution and women have
helped mitigate the effect of the crises for the household, the traditional division
of labor continues and now with even more social burden placed on women.
Migrant women express increased anxiety while managing their multiple roles.

Transnational migrant women deconstructing gender ideologies of mothering

Transnational mothering refers to "the organizational reconstitution of motherhood that accommodates the temporal and spatial separations forced by migration"
(Parrenas, 2010, p. 1827). This new form of motherhood expands the concept of
just mothering or hegemonic mothering[2] by including breadwinning as well (Ibid.).
Having a child and working long hours was not possible for many undocumented
migrant mothers in Greece. Studies have found that employer is more likely to fire
mothers with little children because of mother absences when little children get
sick, a phenomenon called differently 'motherhood penalty' (Corell et al., 2007).
Studies have shown that motherhood experience is a disadvantage in the workplace
and mothers are judged by harsher standards than non-mothers (Ibid.). Childless
women are seen as more advantaged and competent than mothers and more likely
to be recommended for hire, even though no higher salaries were offered (Ibid.).

---

2   Hegemonic mothering ties women's identities to their role as caregivers and nurturance
    (Arendell, 1999).

Almost all the working mothers we interviewed have, at least once, during their migration history left the children back in Albania with their relatives or familiars as the only possible solution for many working mums has been to leave or send children back home. Entela, (41) domestic worker, talks about her experience:

> *I started to work, when she (her daughter) was 40 days old. Therefore I was obligated to send my little daughter back to Albania to my mom, for around one year as I had to work as a domestic worker from the early morning to the evening and then in pizzeria from 7 to 2 at night.*

Such choices were not easy for working mothers and they expressed their difficulties in many instances. Orjana (35) is one of the circular migrant's women that work as seasonal agricultural migrant in Greece and Italy. Leaving her 3 children alone every three months was very difficult for her. Sometimes she felt anxious for not performing her role of the "good mother". The work in agriculture was physically demanding as well, as she had to lift more than 20 kg, harvest the fruits even in bad rainy weather. Inability to stay with their younger children was a source of "motherhood anxiety and guilt", a phenomenon explained in more details in the section below. In this respect, one Orjana said: "*I lived up to 2 years without seeing my children. I was almost experiencing a nervous breakdown. I was in very bad conditions. I was wondering how I could live [without them]. I was getting crazy*".

The whole experience of migrating motherhood, dilemmas, sense of guild, work-care strategies, and motherhood anxieties are best expressed by the case of Miranda, 55 years old women with three children, who worked as house cleaner in Greece.

> *I left my little son in Albania. .. I had to sacrifice him for improving our economic situation. It was quite a difficult time and I regret it… It's not about getting rich, it's about surviving. I had to sacrifice my 1-year-old son, the dream of my life as I could not wait for him to grow up and call me "mum". I was not sure of what I was doing. I planned to leave him [at my parents in Albania] for one 1 year, but it lasted longer. He stayed there for around 2 years without seeing me. I had to go through a severe psychological torture and worst of all, it was so difficult to find a job and I realized the child was not the real obstacle. I was suffering and worst of all I could not see my child. My son was 3 years old when I went back to take him with me, but when I went there he didn't want to go with me, he did not know who I was. He was fond of my mother and sister. I was trying to compensate for the missing time but that time would never be re-compensated. He did not know who we [me and his dad] were. In the beginnings he felt like a foreigner. I felt guilty in front of my son… I felt enormously sad…and I cried. I was trying to regain him by buying him plenty of toys. He was asking to go home with my mother in Albania. Once, he felt asleep in our bed, but I wake up in the middle of the night and I saw him sleeping on the floor. He did not feel us as his parents, he was afraid, he did not know us. When I saw him on the floor I cried…cried and I put him in his bed and then I cried again. When he was growing he kept asking "Why did you do that*

thing [leaving him at my parents], why this way? There are no words to explain him what I
did and why I did it (Tina, 52, domestic worker, Greece)

Our study found that transnational working moms were predisposed to mental vulnerabilities, anxieties, regret and hopeless thoughts while they leave behind or send back in Albania their children. Similarly, in trying to map out the emotional wounds imposed by geographical distance on Philippine mothers and children in transnational households, study of Parrenas (2010, p. 386) explains that the "root causes of these wounds extend beyond the individual female migrant to larger structural inequalities that constrain the options that they have to provide their children with material, emotional, and moral care to the fullest. Various structural inequalities of globalization force them to sacrifice their emotional needs and those of their children for the material needs of the family. Our stories of transnational motherhood transform the notion of traditional motherhood where mothers are supposed to behave in cultural and socially acceptable ways, thus challenging the old patriarchal norms and kinship structures of the past that strongly preserve a traditional gender role expectations and division of labor for men and women in the family (Xhaho, 2014). This new model includes breadwinning (Hondagneu-Sotelo and Avila 1997).

Conclusion

This research, based on 42 interviews with working parents in Greece (out of which 11 are return migrants from Greece), suggests how demanding and stressful was for migrant working parents in the host country in trying to balance their work and family life at the same time. Moreover, such findings add weight to a considerable body of previous research on 'time-based conflict'- with migrant parents investing more time on working, while leaving behind parental roles. Our study found that parental child-care obligation reflected on migrant's socially embedded gender roles and traditional division of labor within the household. It was shown that a "good mother" was supposed to fit to maternal roles of "hegemonic mothering" and provide daily emotional and physical care for their children (though the reality of our transnational working mothers in Greece did not fit in this model), and the "good father" was supposed to be the breadwinner model, who at the extend of family incomes might endure physical and temporal separation from his children. The study found that working mothers were more likely than working fathers to experience pressure[3] to perform their dual role as

---

3   The pressure might not necessary come from the society but even from themselves.

dutiful mother and prosperous worker. Moreover, migrant mothers experience the work-family conflicts to a greater extent than their male counterparts and they felt much guiltier for not fulfilling what they perceived to be the "social expectation of motherhood". Furthermore, we found out that even in dual earning families, women were seen as the main responsible parent for managing childcare and domestic work, which put them in a more vulnerable position. Women were ambiguously shifting between the need and willingness to work and earn money and the need and desire to perform her "naturally" given role of the mother. What is seen as more problematic is that at some extend women themselves have difficulties in challenging and moving beyond these traditional gender role schemas that construct the "ideal motherhood" as women's primary identity. As it is shown in our findings, women's economic independence in the labor market is not articulated in terms of personal autonomy, but rather as sacrifices to support economically the family and have a better future.

The study found that in the situation where Albanian men were left jobless, in time of the Greek economic crises, Albanian migrant mothers managed the situation by becoming simultaneously the primary providers and care givers. At the same time they become more vulnerable due to double exploitation - inside and outside home. Reconciliation of work and family demands are hardly done especially from migrant mothers employed in domestic sector, who are often obligated to work in precarious work arrangements, long working hours and unpredictable demands and shifts, making them facing a triple disadvantaged status, as migrants as women and as mothers. Therefore, by being both the breadwinner and caring wives, migrant mothers in Greece are forced to endure a double burden, that of reproductive (unpaid work of caring and domesticity inside private domain) and productive labor[4] (waged labor outside home), which makes them mentally and physically vulnerable to double exploitation.

Trying to negotiate their identity as mothers and workers, they articulated the "care gap"[5] in terms of economic survival in the host country. In the light of such analysis our transnational mothers expand the concept of merely caregivers - giving daily and face to face care to their children - to the breadwinning responsibilities at the cost of temporal and physical separation from their children (Hondagneu-Sotelo and Avila 1997). Our transnational mothers create new

---

4   Productive and unproductive labor is a term coined by feminist Marxist scholar such as Margaret Benston and Peggy Morton perspective on work and class.

5   Author's definition for explaining the gaps created from the lack of time to care for their children.

definitions of mothering practice, which deconstruct the discourses of "hegemonic mothering" and Betty Friedan concept of "feminine mystique"[6].

References

Ackers, Helen. L. / Stalford, Helen E.: "Managing Multiple Life-Courses: The Influence of Children on Migration Processes in the European Union". In: Clarke, Karen/ Maltby, Tony /Kennett, Patricia (eds.): *Social Policy Review 19: Analysis and Debate in Social Policy*, Policy Press: Bristol 2007, p. 360.

Anthias, Floya/ Cederberg, Maja/ Barber, Tamsin/ Ayres, Ron: "Welfare Regimes, Markets and Policies: The Experience of Migrant Women". In: Anthias, Floya/ Kontos, Maria/ Morokvasic-Müller, Mirjana (eds.): *Paradoxes of integration: Female Migrants in Europe*. Springer: New York 2013, pp. 37–58.

Anthias, Floya/ Kontos, Maria/ Morokvasic-Müller, Mirjana.: (Eds.) *Paradoxes of Integration: Female Migrants in Europe*. Springer: New York 2013.

Arendell, Teresa.: *Hegemonic Motherhood:* Deviancy Discourses and Employed Mothers' Accounts of Out-of-School Time Issues. Working Paper No. 9, Center for Working Families, University of California: Berkeley 1999.

Becker, Joachim/ Jäger, Johannes: "Integration in Crisis: A Regulationist Perspective on the Interaction of European Varieties of Capitalism". *Competition and Change* 16 (3), 2012, pp. 169–187.

Bettio, Francesca / Simonazzi, Annamaria /Villa, Paola: "Changes in Care Regimes and Female Migration: the 'Care Drain' in the Mediterranean". *Journal of European Social Policy* 16 (3), 2006, pp. 271–285.

Bonacich, Edna: "A Theory of Ethnic Antagonism: The Split Labor Market". *American Sociological Review* 37 (5), 1972, pp. 547–559.

Caro, Erka/Bailey, Ajay/ van Wissen, Leo:"I am the God of the house': How Albanian rural men shift their performance of masculinities in the city?". *Journal of Balkan and Near Eastern Studies*, (forthcoming).

Caro, Erka / Lillie, Nathan.: *Feminized Migrant Labor in Austere Times: The case of Albanian migrants to Greece and Italy. Marketization and neoliberal restructuring in Europe,* ILRShool, Cornell University: USA, 2016.

Caro, Erka / Berntsen, Lisa / Lillie, Nathan/ Wagner, Ines: "Posted Migration and Segregation in the European Construction Sector". *Journal of Ethnic and Migration Studies*, 2015.

---

6   Betty Friedan book on "The Feminine Mystique", which give raise to the second wave of American feminism in the 20th century, revealed about women who would find fulfillment in their role as happy and passive housewives and nurturing mothers.

Caro, Erka/ Bailey, Ajay/ Van Wissen, Leo: "Negotiating between patriarchy and emancipation: Rural-to-urban migrant women in Albania". *Gender, Place and Culture* 19(4), 2012, pp. 472–493.

Castles, Stephen/ Hein de Haas / Mark J. Miller.: *The Age of Migration: International Population Movements in the Modern World.* 5th ed. Palgrave Macmillan: Basingstoke, 2014.

Chesley, Noelle.: Stay-at-home fathers and breadwinning mothers: Gender, couple dynamics, and social change. *Gender & Society,* 2011, 25(5), pp. 642–64.

COFACE: *Transnational Families and the Impact of Economic Migration on Families,* 2012, Brussels. Retrieved 5.4.2016 from http://cofaceeu.org/en/upload/03_Policies_WG1/2012%20COFACE%20position%20on%20Transnational%20Families%20en.pdf.

Craig, Lyn/ Sawrikar, Pooja: "Work and Family: How Does the (Gender) Balance Change as Children Grow?". *Gender, Work and Organization,* 16 (6), 2009.

Cuddy, Amy. J. C./ Fiske, Susan T./ Glick, Peter: "When Professionals Become Mothers, Warmth Does not Cut the Ice". *Journal of Social Issues* 60 (4), 2004, pp. 701–718.

Doyle, Martha/ Timonen, Virpi: "Obligations, Ambitions, Calculations: Migrant Care Workers' Negotiation of Work, Career and Family Responsibilities", *Social Politics: International Studies in Gender, State & Society 17 (1),* 2010, pp. 29–52.

Dushi, Mimoza: "Influence of Migration in Women Emancipation. Case Study from Kosovan Albanian Diaspora". *International Letters of Social and Humanistic Sciences 58, 2015,* pp. 91–103.

European Network of Migrant Women and European Women's Lobby, 2012. Retrieved on 4.4.2016 from http://www.migrantwomennetwork.org/.

Fullin, Giovanna: "Labor market outcomes of immigrants in a South European country: do race and religion matter?. *Work; Employment and Society 28, 2015,* pp. 1–19.

Ghosh, Jayati: *"Migration and gender empowerment: Recent trends and emerging issues".* In Human Development Research Paper No. 4. New York: United Nations Development Programme, Human Development Report Office, 2009.

Greenhaus, J.H, Beutell, N.J. Sources and conflict between work and family roles. *Academy of Management Review,* 10, 76, 1985.

Hochschild, Arlie. R.: *The Second Shift.* Benguin Books: United States of America 2003.

Hochschild, Arlie: *The Time Bind: When Work Becomes Home and Home Becomes Work.* Owl Book: New York 1997.

Hondagneu-Sotelom Pierrette / Avila, Ernestine: "I'm Here, but I'm There": The Meanings of Latina Transnational Motherhood". *Gender and Society* 11, 1997, pp. 548–571.

Judge, Timothey. A./Ilies, Remus/ Scott, Brent A.: "Work –Family Conflict and Emotions: Effects at Workand at Home". *Personal Psychology*, 59, 2006, pp. 779–814.

Kamburi, Nelli: "Gender equality in the Greek labour market: The gaps narrow, inequalities persist". Friedrich Ebert Stiftung. *International policy analysis*, 2013.

Karamessini, Maria: "Life stage transitions and the still-critical role of the family in Greece". In Anxo, Dominique / Bosch, Gerhard / Rubery, Jill (eds.): *The welfare state and life transitions. A European perspective,* Cheltenham: Edward Elgar, 2010, pp. 257–283.

King, Russell: "Southern Europe in the Changing Global Map of Migration". In King, Russell/ Lazaridis, Gabriella/ Tsardanidis, Charalambos. (eds.): *Eldorado or Fortress? Migration in Southern Europe.* Basingstoke: Macmillan Press, 2000, pp. 1–26.

King, Russell/ Castaldo, Adriana/Vullnetari, Julie: "Gendered relations and filial duties along the Greek-Albanian remittance corridor", *Economic Geography* 87(4), 2011, pp. 393–419.

Kofman, Eleonor: "Family-related Migration: A Critical Review of European Studies." *Journal of Ethnic and Migration Studies* 30 (2), 2004, pp. 243–262.

Lazaridis, Gabriella "Filipino and Albanian women migrant workers in Greece: Multiple layers of oppression". In: Anthias, Floya / Lazaridis, Gabriella (eds.): *Gender and migration in Southern Europe.* Berg: Oxford, 2000, pp. 49–79.

Mankki, Laura/ Caro, Erka. "Paradoxes of feminization of labour: Working migrant women in the service sector context of Finland and Italy" paper presented at the Conference on Migration, Citizenship and Development in a neoliberal era. 25–27 June 2015, Amsterdam, The Netherlands.

Maroukis, Thanos/ Gemi, Eda.: *Circular Migration between Albania and Greece, Case study report for the METOIKOS Project* funded by the European Fund for Integration of Third Country Nationals, 2011, available at http://metoikos. eui.eu.

Masselot, Annick.: Highly Skilled Migrants and Transnational Care Practices: Balancing Work, Life and Crisis Over Large Geographical Distances. *Canterbury Law Review,* 17(2) 2011, pp. 299–315.

Moreli, Anne: Les servantes étrangères en Belgique comme miroir des diverses vagues migratoires, Sextant, 15–16, 2001, pp. 149–164.

Mrozowicki, Adam.: Coping with Social Change: Life Strategies of Workers in Poland's New Capitalism. Leuven: 2011, Leuven University Press.

Parreñas, Rhacel S.: "Transnational Mothering: A Source Of Gender Conflicts In The Family", *North Carolina Law Review,* 88, 2010.

Pearson, Ruth/ Sweetman, Caroline (eds.) (2010) The Economic Crisis. Special Issue of Gender & Development 18 (2), July 2010.

Peck, Jamie.: *Work, Place: The Social Regulation of Labour Markets.* Guilford Press: New York 1996.

Peterson, Elin.: "The invisible carers: Framing domestic work(ers) in gender equality policies in Spain". *European Journal of Women's Studies,* 14 (3), 2007, pp. 265–280.

Poduval, Jayita/ Poduval, Murali: "Working Mothers: How Much Working, How Much Mothers, and Where Is the Womanhood". *Women's Issues,* Mens Sana Monographs, 7(1) 2009.

Powell, Gary N./ Greenhaus, Jeffrey H: Sex, gender, and the work-to-family interface: exploring negative and positive interdependencies.: *Academy of Management Journal,* 53(3), 2010, pp. 513–534.

Scrinzi, Francesca.: 'Cleaning and ironing… with a smile', Migrant workers in the "care industry" in France. *Journal of Workplace Rights* 14(3), 2009, pp. 271–292.

Shelley, Correll J./Stephen, Benard:" Getting a Job: Is There a Motherhood Penalty?" *American Journal of Sociology* 2007, 112 (5), pp. 1297–1339.

Tammelin, Mia.: Working Time and Family Time: Experience of Work and Family Interface among Dual Earning Parents in Finland. Jyvaskyla Studies in Education, *Psychology and Social Research,* 2009, Jyvaskyla.

Tézli, Annnette/ Gauthier, Anne H.: Balancing Work and Family in Canada: An Empirical Examination of Conceptualizations and Measurements. *Canadian Journal of Sociology/Cahiers canadiens de sociologie* 34(2), 2009.

Xhaho, Armela: *"Albania gender inequality in workplace: expectations of femininity and domesticity"* Revista Haemus, 2014, pp. 45–50.

Xhaho, Armela: "Sworn virgins, male and female *berdaches*: A comparative approach to the so-called 'third gender' people", *Gender Questions,* 1 (1) 2013, pp. 112–125.

Wall, Karin/Jose, Jose S.: Managing Work and Care: A difficult Challenge for Immigrant Families. *Social Policy & Administration 38 (6),* 2004, pp. 591–621.

Couples within the Context of Migration

Magdalena Żadkowska, Tomasz Szlendak

Egalitarian Capital Gained in Norway or Brought from Poland? Experiences of Migration and Gender Equality among Polish Couples in Norway

Abstract *We compare the family life of Polish couples in less gender egalitarian Poland and in Norway. After analysis of the differences, we find a specific characteristic related to gender relations, values and practices we call egalitarian capital – shaping the dynamics of integration with new societies. But is it gained in Norway or brought from Poland?*

Introduction

It is known that the migratory environment does not influence every single activity or social attitude of migrants in the same way. It changes some of them, and some are only touched by it. Multitudes of research show that migratory environment seems to affect values, standards and attitudes as far as conscientiousness at work is concerned (DaVanzo 1981, Kalter 2011). Still when we look at "packets" of values, standards and attitudes, which are so much rooted in migrants' culture, it seems to affect them and to shape the dynamics of integration with new societies (Cao, Galinsky & Maddux 2013, Diehl, Lubbers, Mühlau, Platt 2014, Kalter, Kogan 2014, Kalter, Will 2016).

Polish couples in Norway quickly encounter Scandinavian, gender equality-oriented normative system, whereas they come from a far less egalitarian country in that matter (Warner-Søderholm, 2012), being very different in comparison to Norway also by the standards of welfare state' characteristics.

In Europe there are several typologies of welfare state differing with regard to familialization/ defamilialization of existing policies (Esping-Andersen 1990; Korpi 2000; Thévenon 2011; OECD 2011; 2013, Oun 2013). The "world" of the welfare state directly influences different policies offered by the state, among them is the family policy. We use Korpi's typology of countries to analyse the influence of macro agents (Korpi 2000) on practices and values of couples in modern Europe. It is based on various policies towards men, women and families pursued by state. Thus, there are three different state approaches to family: (1) policies that enhance the implementation of the egalitarian model of parenthood and career, (2) policies directly encouraging women to come back to professional life after the childbirth, and (3) policies generally promoting family. Accordingly, this typology distinguishes liberal systems giving families only minimal support (e.g. UK, Ireland, the Netherlands), social democratic systems supporting double careers and encouraging women to come back to labour market after the childbirth (e.g. Scandinavian countries), and conservative systems supporting families but not supporting women's return to labour market directly (e.g. Spain, Greece, France, Italy) (Korpi 2000). Buhlmann et al (2010) adds the fourth category to this set of three different groups of states, the post-communist states, which transited from the socialist to the capitalist system at the beginning of 1990s (e.g. Poland, Czech Republic, Slovakia, Hungary). This fourth category places the market and the family as the central role players and the state as marginal player (Żadkowska 2016 et al.). That is why post-communistic countries tend to support coming back to equality as far as making a career is concerned (Bühlmann et al. 2010: 63), but not in the domestic, private sphere.

The analysis of values and practices along Europe done by Bühlmann et al. (2010) shows that there are four types of relationships[1]:

1. **egalitarian practices and egalitarian values,** typical situation for parents with two children
2. **stereotypical (gendered) practices and stereotypical (gendered) values;**
3. **egalitarian practices and stereotypical (gendered) values;**
4. and also - **stereotypical (gendered) practices and egalitarian values,** typical for young parents with two children (Bühlmann 2010: 53).

According to the research done by Bühlmann's team (2010), the type of relationship very much depends on the country the couple lives in. In social democratic countries less people of both sexes will hold to stereotypical (gendered) values and less people will practice stereotypical (gendered) practices in their domestic lives

---

1   Using The European Social Survey (ESS) data from 2004–2005 and data of 20 countries, Bühlmann et al. coded couples according to following scheme: (i) the man dedicates more than 3h more than his partner to housework (atypical domestic practices); (ii) both partners dedicate the same time (plus/minus 3h) to housework, and the gendered values are below the median (egalitarian practices and values); (iii) the woman devotes weekly more than 3h more than her partner to housework, and the gendered values are below the median (gendered practices, egalitarian values); (iv) the woman devotes weekly more than 3h more than her partner to housework, and the gendered values are above the median (gendered practices and values); and (v) both partners dedicate the same time (plus/minus 3 h) to housework, and the gendered values are above the median (egalitarian practices, gendered values).

(Bühlmann et al. 2010: 57). If strong egalitarian values and state support stand behind them, emerging non-egalitarian practices have smaller chances to perpetuate.

Overall, these results suggest that the configuration of tension between egalitarian values and gendered practices is biographically rather unstable. It seems to irritate the young parents, and, in consequence it triggers a reaction to reduce it (i.e. towards return to a configuration of coherence). This coherence can be found either in a return to an egalitarian coherence (example of Norwegian parents – see also Kjeldstad i Lappegård (2012)) or in a definitive farewell to egalitarianism and a turn to a coherent gendered configuration – example of Polish parents in Poland – see below (Bühlmann et al. 2010: 59).

Bühlmann et al. (2010) as well as Kjeldstad and Lappegård (2012) propound the necessity to study couples, getting to know the configurations of four-field matrix (practices-values) in a couple and longitudinal and quality research. "Broader reflections relating the development of theory with empirical analysis would certainly contribute to a more thorough understanding of the dynamic interplay between values and practices and their significance for social change (Bühlmann et al. 2010: 64)".

So we were interested in how are things with emancipation and gender equality measured by the analysis of practices (gendered or egalitarian?). Is it like the same with conscientiousness and diligence, i.e. migratory environment changes attitudes towards gender equality? Or is it the same with trust: migratory environment changes it a little or not at all? Clearly one of the key factors here is egalitarian capital.

Since Pierre Bourdieu social capital theory, there are different capitals being titled. The equality capital notion derives from Łukasiuk's migrants' capital (Łukasiuk 2007, see also Da Vanzo 1981 and Kalter 2011), cosmopolitan capital (Wagner 2007; Buhlmann et al. 2010; Gudmundsdottir 2015), bodily capital (Wacquant 1995), sexual/erotic capital (Martin, George 2006; Green 2011). We claim that egalitarian capital is a kind of resource composed of individual's social characteristics (generalized trust radius, gender equality attitudes and probably other factors) in disposition of an individual when encountered with social receiving environment of different characteristics (more egalitarian and equal regarding gender division of labour, including domestic labour) from those of the country of origin.

Polish migrants have been the largest immigrant community in Norway since 2009. The majority of migrants would be afraid of egalitarian values and practices they face when coming from less egalitarian country to more egalitarian one. Poland is a mono-cultural country. Socialization is not based on tolerance towards the Other, Norwegian multiculturalism and male-female relation rules are very different. Polish migrants in Norway are labour migrants. They come to achieve social promotion in the country that has civilization, cultural and economic growth to benefit from. They are open to implement available patterns. They want to achieve financial, professional and social success. Norwegian culture, social system and social patterns presented in media and workplace seems to encourage them when they implement partnership model of family and egalitarian practices both at home and at workplace. Polish men and women apply "superficiality tactics" most often. It means they turn into migratory hybrids selectively accepting Norwegian labour and rest standards, but rejecting Norwegian gender equality standards. There are, however, some migrants who see profits when practicing egalitarianism. Thanks to that, they become the migrants with successful story, assimilated ones. When interviewing Polish couples in Norway we have come across some new patterns of organizing a household with dual careers and children, which appeared because of mobility and migration.

Our findings from Par Migration Navigator Project (Żadkowska et al. 2016, Kosakowska et al. 2016) show strong influence of the country of residence. Polish migrants from our study are open to change their practices of everyday life due to social policy and work-life balance priorities. On the other hand the attitudes do not change that quickly as practices, though Polish men in Norway feel less backlash when doing domestic duties and being involved in childcare comparing to those in Poland. For example in comparison to their colleges in Poland they follow the Norwegian way of dealing with new-born child (first and second). They take this chance, negotiate the dates, stay at home and then encourage the others. Polish fathers in Poland admit they would suffer from social opinion; they would be the objects of jokes coming from their friends and from their family. For them being a father is a matter of private sphere and the couple is left alone to take this challenge. That is why we come up with the idea of **egalitarian capital**. We define the notion so that it becomes a kind of cultural rucksack that one brings which can be a key factor to an integration or even assimilation success.

Methodology

We (University of Gdańsk, University of Stavanger, Polish Academy of Science, International Research Institute of Stavanger and Centre for Intercultural Communication in Stavanger) conduct a sociological and psychological research project Par Migration Navigator[2] in Poland and in Norway, in two regions: Pomerania

---

2   The project Par Migration Navigator is funded by Norway Grants in the Polish-Norwegian Research Programme operated by the National Centre for Research and Development.

and Rogaland since October 2013. The participants of our studies are Poles that migrated to Rogaland, Polish citizens from Pomerania region, and Norwegians from Rogaland. The benefit of this regional dimension is that it enables better control over complicating factors related to the Polish origin. This design leads us into obtaining very precise image of Polish labour migration to Norway and to depict differences between two similar groups – couples/families in Pomeranian region and couples/families in Rogaland.

In the first round of research (conducted by University of Gdansk) we have analysed the changes in everyday-life choices made by men and women when dealing with career involvement, domestic duties division, work-life balance and parental behaviours. 150 in-depth interviews (both joint and individual) were conducted with fifty Polish couples living in two regions (Rogaland and Pomerania). We have analysed what are advantages and disadvantages of involvement in childcare, domestic duties division, parental and care leaves. The results obtained show the dynamics of changes of gender roles fulfilment and work-life balance strategies fostered by migration experience.

In the second round of research we have analysed the changes in leisure and sport activities experienced after migration. We also have compared fertility decisions, giving birth standards and childcare facilities. We have conducted another 48 joint interviews with the same couples living in two regions (Rogaland and Pomerania). We have also studied 96 psychological questionnaires designed to study respondents' attitudes towards gender stereotypes at home and at workplace.

In the third round of research, in February 2016, we have analysed religiousness (practices and spirituality), intimacy and sexuality. We have also analysed attitudes towards gender roles. We have conducted 120 in-depth interviews (both joint and individual) again in the same group of couples living in two regions (Rogaland and Pomerania).

Interviews were conducted during both joint and individual meetings in which respondents provided a possibility to get to know the decision-making process, the integration into both the new country of stay and new phases of relationship as we observed with special care any changes appearing in family life (new child, change of flat, workplace etc.). By the three years long cooperation with couples we did also became familiar with respondents and their relationships' dynamics.

Therefore from all 43 couples present in the longitudinal study we have selected four for this article purposes. While discussing the concept of egalitarian capital and answering the question: gained or brought, we want to present them in detail way. All four couples we have chosen are similar. They are in their thirties. They have higher or average (in one case – a man from the couple number 15) education degree, represent dual earning family model. Both partners are Polish. All of them have children; two couples have become parents for the second time during the project, one couple has one child, one couple has two children from the beginning of the project. Two couples live in Stavanger and two live in Gdansk. All of them have just experienced (or are still experiencing) the moment of tension while changing egalitarian family of two partners into family of three and then of four – they are in crucial moment.

All of them were qualified after psychological test and analysis of gender attitudes as pro egalitarian, declaring to construct the partnership model of their relation (Kosakowska & Żadkowska, forthcoming 2016).

Factors creating egalitarian capital

In four analysed cases we will present all the data we receive and will show where the egalitarian capital is constrained and which characteristics of environment encourage it to develop.

First couple is Monika and Przemyslaw. **Monika** (34 years old) is an exploration geophysicist and **Przemyslaw** (34 years old) is a senior petro physicist. They have lived in Norway almost seven years (due to the date of the first interview). Monika and Przemyslaw have been a couple for 14 years. They got married after 7 years of their relationship. They have one child. Both of them have higher education background.

Asked about the family of origin that is one of factors for future relationship model of adult siblings (Żadkowska, 2016b) they say:

Przemyslaw: Well, dad also cooked, he even took care of me, but mum was supposed to do the majority there.

Researcher: And did your mums work?

Przemyslaw: I mean, my mum - yes, all the time, even now she also worked, she's just given up her work, but it wasn't a kind of challenging job.

Researcher: But still, it was eight hours, wasn't it?

Przemyslaw: Yes, yes, yes.

Monika: And my mum, I remember there were ups and downs. There were times she worked and then she didn't, so there were different stages, so... when I was very little they worked together, my mum and dad at one company, then, I suppose, I was finishing my primary school and she didn't work, then she worked again, so it was fluctuating this way. As far as I can remember, dad worked all the time, there was a time he didn't work for about a year because the company was closed down or something, but he found a new job quickly, so dad worked all the time; as for mum - there were various things, but she also, when she was with us, with my brother, I think she took maternal and parental for three-four years ...

Przemyslaw remembered his cooking father. It is strong figure to give potential for future egalitarian practices at home (Żadkowska 2013, Żadkowska 2016b). While discussing the division of domestic duties the idea was always to share them.

Monika: I mean we always have a division, so it isn't like I am at home and he does nothing, it is like, with cooking for example, it is always like, for example, one day him, when there isn't a kid, he says he cooks today, or me, because he is a specialist on some subjects, like for example spaghetti or sauces - he makes them. For example other things, the rest, or some things sweet - I make it and it isn't a problem [...]

Przemyslaw: officially we have no division, there's any, none, it's just who cooks? Yeah, I can today, because I'm just in the mood...

Przemyslaw and Monika admitted that their marriage was egalitarian before the child appeared. They said that their situation in Norway (good job opportunities, work-life-balance achieved, social and family policy) made them decide about the baby "In Poland we wouldn't have made this decision, and have no child" Monika said. In the process of returning to equality after the birth of their first child, the Norwegian welfare plays important role.

The second couple is Sara and Stanislaw. **Sara** (34 years old) and **Stanislaw** (37 years old), married, have been a couple for 16 years. They are parents of two daughters. They came to Norway almost 7 years ago. Sara joined Stanislaw after two months. Sara works as an accountant; she has a higher education background. Stanislaw is a bus driver with average education background. They have pointed out different reasons for coming to Norway. Sara claims she wanted to change their environment, while Stanislaw believes that the improvement of financial conditions was on top of their decision.

While asked about the division of duties among their parents they say:

Sara: I grew up with my mum only, so we lived together, me and my mum, she virtually did all the chores and I helped her but I could not say I was burdened with some hard duties. (...)

Sara: Well, she virtually had to bring her daughter up by herself, but as there were only two of us there weren't that many of these chores. Because I was that kind of a kid who took care of her room and I would not need assistance, the same with homework, so she was not very burdened with that. I also helped with taking out the rubbish and washing up for sure. And cooking wasn't a problem for her, and so with most duties. Mum never complained and me neither, so living together was nice. I recall these times with delight.

Stanislaw: Mum did not work all her life, dad worked and so, involuntarily, mum worked at home and dad - outside. (...)

Stanislaw: Yes, because we always had some part of farm, there were pigs, rabbits - there are rabbits still, there's a big plot, but again, only dad takes care of it.

In Sara's situation there is no image of gender roles played in her family. She has a figure of a strong mother dealing with all domestic and parental duties. Her mother was also devoted to her professional life. For a woman this is a "rucksack" of alternative practices she can choose in her adult life. Stanislaw was socialised in a traditional family (no working mother), but also in the family involved in the family farm. Division of duties was visible, duties were even divided according to gender into male and female ones.

Similar to Monika and Przemyslaw, Sara and Stanislaw represent the evolution of an egalitarian relationship model. Both couples (along with many others from our study) claim that Norway is a very good place to balance work and family life and behave in de-gendered way.

Sara: Well, perhaps our division is a bit unequal, but that's ok with me. Due to my husband's work, he nearly always has a break during the day. If he starts, let's say, at 5 or 6 in the morning, he has a break from 9 to 12. And during that time he gets back home and always cooks dinner. And this is a huge bonus for me, as when I get back home at 16:15 or 16:30, my only duty is to heat the dinner up, whether it is a soup or prepared potatoes, but the salad is already done, and chops - I just have to put them on the pan. I don't have to think that before I manage it, it is already 6 in the evening. It's almost ready, already. In regards to cleaning, my husband also gains when we're out, no children, no me, he cleans the floors then, in the whole house, so cleaning so many square meters of floors is not on me. I am supposed to do the laundry for kids and for myself. This dinner and cleaned floors - these are the most important things, I don't have to do them and they do not concern me [laugh] (…).

Sara: I don't know if it can be called a household chore but we have a division that when my husband comes back after dinner, e.g. cleaning is his duty, he loads the dishwasher, all these dishes, and I dedicate time to help our daughter in learning.

Stanislaw: My duties? To clean in the kitchen. To load the dishwasher, because I don't like when kids do it, I prefer to do it myself.

Stanislaw: But it applies to weekdays. My wife does it on weekends. I prepare kids' breakfasts to take to school, in the morning, when I get up before going to work. Basically cleaning there isn't as much, and when my wife comes, she takes care of kids, homework, doing their laundry, God forbid she would touch mine, I prefer to do it myself. Because when I do it myself, I know how and where things end.

Along with higher education there are other important factors to build the egalitarian capital: habits coming from family of origin, attitudes towards egalitarian division of labour (at home and in workplace), dual career family model. There are also determinants that are present in the environment the couple lives. Every

Polish couple, from our study, that expressed the value of egalitarianism in relationship stressed the opportunities for women in professional career and for men in parental curriculum. These outcomes confirm the Bühlmann's theory about the welfare state's determinism (Bühlmann et al. 2010).

Third couple is Jaggosa and Sebastian. **Jagoda** (33 years old) and **Sebastian** (33 years old) are married since 2009. They have a 10 – months – old – son (due to the date of first interview in 2014). They have never been in Norway but they lived in Great Britain for one year. Both Jagoda and Sebastian are EU project specialists. Jagoda is also a business coach. She organizes and conducts workshops. Sebastian is also a photographer. In 2015 they became parents for the second time (a daughter was born). They began with their own business as well (they opened a photographic studio).

Jagoda remembers in her childhood the division of domestic duties was done whenever it was possible.

Jagoda: In my family generally my mother ran most things, whilst dad was very active regarding cleaning if he was at home; there was a great cleaning on Saturdays, there isn't this rhythm of cleaning at our place which makes me pissed a little but at my parents' home it was always a cleaning starting on Saturday morning, if my dad was home, because he regularly worked on weekends, but if he was at home it was clear that dad was cleaning and at this moment mum was taking care of the kitchen in a minimal way or she didn't touch anything. Dad was cleaning and we were cleaning and mum - nothing, but on the other hand mum was responsible for cooking, provisions regarding kitchen and for washing - yes. Well we helped her if needed, dad did not deal with it, he made some fixing, and some stuff in the garden.

Researcher: And who was taking care of home?

Jagoda: Well, generally mum was the main boss at home, dad was more like a kind of a tag.

(...)

Jagoda: Dad was a vet, Mum was a teacher, perhaps this chores division was a result of the fact that Mum was just more at home and she had more time.

While Sebastian is remembering his childhood, he also sees sharing duties but under his mother management:

Sebastian: I think it wasn't so flexible as it is at our home, but it also wasn't like Father didn't do anything, perhaps as we, when we make decisions, we do it together - yes, we do it together, at our home it was sometimes more like Mum was ruling - yes, she was kind of forcing or persuading - yes, and she was dividing duties, so maybe such a change - yes.

Both of them admit their relationship is more about egalitarianism than their parents' one. But two small children at home make managing the family a very difficult thing. There is little help coming from the state. It is very difficult to have a place in a public kindergarten. Men have difficulties at workplace when communicating about parental leave plans. When it comes to your own business (which is the case of Sebastian) you have to manage both at once – family and business or resign from … family duties.

> Jagoda: We share duties rather **chaotically**, which means Sebastian is generally responsible for cooking, provisions, kitchen, it's his department, he is also responsible lately, since the baby was born, he usually does the laundry, so he does the washing. I am responsible for tiding up, although actually we tidy up together, but generally I usually run and tidy up and that's how it looks like.

> Jagoda: You know, I am fully responsible for tiding up, **sometimes** I try to put it on Sebastian, hey, vacuum there, but generally when it's pushed all the way down and, for example, we have to prepare a party and everything needs to be cooked and tidied up, it's obvious Sebastian will cook and prepare everything and I will tidy up during this time - no - it is not based on the fact that it is my main department, tidying and taking care of the baby - we divide it in half more or less, though it depends, doesn't it? When we are together, Sebastian is less eager to change diapers, I do it more often then [laugh]. (…)

> Jagoda: You know, what he is totally, generally one can say, he is totally responsible, almost totally responsible, with few exceptions when he is out, for cooking and provisions, because I do it rarely, only if something somewhere rarely, he provides mainly. Sometimes I buy bread, things needed suddenly, and he's responsible for complete provisions for us and for all things that need to be fixed, hammering, screwing, doing something, I don't go into this. (…).

> Jagoda: You know, what comes from that, what is more suitable for someone to do, what does one like more, Sebstian prefers to cook, I prefer to tidy up so I tidy up more often, especially as mess disturbs me more than him, perhaps I am exaggerating but I get this idea of tiding up quicker than he does.

In Jagoda stories about their home organization, especially after the birth of second child, we can "hear" the tensions Bühlmann portray to be very symbolic for young parents. These tensions will make the couple try to return to a configuration of coherence. Instead of a configuration of egalitarian coherence there is a risk to finish with coherence of gendered values and practices.

> Sebastian: I guess everyone is capable of doing everything, yes, but, well, we plan, you take care of the baby today, I do shopping, cook dinner, do the laundry, so it isn't like one person just sits doing nothing and the other tries to deal with everything, we share the duties, and we don't do it like only I do something, only I cook and only Jagoda tides up.

> Sebastian: **Perhaps it comes from the background** to some extent, perhaps if I had everything done for me at home and I wouldn't have to do anything, then perhaps, **I would either try to duplicate this pattern**, and everything just came naturally, it wasn't like that, I don't know what can you do, ok, you'll do this and that, no, **it was so natural** - yes.

Sebastian admits the role of the egalitarian capital origins from his family. He says the division of duties he and Jagoda have is designed in a "natural" way – reproducing some ideas from childhood. And "natural" means egalitarian not gendered. Against welfare state determinism – forcing familiarization of parental practices and gendered division of domestic duties - they try to be coherent with egalitarian values and practices.

The forth couple is Nina and Patryk. **Nina** (32 years old) and **Patryk** (30 years old), married since 2008. They have a 4 – year – old daughter (due to the first interview in 2014). Nina is an academic teacher, Patryk in an entrepreneur. Patryk has his own business. Both Nina and Patryk worked in USA while they were studying. They have not been in Norway. In 2015 Nina and Patryk became parents for the second time (a son was born). In the end of 2015 Nina defended her PhD thesis. Coming back to her childhood Nina remembers traditional family relations:

> Nina: Well, typically as they say. As it was in the old days, meaning everything's on mum. Mum-strongwoman and I inherited that from her, because professional work, three kids, little money at home. Father rather not thrilled with family life. Lots of work, tired after work, well, **he was sitting in front of the TV** and during this mum did not foist anything on him, but she was doing her stuff. And she also took it from granny's home, her parents' home that it was her who always helped granny. They, they were doing everything in the house together, and men was just sitting there.

> Researcher: And did both your parents work professionally?

> Nina: Yes, yes, yes. Mum was a teacher, not full-time but she had much overtime, tutorials, because money was scarce, she had to do these tutorials somehow. Well, a dinner, we were here, and she made these tutorials, or she was going somewhere to teach, so it was hard. Actually she did not care for herself during that time. She was always tired. It took its price on us... I do not like to recall it, as it is concerned I did not enjoy it, and I did not help her because I was one of these rebellious ones. And she also did not force it on me. Complaining probably, that I do not help, because she probably had this vision that the daughter would act like her...

Patryk has similar memories:

> Patryk: (...) ...my father... was a sailor by education, but he probably... he did not graduated at Naval Academy, that is he was studying for a couple of years but then he got busy with something private, private enterprise as he said. On the other hand, my mother was a physiotherapy technician. She worked in this profession for a very short period of time. When I was born, she never came back to professional life.

When it comes to domestic duties, the proportions of work are imbalanced after the children were born. Nina defends her husband, as equal partner at home but then admits he only helps and waits to be asked for help. Nina recalls also the importance of family of origin in shaping domestic patterns.

*Nina: No! I just laughed like that, because someone says - well, we share very strictly. You, we do it like, Patryk vacuums, though I vacuumed lastly but as I say - damned, how long I haven't vacuumed, it's been two years. And so, who does what, it just made itself. There is of course time and there we have an understanding with each other, e.g. it's nice that we don't do. Well, it's me more, **I sometimes turn into housewife**. Hey, a mess, go on, tidy up a little! Patryk no, Patryk sees e.g. that when I'm busy he will never tell me - You sat all day doing nothing - no, he won't. It is, It's nice in that matter, that, and, and, and it's not like we make a specific division. But it has already got customary, who does what.*

*Nina: Yes! Though there are things, that I laugh, that it is as if it got customary, but if Patryk has already took it, then it's like male, I laugh. If he has vacuuming, than it's vacuuming, and it's something like that. I, I really see it in upbringing. Still men grow up, they have often grown up at homes, where mothers were doing everything. So I see it in my brother, or someone else too. **It was my mum doing it, mum was also pointing what if you already have**. I will do it if someone shows it to me. If I show something to Patryk, then he will do something, but **I have to show it to him**.*

Patryk has one visible duty. This division shows the tendency of adaptation to inequality (Buhlmann et al, 2010: 57). Nina confirms it when saying: "I have become more **mummy style** lately". It perfectly confirms observations of Buhlmann. The couples in former communist countries display higher frequencies of gendered values, in particular, when having children (Buhlmann et al, 2010: 57–58). Although they played egalitarian couple before children were born, the mechanism to return to gendered coherence is strong and the state's characteristics do not help.

Patryk: My duties, … so: duties are from the group, let's call it, maintaining tidiness, helping us not to overgrow with dirt here, I generally have my vacuum cleaner. I am the operator and I vacuum once a week.

Patryk: You know what, I think Nina used to do something with this vacuum cleaner, when we started to live together, I suppose she doesn't like vacuuming, and it doesn't bother me, so I, so I just do it.

Nina and Patryk come from the most traditional families of origin comparing all four cases. It might be one of the reasons for the tensions in their relation when it comes to domestic and parental duties. We might only suspect that migration to any country would help them to escape from familiar patterns. The new environment might have been helpful in inventing couple's own patterns (there are other migrant couples in our study who show this tendency). According to Bühlmann's theory, Norway might be one of the countries that would facilitate "return to equality" and stop "adjusting to inequality" process (Bühlmann et al., 2010: 53) for Nina & Patryk and Jagoda & Sebastian as it is for Monika & Przemyslaw and

Sara & Stanislaw along with other coherent egalitarian couples living in Norway that took part in our study.

Conclusions

As we observed in Bühlmann study: 1) Couples without children (including those who expect the first child) declare more egalitarian values and practices in both countries Poland and Norway (Bühlmann et al., 2010: 58), 2) There are more gendered coherent couples in Poland than in Norway and there are more egalitarian coherent couples in Norway than in Poland (Bühlmann et al., 2010: 58). Our goal was to show why and what happens to the egalitarian rucksack when a couple starts to create the family in Poland and what happens when they live in Norway when both men and women value egalitarianism and declare egalitarian practices. We called this rucksack the **egalitarian capital** and explained that this capital is a kind of resource composed of individual's social characteristics (generalized trust radius, gender equality attitudes and probably other factors like: habits coming from family of origin, attitudes towards egalitarian division of labour [at home and in workplace], dual career family model) in disposition of an individual when encountered with social receiving environment of different characteristics (more egalitarian and equal regarding gender division of labour, including domestic labour) from those of the country of origin. We tried to show that it is a result of different factors put together and that is why it can be gained during socialisation processes and then reproduced and developed in special circumstances. The migration to egalitarian country encourages and facilitates this process.

In the article giving four case studies, we have discussed the difference in life cycle of a couple determined by the welfare state the couple lives in the examples of two Polish couples living in Gdansk (Poland) and two Polish couples living in Rogaland (in Norway). Two partners present egalitarian values, including attitudes toward gender roles. An egalitarian country like Norway is the place to make their plans come true. The egalitarianism and sameness are two factors that strongly encourage the couple's life choices and decide their migration success. In Norway, Norwegian environment, social system, workplaces and social patterns play an important and encouraging role when implementing partnership family model and making motherhood and fatherhood decisions. It works also for migrant fathers motivated to raise a family in Norway. Stories of this type of couples show not only façade, out-door success, but also internal successful couple life story. As our case studies show, couples of this type have more chances to survive coherent and save their **egalitarian capital** in Norway than in Poland.

According to these outcomes, our research also gives strong arguments to discuss future social and family politics regarding parental leaves and discrimination on labour market among employers, politicians, journalists and decision makers. It will be always an outcome of a puzzle – the type of welfare state, family policy of destination country and individual choices based on cultural rucksacks brought from the country of origin.

References

Bourdieu Pierre: *Dystynkcja. Społeczna krytyka władzy sądzenia*, Wydawnictwo Scholar. 2005.

Buhlmann Felix/Elcheroth Guy/Tettamanti Manuel: "The Division of Labour Among European Couples: The Effects of Life Course and Welfare Policy on Value–Practice Configurations", *European Sociological Review* 26 (1). 2010, pp. 49–66, DOI:10.1093/esr/jcp004, Retrieved: 15.08.2016 www.esr.oxfordjournals.org

Cao Jiyin/Galinsky Adam D./ Maddux William M: "Does Travel Broaden the Mind? Breadth of Foreign Experiences Increases Generalized Trust'" *Social Psychological And Personality Science*, 5, 5, 2014, pp. 517–525.

Da Vanzo Julie: "Repeat migration, information costs, and location-specific capital" *Population and Enviroment* Volume 4, Issue 1, 1981, pp. 45–73.

Diehl Claudia/Lubbers Marcel/Mühlau Peter/Platt Lucinda: "Starting out: New migrants' socio-cultural integration trajectories in four European destinations" *Ethnicities* April 2016, pp. 157–17 doi:10.1177/1468796815616158

Esping-Andersen Gosta: *The Three Worlds of Welfare Capitalism*, Cambridge: The Policy Press. 1990.

Green Adam Isaiah. "Playing the (Sexual) Field: The Interactional Basis of Sexual Stratification." *Social Psychology Quarterly*. 74. 2011, pp. 244–266. access: 15.08.2016.

Gudmundsdottir Solrun H.: *Developing Cosmopolitan Capital. Gaining Cosmopolitan Capital Through Study Abroad* (University of Iceland School of Humanities MA in English Teaching) 2015. Retrieved: 15.08.2016 http://skemman.is/stream/get/1946/20849/47889/1/SHG_CC_and_study_abroad_done.pdf

Kalter Frank: *Social Capital and the Dynamics of Temporary Labour Migration from Poland to Germany*, Oxford University Press, 2011.

Kalter Frank/Kogan Irena: "Migrant Networks and Labor Market Integration of Immigrants from the Former Soviet Union in Germany". *Social Forces* June, Vol. 92 Issue 4, 2014, pp. 1435–1456.

Kalter Frank/ Will Gisella: "Social Capital in Polish-German Migration Decision-Making: Complementing the Ethnosurvey with a Prospective View"*Annals of the American Academy of Political and Social Science*, 666 (1), 2016, pp. 46–63.

Korpi Walter: "Faces of Inequality: Gender, Class, and Patterns of Inequalities in Different Types of Welfare States". *Social Politics,* Oxford University Press. 2000, pp. 127–191. Retrieved: 15.08.2016

http://www.medicine.gu.se/digitalAssets/1453/1453386_127.full.pdf

Kjeldstad Randi/Lappegard, Trude: "How do gender values and household practices cohere? Value-practice configurations in a gender egalitarian context" *Discussion Papers* No. 683, Statistics Norway, Research Department. 2012. Retrieved: 15.08.2016

https://www.ssb.no/a/publikasjoner/pdf/DP/dp683.pdf

Kosakowska-Berezecka Natasza et al.: „Changing country, changing gender roles—migration and transformation of gender roles within the family—a case of Polish migrants in Norway" in: *Parenting From Afar: The Reconfiguration of the Family Across Distance,* Eds. Maria de Guzman et al. Oxford University Press. 2016.

Łukasiuk Magdalena: *Obcy w Mieście Migracja do Współczesnej Warszawy.* Wydawnictwo Akademickie ŻAK. 2007.

Martin John Levi/ George Matt: "Theories of Sexual Stratification: Toward an Analytics of the Sexual Field and a Theory of Sexual Capital." *Sociological Theory.* 24, 2006, pp. 107–132.

OECD 2011 and OECD 2014. Retrieved: 15.08.2016

http://www.oecd.org/els/soc/PF2_1_Parental_leave_systems.pdf, PF2.1: Key characteristics of parental leave systems.

Szlendak Tomasz: *Socjologia rodziny.* Warszawa: Wydawnictwo Naukowe PWN 2010.

Thévenon Olivier: "Family Policies in OECD Countries: A Comparative Analysis". *Population and Development Review* 37(1), 2011, pp. 57–87.

United Nations: *Men in Families and Family Policy in a Changing World.* 2011. Retrieved: 15.08.2016.

http://www.un.org/esa/socdev/ family/docs/men-in-families.pdf.

Wacquant Loic J.D.: "Pugs at Work: Bodily Capital and Bodily Labour among Professional Boxers" *Body & Society* 1: 65 1995: pp. 65–93.

Wagner Anne-Catherine: *Les classes sociales dans la mondialisation.* Paris: Découverte. 2007.

Warner-Søderholm Gillian: But we're not all Vikings! Intercultural Identity within a Nordic Context *Journal of Intercultural Communication,* 29, 2012, pp. 19–32.

Żadkowska Magdalena: „O pułapkach tradycji podczas przygotowań do świąt wielkanocnych", pp. 282–295. In: Eds. Dorota Rancew-Sikory, Grażyna Woroniecka, Cezary Obracht-Prondzyński. *Kreacje i nostalgie. Antropologiczne spojrzenie na tradycje w nowoczesnych kontekstach.* Warszawa: Polskie Towarzystwo Socjologiczne. 2009.

Żadkowska Magdalena: „Para w praniu. O współczesnej rodzinie i codziennych czynnościach w socjologii Jeana-Claude'a Kaufmanna," *Sudia Socjologiczne*, 2012, pp. 143–165.

Żadkowska Magdalena/Kosakowska-Berezecka Natasza/Ryndyk Oleksandr: "Two worlds of fatherhood—comparing the use of parental leave among Polish fathers in Poland and in Norway" in: *Migration - Ethnicity - Nation: Studies in Culture, Society and Politics* Eds: K. Slany, E. Guribye, P. Pustułka, M. Ślusarczyk. Peter Lang International Publishing House. 2016a.

Żadkowska Magdalena: *Para w praniu. Codzienność, partnerstwo, obowiązki domowe.* Gdańsk: Wydawnictwo Uniwersytetu Gdańskiego. 2016b.

Nóra Kovács

Global Migration and Intermarriage in Chinese-Hungarian Context[1]

Abstract *The paper scrutinizes life events narrated by a Hungarian woman married to a Chinese wholesale tradesman for almost thirty years. Their relationship was challenged regularly by apparently irreconcilable notions of marriage, family, and love; notions shaped by their different sociocultural backgrounds. Their experiences are integrated into the results of an anthropological research on Chinese-Hungarian mixed couples.*

Introduction

This anthropological paper scrutinizes life events narrated by a middle aged Hungarian woman married to a Chinese wholesale tradesman for almost thirty years. The conversation with her opened up a window to several decades of the life of a Chinese-Hungarian mixed marriage and mixed family challenged regularly by apparently irreconcilable notions of marriage, family, and love; notions shaped by the spouses' different sociocultural backgrounds.

I shall call this woman Susan and I refer to her husband as Zhang. These are not their real names. In an attempt to protect their identity I changed their names as well as some other particularly revealing details of their lives. The interview with Susan had two sessions, provided a large and rich text that sheds light on a so far unexplored group of phenomena. This interview provided deeps insights into the intimate borderland between Chinese migrants and members of the Hungarian host society.

Tracing Susan and Zhang's relationship from its genesis in the isolated cold war era to the globalised present, migrants' transnational practices appear as factors shaping mixed marriage experience and intimacy in a fundamental way. Susan's ethnographically rich account reflects elaborately on how distance and closeness is created and manifested in cultural terms revealing the dynamics of exchange and emotion in their relationship.

The wider context of the topic is inseparable from the contemporary phenomenon of international migration. The interpretation of this particular couple's

---

1 The project received support from Hungarian National Research Fund – OTKA K-112282.

experiences are combined with and integrated into the results of a piece of anthropological research on Chinese-Hungarian mixed couples, an inquiry that explores an intimate aspect of Chinese migrants' presence and integration in Hungary (Kovács, 2015). The discussion is based on data gathered through fieldwork and semi-structured interviews with members of married, cohabiting and dating couples as well as members of separated or divorced couples, and to a lesser extent on online ethnography and online content analysis. Referring to similar attempts in the EU (Gaspar, 2011) the research project has aimed at setting up a relationship typology. It studies how spatial mobility and transnational practices shape the lives of mixed marriage-based families. Furthermore, it has explored notions and values that are at play in shaping the dynamics of these relations.

Susan and Zhang's story

By the time Susan met her would-be husband Zhang in East Africa in 1987 she probably kept no memory of the vow she made at age thirteen never to marry a Hungarian man. Susan, a highly qualified and reflective intellectual graduated from a top Hungarian university, recalled it later when she was trying to make sense of her nearly three decades of married life.

It was her second study period in East Africa when she, 27 at the time, entered in a relationship with Zhang, a twenty-year old man from Southwest China, sent there by the PRC as part of his training to become a Chinese diplomat in Africa. Susan got pregnant shortly after they met. Chinese authorities considered Zhang's intimate affair with Susan a potential jeopardy and sent him back to Beijing where, according to Susan's story, he was kept in home custody for nearly a year. Susan returned to her parents' home from Africa and she gave birth to their first child in 1988. Zhang's escape from China to Hungary in January, 1989 coincided with the beginning of the three-year period when Hungary's borders were opened to Chinese citizens and when tens of thousands of Chinese migrants arrived in Hungary with an entrepreneurial spirit.

Susan's young Chinese partner, Zhang, also moved in with her parents in a small town close to the capital in 1989. Their coexistence started badly and continued worse. Susan's mother disliked Zhang from the moment he arrived. Susan recalled her mum slapping at Zhang's hands when he opened the pantry door or the chest of drawers. Susan, Zhang and their one-year-old moved to a rented apartment, the first in a long series of temporary homes in the suburbia of the capital city.

According to Susan's story, it was a piece of advice from Chinese acquaintances of Zhang's in Hungary and a subsequent family mobility decision that made eight-month-pregnant Susan the very last Hungarian refugee in an Austrian refugee camp in September, 1989, months after the 1951 Geneva refugee convention was signed by Hungary. Two other important life events occurred during their stay in Austria: she had their second child in the camp and, under some pressure from camp authorities, they got married officially. After a physically, mentally, and emotionally challenging year of married life in the refugee camp, Susan returned to Hungary with their children, while Zhang stayed on in Austria to work as a blue collar employee of a local company, visiting his wife and children on a regular basis.

Back in Hungary Susan earned the family's living, including their rent, as a freelance professional. While working in Austria Zhang made efforts to learn German and tried to convince Susan to send their children to China to live with his parents for a couple of years, a proposal Susan kept rejecting categorically whenever the issue came up. The couple's third child was born in 1993.

It was the arrival of his brother from China in the same year that set Zhang on the career track of the typical Chinese entrepreneur of the 1990s in Hungary. Together with his brother they opened a series of shops all over the country and beyond its borders, and their business prospered. The brothers' father aged 68 at the time arrived from China to live with Zhang's family and to assist his sons in their enterprise. Coexistence with her father-in-law resulted in a never ending conflict for Susan. As a result, Zhang and his father left the family home and moved to a nearby small town characterized by a dominantly working class population, a feature Susan considered relevant in their choice of location. This incident loosened the link between Zhang and his Hungarian family to a certain extent; nevertheless he paid regular visits to the family and the couples' twins were born in 1998. According to Susan's account, these visits often led to confrontations between Zhang and his wife or children, often about issues related to what to spend money on. It was years later when Susan learned that Zhang had a series of liaisons, mostly with Hungarian women, following the years he and his father moved out.

An important episode took place the year after the twins were born. In 1999 Zhang made an attempt to move his wife and children to China for at least one year, possibly longer, as he planned. Zhang's reasons and considerations behind this project are also known from Susan's side. It seems that he wanted to make up for his children's Chinese language education, an area abandoned up to that point. Suitcases packed with Hungarian schoolbooks for a year, Susan took a plane to China with her children to meet Zhang at Beijing Airport. The family returned to Hungary in less than three weeks. Susan's elaborate sub-narrative gives a detailed account of how and why the project failed.

Having returned from China, Zhang continued to reside away from his family and his visits became more sporadic and less foreseeable. However, until about

2004 he did have a bed in the family home that Susan managed to purchase in the end. Susan and her children's relationship with Zhang was continually deteriorating until another significant event occurred. In 2011 Susan's father-in-law aged 85 decided to move back to China definitively. One of Zhang's employees encouraged him to attend the church services of a neo-Christian sect in his town of residence, a development that may be associated with his renewed interest in visiting his practically separated wife and children more frequently. Shortly before our last interview was made in 2014 Zhang made an explicit attempt to reconcile with Susan.

Table 1. Susan and Zhang: Key dates and events

Year	Events in Susan and Zhang's lives
1959	Susan is born in a small conservative town into a lower-middle class family, her parents originating from small, remote village communities.
1967	Zhang is born in Southwest China into a poor, lower class family of workers living in a marriage preceded by forced divorces and arranged forcefully by state authorities.
1987	Susan and Zhang meet in Africa, engage in a relationship, Susan gets pregnant and returns to Hungary, Zhang is sent back to China and kept in home custody in Beijing.
1988	Their first child is born in Hungary.
1989	Zhang joins Susan and his child in Hungary. They go to Austria as refugees, they marry and their second child is born in a refugee camp.
1990–1994	Zhang is employed in Austria as a blue collar worker, commutes monthly to Hungary.
1990	Susan returns to Hungary with their children.
1993	Zhang's brother migrates to Hungary to start a business and suggests to his brother that they work together. Zhang returns to live in Hungary and the brothers open a series of shops. Susan and Zhang's third child is born.
1995	Zhang's father arrives to live with Susan and Zhang. This generates a serious conflict and Zhang and his father move out. Susan alone provides for her children although Zhang's business prospers.
1998	The couple's twins are born.
1999	The family makes a failed attempt to get settled in China.
1999–2011	Zhang has a series of love affairs with Hungarian women.
2011	Zhang's father returns to China.
2014	Zhang joins a neo-Christian religious sect and makes attempts to reconcile with his wife and family.

Chinese migrants in Hungary

Several aspects of the Chinese diaspora, the most numerous visibly non-Hungarian immigrant group in Hungary, had already been explored by the mid-2010s. What differentiates this population from other Chinese diasporas in Western Europe or North America is its less than three decades of history and its specific business profile that can be associated with much lower levels of integration and local language acquisition, particularly so in the case of the first generation. Chinese citizens needed no visa to enter Hungary between 1989 and 1992 and their numbers reached neared forty thousand by the late 1990s. Establishing retail networks they provided Hungarians with cheap consumer goods, a process described by Pál Nyíri (2007). He interpreted Chinese tradesmen's role played in Hungarian society as that of a "middleman minority", a concept introduced by Jonathan Turner and Edna Bonacich in 1980. The concept of middleman minority refers to migrants who, based on cross border ethnic networks, occupy institutionalised positions in certain well-defined areas of the economy between the highest and the lowest strata of society, while they stay outside social hierarchy since they are foreigners. This is an important idea that has a bearing on the formation of partner relationships between Chinese migrants and members of the host society (Nyíri, 2007). According to a more recent study focusing on the Chinese business model in Hungary, regional wholesale activities have become dominant in case of the more successful Chinese entrepreneurs (Várhalmi, 2013).

The changing economic and legal environment in Hungary may have contributed to a substantial drop in their numbers by the mid-2010s. In 2015 there were an estimated fifteen thousand Chinese citizens living and working in Hungary. Demographically, the Chinese migrants formed a relatively young and educated, gender-balanced population in Hungary equipped with the social capital of transnational networks. Thus the "typical" Chinese migrant of the early 1990s to Hungary could be of either sex, aged around twenty five coming from any part of mainland China, likely to have completed some formal education including a college degree. But she or he would pursue commercial activities and would show limited interest in learning Hungarian. Most of them chose the capital, Budapest as their place of residence. Besides commercial units, shops, markets, food stands and restaurants, dozens of immigrant Chinese organisations and institutions have been formed since the early 1990s (Kováts, 2012, p. 60).

The linguistic position and degree of integration of the second generation of Chinese migrants in Hungary are very different from that of their parents. A piece of anthropological research has recently explored several aspects of second generation Chinese identity in Hungary, with a special emphasis on the hybridity of the second generation's so-called banana identity (Beck, 2015, p. 59). Using life history interview as a technique, a comparative international project focused on the patterns of integration and attitudes towards migrant women, including a sample of Chinese migrant women in Hungary (Kovács and Meleg, 2010). The school experiences of Chinese children in Hungary have also been studied in a comparative context by a group of anthropologists (Feischmidt and Nyíri, 2006).

Chinese-Hungarian partner relationships – background

Until recently the intimate relationships between Chinese migrants and Hungarians have not been targeted specifically. A first research report of the current research project on intimate relations between Chinese migrants and Hungarians discussed interethnic partner relationships (Kovács, 2015).

There is extensive literature in demography, sociology, social anthropology and migration research that discusses issues relevant to the study of Chinese-Hungarian mixed relationships. Three branches of literature have proved to be particularly helpful in the attempt to understand and handle this phenomenon: studies on Chinese society, especially on changing family relations; migration studies with a focus on mixed marriage as a factor of migrants' integration; and sociological relationship studies that include notions of race, culture or transnationality in their analyses.

An attempt to understand the inner dynamics of Chinese-Hungarian mixed partner relationships in Hungary is inseparable from the conceptual framework of "transnational anthropology" with a simultaneous focus on two or more locations, social networks, and discourse and symbol systems affecting migrants' lives. The focus in migration research thus shifted from assimilation models, the melting pot theory, and second generation culture change towards the study of simultaneous economic, family and cultural ties of diasporas with two or more locations or countries (Basch et. al., 1994), a daily reality of migrants' ethnically mixed marriages.

Matthijs Kalmijn found that theories of partner choice provide important clues to the causes of intermarriage (Kalmijn, 1998). Literature has also approached intermarriage as a channel of immigrant integration. A study based on registry data from thirty-nine immigrant groups in Sweden stresses the differences between immigration patterns and immigrant integration in the US and Europe (Dribe, 2008). Two of their statements draw the attention to important aspects of the phenomenon studied. They emphasize that there are differences between immigrant groups in terms of family culture, family systems, kin relations, and marriage customs; and that these are highly persistent over time (Dribe, 2008).

The results of Kalmijn and van Tubergen (Kalmijn, 2005) concerning the role of cultural factors in endogamy are in line with those of Dribe and Lundh (2008). Sofia Gaspar's (2011) attempt to elaborate an international migrant marriage typology for a Western European context proved to be a good point of departure to set up Chinese-Hungarian relationship typology.

By surveying nearly two thousand Chinese married couples about their marital relations and the quality of their marriage, Ellen Efron Pimentel (2000) provides a vivid picture of Chinese marriages in an urban setting at the end of the 20th century (Efron Pimentel, 2000). "Can a common set of assumptions about the marital relationship be applied to different societies?", she formulates one of her central questions regarding Beijing marriages (Efron Pimentel, 2000, p. 32). Pimentel points out that "historically the conjugal bond took a distant second place to intergenerational ties between parents and children, especially sons", and that "marriage was universal and utilitarian, conducted for the purposes of having children and furthering the larger family group" (Efron Pimentel, 2000, p. 33). During the 20th century, however, ideas about marital relations in China have changed greatly. Pimentel concludes that parental approval seemed to affect marriage quality strongly and the Chinese couples seemed to share a relatively unromantic vision of love (Efron Pimentel, 2000, p. 44).

Chinese-Hungarian partner relationships – a project overview

The research on Chinese-Hungarian inter-ethnic partner relationships discussed in this paper was driven by the general assumption of literature on Chinese migrant entrepreneurs in Hungary that there are few of such bonds in spite that there is no explicit norm of endogamy valid among Chinese migrants (Nyíri 2006, p. 44). It has to be noted that practices related with the norms of endogamy should be seen differently in the partner choice of first generation young adult migrants arriving and living on their own in Hungary than those of the second generation Chinese youth living in Hungary under close surveillance of their family. Moreover, a distinction has to be made between temporary dating periods and formalised long-term commitment. My fieldwork data suggests that the former is often allowed whereas the latter is often discouraged by parents of Chinese youth in Hungary.

One aim of the current research was to explore whether the assumption concerning the low incidence of this phenomenon held, and if it did what factors accounted for it. My principal focus of interest was the first generation of Chinese migrants. Until January 2016 I spotted thirty-nine such bonds through my personal network of acquaintances and as part of a fieldwork conducted in the

Chinese-Hungarian encounter zone where Chinese migrants and Hungarians meet outside spaces of commerce, at universities and in language schools, tai chi and kung fu trainings, tea houses, and Chinese medical service providers. Online fieldwork was also conducted. I tried to gather as much basic demographic data on the persons and relationships as possible and also attempted to make interviews. Up to the present fifteen formal interviews concerning Chinese-Hungarian mixed partnerships were conducted. In three cases both partners in a relationship were willing to participate. More persons were contacted from the list and some information was obtained from them regarding their relationship without actually conducting an interview. Out of the un-interviewed relations, uneven and fragmented but rich qualitative information was gathered on eighteen couples from third parties and from the internet; and uneven, fragmented and scarce information became available on twelve relationships.

Talking to Hungarians connected in one form or another with Chinese persons in Hungary I encountered two contradicting stereotypes about the composition of these relationships. Some were convinced that it was exclusively Chinese women dating Hungarian men; others held the view that it was always Chinese men forming unions with Hungarian women. My accidental sample turned to be gender balanced with nearly half of the Chinese partners being men. The interviewees belonged to very different age groups from twenty-seven to eighty-three, the relationships ranged from a shorter dating period to an exceptional case of fifty years of marriage. There were cases of marriage, divorce, separation, distance relationship among the interviewed partnerships. The majority of the thirty-nine Chinese partners do not represent the "typical Chinese migrant entrepreneur" of the 1990s, only sixteen out of the thirty-nine dedicate themselves to commerce or restaurants. Most of the others are educated professionals who are employees or work freelance.

To sum up some of the results, the persistence in time of a relationship seems to be different depending on whether the Chinese member of a couple is male or female. Based on the cases encountered during this research, the relationship is more persistent in time if the Chinese partner is female. Chinese-Hungarian intimate bonds outline two basic categories. Relationships of the "typical Chinese migrant" generally involve not only important cultural, but also large educational and social distance between the parties and are likely to become less successful. Relationships called "student love" provided the majority in the sample of this study. The category was labelled after a shared university study period in Hungary, China, or a third country. Affection and romantic engagement played a role in the Chinese partner's mobility. Chinese-Hungarian "Student love" relationships tend to be more harmonious and more persistent in time (Kovács, 2015).

Methodological considerations about the presentation of research results

A unique story

Susan and Zhang's story is a very special one among the cases of Chinese-Hungarian partner relationships encountered during this research project. It started years before the first wave of Chinese migrants arrived in Hungary. Susan and Zhang met in an exotic third world country as fellow students before the fall of the iron curtain. Pressed by family circumstances, at one point they chose to become refugees, a decision the overwhelming majority of Chinese migrants to Hungary would never have made. Although heavily loaded with conflict and periodical separation, and likely to finally end in divorce, their marriage produced five children and lasted nearly three decades.

In spite of its uniqueness and its extreme features, it offers itself for the discussion of several issues considered relevant to the understanding of the workings and dynamics of intimate relationships between Chinese migrants and Hungarians. The case of Susan and Zhang is an example of the "typical" Chinese migrant's relationship since after the initial attempts to study or work as an employee, Zhang's professional career shows the pattern of Chinese migrant entrepreneurs. Her account of their relationship revealed how cultural and socio-emotive difference and large social distance between a Chinese husband and a Hungarian wife may contribute to a state of extended crisis and uncertainty. Susan's insights may contribute to an explanation of why there have been relatively few successful Chinese-Hungarian mixed partner-relationships between the "typical Chinese migrants" of the 1990s to Hungary and members of the host society. By comparing and contrasting certain aspects of Susan and Zhang's lives to those of the other couples studied, central issues like personal motives to enter into a relationship, transnational practices, language strategies, culturally embedded notions of the family, and the role of filial piety in a mixed marriage and family are going to be discussed.

Missing information

Several types of data insufficiency had to be handled during the analysis and interpretation of research results. Empirical research on the Chinese diaspora has proved to be challenging because of migrants' very long working hours, communication difficulties, and a general preference on migrants' part not to participate in any type of research. Some potential interviewees could not be convinced to talk. Incomplete but in certain areas rich qualitative information was gathered about some of the couples from newspapers, television documentaries, internet sites, and the social media.

In the majority of the cases found it was only one of the partners willing to participate in this research. So the views expressed are often not counterbalanced by the partner's version of the relationship. In Susan and Zhang's case it is obviously "her" version of their marriage that is presented here. I had no better option than presenting a one-sided picture, her version of their story, her lived experiences. I tried to explore the Chinese side, too, but Susan was convinced that Zhang would never agree to have an interview on this topic. Throughout the fieldwork period I found men, and especially Chinese men, less willing to talk about personal affairs.

The narrative process and its interpersonal context

In spite of the relatively high rejection rate, during this research project I made several interviews, but very few of them reached similar ethnographic depths as the sessions of conversation with Susan. I felt I learned much from it but also felt that the customary analysis of lexical content wouldn't help me grab enough layers of this phenomenon. While trying to handle this problem I've been inspired by an article authored by Katherine Pratt Ewing. Drawing on insights from sociolinguistics and psychoanalysis she draws the attention to several factors (contextual cues, indexicals, emotional transference and countertransference in the interview situation) to take into account when the researcher wants to turn his or her intuition about a topic into systematic analysis (Pratt Ewing, 2006).

During our encounters solidarity and attunement were created as she knew of my personal experiences of having lived in a mixed marriage and this counterbalanced our uneven positions of power within the interview situation (me prompting, she revealing intimate aspects of her life). As to how the context of our ethnographic encounter was created and how this interview turned out, it is important to tell that it was a mutual friend and former professor who recommended that I should talk to Susan. The shared part of our academic history and the reference to our mutual friend from academia made Susan to take an academic standpoint and have an objective, somewhat distanced look at her own life experience. She gave the impression that the interview situation created for her a new possibility to reflect on different stages of her life with Zhang by turning them into narrations.

Discussion - some factors influencing the dynamics of Chinese-Hungarian partner relationships

Personal motives to enter relationship

In her own interpretation of her marriage Susan's choice of Zhang as her husband is inseparable from her family context of racism and prejudice and her opposition to it. She started her lifelong dispute with her father who came from a closed traditional village community where Susan and her sister were sent regularly for summer holidays. She was categorically banned from playing with Gypsy kids in the village. She and her father argued about issues of racism and discrimination against Gypsies and Jews all their lives, at one point cutting off communication for more than a decade.

Rebellious attitude or not and regardless of the tradesman's career that Zhang finally followed, Susan and Zhang first met in a university context similarly to the majority of the cases interviewed and similarly to the majority of those relationships in the sample that are relatively persistent in time and relatively more harmonious. A typical Chinese tradesman in his early fifties living in Hungary found his younger Hungarian partner at an online Hungarian dating site where they kept corresponding for more than a year before they first met. Although previously considered an important motive behind mixed partner relationships, the attraction of the "exotic other" as a motivating factor appeared only once, in the account of a middle-aged Hungarian man who found perfect beauty when he first cast eyes on his Chinese partner and decided to conquer her. Contemplating the choice of Chinese tradesmen as potential partners one of my Hungarian female informants referred to the constraints of the partner-market saying that "they [Chinese men at the markets and stores] are at least different from the typical Hungarian guy with a bear in one hand and television remote control in the other. It's something new you may find in him."

Susan, three other Hungarian female interviewees, and also a Hungarian male interviewee spontaneously referred to themselves as inherently conservative in terms of traditional gender roles in the family and in terms of values related to the unity of the family and personal efforts to achieve it. All four of them connected their conservative family background to their choice of a Chinese man as partner. Likeness regarding these values, one of the bases of initial engagement in a relationship, turned out to be a double-edged blade working against the integrity of these interethnic bonds in several cases.

Filial piety, family and marriage in the context of interethnic partner relationships

Various aspects of the influence of the Chinese indigenous ethos of filial piety and the related norm of respect to be paid to elders and authorities are discussed widely in literature on Chinese society and family (Cong and Silverstein, 2008; Naftali, 2009). This norm holds differently in the behaviour of different social and geographical groups in China (Naftali, 2009). Filial piety seems to have an important bearing on the formation, development, persistence and quality of Chinese-Hungarian intimate bonds, the more so, the larger the socio-cultural gap is between the partners. Susan and Zhang's case provides an extreme example of this. From Susan's viewpoint Zhang's filial duties towards his elderly father, a bond apparently unaccompanied by European versions of affection and closeness between father and son, became Zhang's highest priority ever since his father arrived to stay in Hungary. Accompanying, housing, financing his father and prioritising his wishes and needs against those of his wife and children resulted in conflict, separation, and a trust deficiency not only between the spouses but also between Zhang and his children.[2]

Duties towards the Chinese partner's parents appeared in some of the interviews, although they were seen and treated differently depending on what relationship category the bond fit. Let me refer again to the two categories, "student love" and the "relationship of the typical Chinese migrant", mentioned earlier. Practices related to filial piety were reported as causes of family tension or conflict in cases of the latter category. "Student love" migrants handled these duties with more ease and reacted to challenges with close cooperation. In one case where both partners were interviewed the married couple with two children often referred to the preparations they made to be able to house the wife's retired parents who would come to live with them in Hungary indefinitely. A specific subgroup of "love migrants" within the sample is characterized by high qualifications with multiple language skills and a high degree of job-related international mobility. Tensions or conflict related to the duties of filial piety in cases of the couples belonging to this category seem to have been missing altogether.

---

2   During the years Zhang's father resided in Hungary two of Zhang's siblings also lived there, one of them working closely together as an associate, Zhang being the only one with a spouse and family. Susan recalled several incidents when the brothers, well into their thirties, competed violently and on one occasion fought physically over which one of them their father loved most.

Zhen Cong and Merril Silverstein (2008) studied intergenerational assistance and its relation to the well-being of elders in a rural province of China that shows a marked preference for assistance from sons and their families. They reached an interesting conclusion. Elders' depressive symptoms were reduced when they received assistance from daughters-in-law, and increased when assistance came from sons, suggesting that the benefits from intergenerational support was conditional on culturally prescribed norms (Cong and Silverstein, 2008). Culturally prescribed norms influencing the quality of and happiness in a relationship are also discussed by Catherine Charsley (2005). Approaching her topic from husbands' point of view she found that relationship quality and happiness are affected by factors associated with migration and culturally conditioned expectations. Considering Cong and Silverstein's result alongside with Pimentel's results on the importance of parental approval of a marriage as a key factor in marriage quality, it would be tempting to associate these findings with one of the results on the research on Chinese-Hungarian relationships. Actions taken by daughters-in-law may have an important influence on the extended Chinese families' well-being and it may have a negative effect if they do not or cannot meet certain cultural expectations. Another culturally conditioned norm related to the behaviour of daughters-in-law (and also sons-in-law) is their willingness to send their very young children to stay with grandparents in China for longer time periods. Sending children is an important step in the exchange process within the family where it consolidates grandparents' role and position. These considerations may give clues to the reason why bonds between Chinese men and Hungarian women are less persistent and why a lower success rate can be associated with them.

While talking to members of "relationships of the typical Chinese migrants" in Hungary, issues related to filial duties were frequently connected to Chinese migrants' culturally different notion of the family. The following excerpt from the conversation with Susan provides an extreme case yet highlights some of the central problems that may arise:

S: *The way I see it, no matter how many foreign languages my husband speaks, certain concepts would simply have different meanings in any language we would use to communicate. So, when I say my family, and when he says my family, it is a different thing that appears in his mind. (…) My family refers to his parents first of all. And his ancestors. And in a way we are somehow also included in the extended family as appendices, but we are of no primary interest. A completely different idea of the family… Most of his energy and efforts go into showing his parents how good a son he is and into supporting his parents in a maximal way. Well, now I am going to give you an extreme example: one of the reasons why our marriage failed was that he never supported us in any way. He thought that since I earned relatively good money, he had no reason to support his children financially. So I was*

supposed to maintain them. And I [referring to Zhang] would accumulate all I earn and buy
a house for my parents in China, and buy a restaurant for my cousin in China, and so forth.

N: Is a cousin a more important family tie?

S: Yes, in the sense that…actually, it isn't. Not from an emotional point of view. That is also
a gesture for his parents. To demonstrate to them how good a person their son is, and not
only personally to his parents, but also to their neighbours, their entire neighbourhood. He
wants to help his parents increase their prestige, so when they talk to the other elderly people
or play mah-jong with them they could tell that their son bought this and that, and helped
the family this way and that way. Do you understand" (Susan)

It is quite clear, that different cultural notions of seemingly universal concepts, like family, would not – and does not – doom Chinese-Hungarian marriages to unresolvable conflict or failure. In this case we have Susan who lives a life of protest against his father's racism and prejudices. At the same time, her conservative religious background makes her have a fatalistic vision of marriage: Zhang is her share of marriage in life and she has felt obliged to persist in her marriage much longer than other Hungarian women I talked to. On the other hand we have Zhang with his different cultural concepts, the austerity of his poor, working class background and a last, very important thing: a family history of lack of affection in intimate family ties. The combination of individual traits and more general cultural notions seem to be important ingredients in how the marriage and family history of Zhang and Susan's bond have developed for nearly three decades.

Exploring causes of why the Chinese work extremely hard by Western standards, Stevan Harrell (1985) makes a point that sheds light on the connection between the notion of family and the notion of Chinese work ethics (Harrell, 1985). He argues that socialization and material incentives alone cannot be held responsible for work-related practices in China. He concludes that the "Chinese have been socialized, after all, not just to work hard, but to work hard for the long-term benefit of the family" (Harrell, 1985, p. 224).

During our conversation about their marriage that we may consider an extreme case Susan questioned Zhang's ability to love, a trait that may have resulted from his austere and unhappy family environment. At the same time several of my interviewees commented upon the role of closeness, intimacy and affection in understanding and accepting cultural otherness through their partner, even in cases of failed relationships.

Transnational practices, language strategies, cosmopolitism

Although Chinese migrants to Hungary can be considered a schoolbook example of a transnational migrant population, the degree of transnationality in the sample in general was relatively low. The patterns of transnational practices of the Chinese-Hungarian couples and families encountered during this research can be related to several factors. Susan and Zhang's case, again, offers a good example of how this has come about. Partners' and offspring's language acquisition is a key issue in theirs as well as in all the other cases, too. Lacking fluency in Chinese language and ways is an obstacle to reaching up to the norms of behaviour expected from close kin. Two of my informants pointed out that grandchildren with no knowledge of Chinese became sources of dissatisfaction and humiliation for their grandparents while visiting them in China.

Although fluent in several languages including an exotic foreign tongue, Susan never studied Chinese formally. She related that at one point when her father-in-law came to live in Hungary she understood quite a bit and could utter some words. When asked for her reasons for not learning she said that in the beginning she was too busy attending her family and later, when conflicts between her and Zhang became more intense, she lost interest in learning. According to Susan, Zhang never spoke Chinese to his children because in Hungary it was his intention to learn Hungarian, and during their stay in Austria he made serious efforts to learn German, goals he finally achieved. According to Susan, their children so far have had no interest in learning Chinese and do not identify with their Chinese heritage at all.

Building a successful and prosperous transnational economy-based enterprise with locally settled Chinese family members and business partners overseas, Zhang fits the stereotypical transnational Chinese businessman. Yet his attempt to move his wife and children to China in 1999 failed. In Susan's account it was not hardships and illnesses nor the lack of comfort the family faced in Zhang's hometown that made the entire family return to Hungary in less than two weeks. Susan highlighted an incident that she thought gave Zhang an ultimate push to change his mind about their mobility decision. Witnessing a husband beating up his wife violently in the bathroom of a local bus station in China, Zhang intervened verbally, indicating to the man that his behaviour was inappropriate. The situation ended in a violent fight in which local men beat Zhang up. When he reappeared with torn clothes and a bleeding face he told Susan that he changed his mind and did not want to move to China with his family after all.

Transnational practices of the other couples in the sample vary according to what relationship category they belong to. "Student love" bonds show two different patterns. The "student love" subgroup composed of highly educated, internationally mobile independent professionals who do not live in Hungary on a permanent basis and have a very high value on the international job market, often use a third language, mostly English, to communicate with their partner while their children become bi- or trilingual. These couples lead a cosmopolitan way of life on which the partners' cultural background does not exert a very tight grip. Other first generation "student love" members in the sample mutually learned to speak their partner's mother tongue, and several of the Hungarian partners had trained to become Chinese language professionals. "Student love" couples' children living in Hungary learn Chinese as one of the languages used at home by their mixed family. "Student love" couples' family economies in the sample are not defined transnationally. They cannot afford to travel to China to visit relatives every year. Children from the "typical Chinese migrants' relationships" with Hungarians – from the least successful group with relatively more cases of conflict and separation - generally know no Chinese at all. This might be connected to several factors: their Hungarian parent's lack of knowledge of Chinese, their parents' general level of education, the deterioration of the relationship between the partners, divorce or separation.

Searching for an explanation why there are few inter-ethnic partnerships between Chinese migrant entrepreneurs and Hungarians in Hungary, and even less such bonds that operate smoothly, we need to see how notions of family and marriage interfere with the operation of migrant entrepreneurs' transnational network-based business model. Why is it much more of a challenge for a Chinese entrepreneur to have a Hungarian partner? This transnational business model has Chinese bridgeheads, often close kin, at all stations of the trading process. According to data in the Hungarian trade registry Hungarian spouses do assist their Chinese partners in establishing the Hungarian bridgehead of their transnational business, nevertheless, they lack knowledge of Chinese and Chinese norms of behaviour towards close relatives and often have a more individualistic vision of intimate relationships. Hungarian spouses, mostly wives cannot and do not want to reach up to the expectations of their partners and their traditional families. The transnational family business-based career is in sharp contrast to the career of the independent professional driven by more individualistic preferences and considerations.

Bibliography

Basch, Linda / Glick Schiller, Nina / Szanton Blanc, Cristina: *Nations unbound. Transnational projects, postcolonial predicaments and deterritorialized nation-states*. Gordon and Breach Science Publishers: New York 1994.

Beck, Fanni: *De ha a tükörbe nézek, az arcom kínai. Másodgenerációs kínai fiatalok hibrid identitáskonstrukciói*. MAKAT Antroport: Budapest 2015.

Charsley, Katharine: "Unhappy Husbands: Masculinity and Migration in Transnational Pakistani Marriages". *The Journal of the Royal Anthropological Institute*, 11 (1), 2005, pp. 85–105.

Cong, Zhen / Silverstein, Merril: "Intergenerational Support and Depression among Elders in Rural China: Do Daughters-in-Law Matter?" *Journal of Marriage and Family*, 70 (3), 2008, pp. 599–612.

Dribe, Martin / Lundh, Christer: "Intermarriage and immigrant integration in Sweden: An exploratory analysis". *Acta Sociologica*, 51, 2008, pp. 329–354.

Efron Pimentel, Ellen: "Just how do I love Thee?: Marital relations in urban China". *Journal of Marriage and Family*, 62 (1), 2000, pp. 32–47.

Feischmidt, Margit / Nyíri, Pál eds.: Nem kívánt gyerekek? Külföldi gyerekek magyar iskolákban [Unwanted children? Foreign children in Hungarian schools]. MTA Nemzeti-Etnikai Kisebbségkutató Intézet / Nemzetközi Migrációs és Menekültügyi Kutatóközpont: Budapest 2006.

Gaspar, Sofia: "Comparing EU bi-national partnerships in Spain and Italy". *Sociologia On Line*, 2, 2011, pp. 101–119.

Harrell, Stevan: "Why do the Chinese work so hard? Reflections on an entrepreneurial ethic". *Modern China*, 11 (2), 1985, pp. 203–226.

Kalmijn, Matthijs: "Intermarriage and Homogamy: Causes, Patterns, Trends". *Annual Review of Sociology*, 24, 1998, pp. 395–421.

Kalmijn, Matthijs / de Graaf, Paul M. / Janssen, Jacques P. G.: "Intermarriage and the Risk of Divorce in the Netherlands: The Effects of Differences in Religion and in Nationality, 1974–94", *Population Studies*, 59, (1), 2005, pp. 71–85.

Kovács, Éva / Melegh, Attila eds.: „*Azt hittem célt tévesztettem" A bevándorló nők élettörténeti perspektívái, integrációja és a bevándorlókkal kapcsolatos attitűdök nyolc európai országban.* KSH Népességtudományi Kutatóintézet: Budapest 2010.

Kovács, Nóra: "Cultures unfolding. Experiences of Chinese-Hungarian mixed couples in Hungary". *Current Issues in Personality Psychology* 3(4), 2015, pp. 254–264.

Kováts, András: *Migráns szervezetek Magyarországon. Kutatási zárótanulmány.* MTA Társadalomtudományi Kutatóközpont, Kisebbségkutató Intézet: Budapest 2012.

Naftali, Orna: "Empowering the Child: Children's Rights, Citizenship and the State in Contemporary China". China Journal, 61, 2009, pp. 79–103.

Nyíri, Pál: *Chinese in Eastern Europe and Russia: A Middleman Minority in a Transnational Era. (Chinese Worlds)*, London and New York: Routledge 2007.

Nyíri, Pál: "Kínaiak és afgánok Magyarországon: két migráns csoport érvényesülési stratégiái". In: Feischmidt, Margit / Nyíri, Pál eds.: *Nem kívánt gyerekek?*

Külföldi gyerekek magyar iskolákban. MTA Nemzeti-Etnikai Kisebbségkutató Intézet / Nemzetközi Migrációs és Menekültügyi Kutatóközpont: Budapest 2006, pp. 39–74.

Ochs, Elinor / Capps, Lisa: "Narrating the Self" *Annual Review of Anthropology,* 25, 1996, pp. 19–43.

Pratt Ewing, Katherine: "Revealing and Concealing: Interpersonal Dynamics and the Negotiation of Identity in the Interview." *Ethos: Journal of the Society for Psychological Anthropology* 34 (1), 2006, pp. 89–122.

Várhalmi, Zoltán: "Vállalkozó migránsok Magyarországon". In: Kováts, András ed.: *Bevándorlás és integráció. Magyarországi adatok, európai indikátorok.* MTA Társadalomtudományi Kutatóközpont: Budapest 2013, pp. 89–100.

Viorela Ducu, Iulia Hossu

Bi-national Couples with a Romanian Partner in the European Context[1]

Abstract *Partners' countries of origin and of residence mold the life modes of bi-national couples, influencing their practices, including the language they use, up to the emergence of a neutral-language strategy. They face different degrees of acceptance, displayed through children's raising and education, religion, tradition and choice of country.*

Theoretical contextualization

Bi-national couples are considered "a desirable by-product of the European project" (Brahic, 2013, p. 699) and in the past years the interest for this research has exponentially grown, being present on the work agendas of many researchers. Through the intensification of Romanians' migration during the last decade, the number of bi-national marriages by Romanian citizens also rose, among all of the eastern European nationalities it seems like Romanians are the most open minded about bi-national marriage (Robila, 2010). This paper aims to analyze the practices (Morgan, 2011a, b) this type of family employs in order to be displayed "as a family" (Finch 2007, 2011, Dermott and Seymour, 2011). The defining trait of the bi-national couples seems to be the choice of the country of residence (Brahic 2013, Gaspar 201). They way of displaying is directly influenced by the public's attitude (Finch, 2011, Morgan 2011a) of which they confront themselves with: like the family/community, and this occurs especially when they are forming as a couple, i.e. when the level of acceptance of the others becomes very important (Ducu, 2016). The essential issues in exposing the differences in the bi-national couple are critical and important moments (Brubaker *et al.*, 2006, Haynes and Dermott, 2011) such as choosing a religion for the matrimony or for children's baptisms, or choosing the children's citizenship. But for these bi-national couples it seems that the practices they have in using the language in their family become the traits that define the manifestation on the bi-nationality (Gaspar, 2009), a happening that not only "happens" (Brubaker *et al.*, 2006: 302) in certain moments

---

1 This work was supported by a grant of the Romanian National Authority for Scientific Research and Innovation, CNCS – UEFISCDI, project number PN-II-RU-TE-2014-4-2087.

that are defining, and this "doing bi-national families" is active, fluid and daily (Morgan, 2011, b).

Romanians in Europe

Romania's adhering to the E.U. in 2007 was followed by a growth in the number of Romanians who have decided to live for a period of their lives in a European country other than Romania. Furthermore, after 2014, Romanians were given the right to work, in Great Britain inclusively, which was a determinant factor in the approach of Romanians leaving for Great Britain.

In broad lines, the approach to the movement of Romanians into other European countries in recent times can be divided into three periods: the Communist period, the period between 1989–2007, the period after 2007.

In the communist era we speak about very few instances of legally moving (persons who were granted exceptional status, such as people liked by the communist system, or the repatriation program of Germans from Romania). Another category of Romanians who moved to Europe were the ones who have managed to flee the country: either never returning from a legal exit path the government had granted when the travel permit expired, or being able to pass the border illegally and then applying for refugee status. But the European countries were not very open to the refugees from Communist Romania, and due to this fact the latter mostly headed to North America.

After 1989 and the opening of the borders, more and more Romanians managed to move and live in longer or shorter periods of time in countries across Europe. The most visible ones were those who have illegally migrated for work, a part of whom managed to legalize their stay through marriage with citizens from other European states. But a large number of Romanians studied abroad in 1989–2007 or have moved to unite with the family. In the 90s there was a trend of marriage with other citizens of other European states and a large number were using dating announcements. Accepting Romania as a part of the E.U. project accelerated the movement of Romanians in between member states. Of course the move was for work, especially the work that required low skills. But a great number of Romanians have also worked as high-skilled workers in many European states or have studied abroad: more and more young people decided to study and graduate at a university abroad.

On the above grounds, we have included into our research participants who are situated in different categories: from Romanian refugees in the Communist era, illegal migrant in 1989–2007 and "free movers" (Favell 2003, Gaspar, 2010) after 2007.

Methodological aspects

The research will be based on the qualitative analysis of data obtained through interviews (individual or couple) with transnational family members living abroad (UK or Belgium). We have analyzed the stories of 10 couples, obtained either through couple interviews with both partners (5 couple interviews) or individual interviews (5 interviews with the woman partner of the couple).

Structure of the interviews
UK
Virginia and Alexander (Romania, UK, 23 years) – couple interview
Cristi and Petra (Romania, Czech Republic, 3 years) – couple interview
Adi and Katarina (Romania, Lithuania, 3 years) – couple interview
Mila and Dragoslav (Romania, Serbia, 25 years) – individual interview

Belgium
Tudor and Stanka (Romania, Bulgaria, 1 year) – couple interview
Gabi and Edin (Romania, Belgium, 9 years) – couple interview
Cristina and Gabyn (Romania, Belgium, 20 years) – individual interview, Cristina
Dana and Otho (Romania, Germany, 2 years) – individual interview, Dana
Lilia and Milos (Romania/Slovak, Slovakia, 19 years) – individual interview, Lilia
Agora and Alonzo (Romania and Spain, 2 years) – individual interview, Agora

Countries of origin and countries of residence

The country in which bi-national couples decide to move (Brahic, 2013, Gaspar, 2010) is especially influenced by one of the partners if the decision is made in favor of that partner's country and this is a major force difference in favor of the majoritarian partner. Few of our couples share the classical story of encounter when a partner goes to the other's country, they form a couple and live together in the country of one of the partners. Gabi and Edin are in such a situation, having met and living in Belgium, as well as Cristina and Gabyn, who met in Romania and live in Belgium. Although they have lived in the UK, Alexander's country, for 20 years, Virginia and her husband met in Ireland and had a relationship from afar, then they married and moved to the UK. However, we observe that these couples, where one of the partners is the member of the majority in the country of residence, were formed a longer while ago, at the beginning of Romanian migration: Virginia, Gabi and Cristina left Romania during the first years after the Revolution.

Even if they met their partners in their country of origin, Lilia and Mila ended up living in a third country. Lilia (an ethnic Slovak from Romania) and Milos have met in Slovakia, where Lilia was having her secondary studies, then they both moved to Belgium. In contrast, Mila met Dragoslav in Serbia, but she has been living in the UK for the last 6 year, hence their relationship has become a transnational one. After establishing a family in Eastern Europe many years ago, Lilia and Mila had to confront a second migration within their life history, ending up living in Western Europe.

The more recently formed mixed couples from our analysis ended up living in other countries than those their members come from.

Agora (an ethnic Aromanian from Romania) also met her partner at home, in Alonzo's last months of stay in Romania, but their careers have changed direction so that for almost 2 years they have had a transnational relationship, he stayed in Argentina and she in Belgium.

Dana and Otho, Tudor and Stanka, Adi and Katarina met in the countries where they also live as a couple, but this is not the country of any one of them. The same is the case with Cristi and Petra, although they met in the UK, they started their relationship through the Internet, while Petra was still at home in the Czech Republic, her migration to the UK having the explicit goal of living with Cristi.

Only three of our couples confirm the "classic model" of the Eastern European (especially one of the women) who marries the West European to accede a better position in life (Gaspar, 2010), more than this, out of the three couples, Cristina left Romania after she met her husband; Virginia and Gabi had left the country for several years and only after that, they met their husbands abroad. At the time these couples were formed Romania was not an EU member.

We have two couples that work transnationally: Mila and Dragoslav; Agora and Alonzo (one partner in the EU and the other outside of the EU). Mila could be placed in the migrant category because of the work and life she had in the UK, out of the necessity of course and Dragoslav is from a non EU country (Serbia), the couple being in the position of living transnationally as a necessity. It is not the same case for Agora and Alonzo, they are from the free movers' category that has moved either for studies (she is in an internship for PhD classes in Belgium) or for a better job (Alonzo moves to different countries in function of the professional opportunities he might have).

Four of our couples: Virginia and Alexander, Mila and Dragoslav, Crsitina and Gabyn, Gabi and Edin; qualify of what Brahic defined in 2013 as a bi-national couple: the term "bi-national" is based on a legal categorisation (individuals' nationality) imposed on individuals by the State. In a strict legal sense and in the context of this study, this term solely acknowledges the difference of nationality between partners. In other words, it does not presuppose the existence of other differences in terms of culture or language, for example." (Brahic, 2013, p. 703). Even when Romania has entered the EU, Romanian – Western-European couples can still be considered bi-national European couples, since European bi-national marriages are defined as marriages between partners with a different European nationality at the time of marriage. (Koelet and de Valk 2013, p. 4)

Six out of the ten couples can be put in a certain category called intra-couples, starting from what Gaspar had defined in 2008 as a "European intra-marriage to refer to marital unions between citizens from different national contexts inside the EU" (Gaspar 2008, 2010).

We use the expression couples and not marriages because Tudor and Stanka, Agora and Alonzo, Adi and Katarina, Cristi and Petra are not married even when the last two couples already have children. On the other hand, Dana and Otto and Lilia and Milos are married, the latter also having children.

Unlike previous research that focused on bi-national European couples, especially in the residence country of one of the couples' members (van Mol and de Valk, 2014; Koelet and de Valk, 2013, 2016), we can observe that all of our six intra-European couples live in other countries than the original ones of one of the partners, including the transnational couple Agora-Alonzo, who, even if living in different countries, none of the partners comes from the country they currently reside in. If four of the six couples could be put in the category of free movers or the high-skilled, in the case of the couples Cristi and Petra and Adi and Katarina, they are more likely to adhere to the category of "migrants who take advantage of welfare": they are migrants for work, and even though each of them has a child, they would rather not get married, in order to benefit of the social support for the "single mother". We can conclude that being a bi-national couple without aiming for the support of the partner in the country of origin is not a phenomenon that is specific for elites. Furthermore, through the growth in the movement of citizens among the EU countries, we can expect that the numbers of these couples would exponentially grow in the future.

Acceptance from the extended family and the community

The way in which the members of the family and the community accepts the mixed couples influences the way the couple is auto perceiving itself (Huijnk, Verkuyten and Coenders 2012). If mixed couples are confronting an opposition from their family members they would rather try to portray the double identity of the partners (Ducu 2016). In the matter of bi-national couples the acceptance degree depends of the perception they have on the country of origin of the other partner.

In our research, couples formed a long time ago, in the country of origin of one of their member, have been accepted more easily by the extended family of the foreign partner, either since they knew too little of Romania, as was the case of Alexander's family, or on the contrary, had had positive experiences with Romanians before, such as the situation of Edin, who used to be friends with famous Romanian tennis men, hosted by his family, before meeting Gabi.

> E.: No, she wasn't the first Romanian person that I knew. The first Romanian person that I knew in my life... his name was Cornel Barbu, was a tennis player, a very impressive tennis player and in the tennis club we had a couple of other Romanian tennis players (...)

> G.: You played together?

> E: Yes. (...) It's true that, for instance, you have Romanian tennis players like Ilie Năstase and Ion Țiriac. You have famous gymnastics and also Romania is one of the most ancient nobilities of Europe, which is also a positive point. In Belgium we have had also other information about Romania, about life there, we know, for instance, that you don't want to be an orphan in Romania, we understand that, we know that. (...) You have some famous linguists in Romania that I came across a little bit during my studies. I read a Romanian novel before I knew G.

> G: Eliade?

> E: No, that came later, but I have read the novel of Gheorghiu, which is called' "The 25th Hour",'. It's about religion. And, of course, I knew George Zamfir before, but you know, you have some aspects of Romania like I would have from other countries probably. Yeah.

> G: So I was not something very, very, very new, exceptional.

> E: No. No. I am also very aware that is also a Romanic language Romania. A Latin language. I didn't know that it was so far in Europe, geographically.

> (Gabi and Edin, Belgium)

In this dialogue between Gabi and Edin we can notice that Edin was positively open towards Romania even before the relationship with Gabi, an openness that Gabi was not aware of up to this interview.

Another situation is that of Mila, who got to live in a Serbian-Romanian-Hungarian multi-ethnic village in Serbia, where mixed couples were not exceptional. Lilia was also well received in Slovakia, being an ethnic Slovak. In what concerns foreign partners from these couples, they also enjoyed a good reception in Romania, since they came from "better" Western-European countries, were generally regarded as superior to Romanians. Mila came from a village in Romania that is close to the Serbian border, where Romanian-Serbian marriages are common, and Lilia brought another Slovak to her family.

In contrast, in what concerns recently formed couples, especially after the wave of Romanian migration to Western Europe, the acceptance of Romanian partners is not so simple anymore.

Dana had to confront the „typical German coldness" of Otho's relatives. While the couple lived in Belgium and reduced the contacts with the German family to a minimum, Dana's mother – with whom the couple maintains a very close relationship – accepted Otho with much warmth, thus he tries learning Romanian words to communicate with his mother-in-law.

In contrast, Agora met the ferocious opposition especially of the female members of Alonzo's family, since they were not ready to accept a Romanian into the family, due to the defamation targeting Romanians in Spain. Alonzo's counter-argument for his family was Agora's level of education, who is a PhD student, in contrast with them who only have mid-level education. In spite of this difference, the relationship still remained tense, the "Romanian woman" being still viewed from a high horse.

> „Yes, here you can register my reaction. They are reserved! And once again they are re-served... The feminine side, so the sisters, the mother... For example, in the community in which my boyfriend lives, there are... so, you can find Romanians, but ones who work...So they are not with a particularly high education, or to see Romanians that can be given as an example. But even if they work in agriculture (...) they are honest people, they are not delinquents or... but still we are regarded by them as „Romanians", so there is a difference... And my boyfriend's argument, the moment he gets criticism, is „Wait a minute, educationally speaking, she is above you!" (Agora, Belgium)

We however saw the gravest disappointment of the partner's family in Tudor's case, when Stanka's family, whose daughter left to different countries of the world at the age of 16 for study, and meanwhile also won the US visa lottery, had difficulties accepting that of all the countries where she was and all the nations she has met, Stanka had to choose a Romanian, just as worthless abroad as a Bulgarian.

> At 16, I won a scholarship and I moved to study in Thailand, in Bangkok, in an international British school. After that, I studied in the UK for 2 years... then I moved for 1 year to Spain, as an exchange student, and then I came back to England for one year. Then I did my Master's in the Netherlands. Then I went back to Bulgaria for a year, then I won the Green Card and I moved to the States...(...)...Actually, the first time I told my mom I was seeing a Romanian guy she told me: "Of all the travels you've done and everywhere you've been you, choose a Romanian guy, which is just across!" (Stanka, Belgium)

The creation of bi-national couples has further impact than the members of the couple, on their families and the community they live in. "When people from different nations join together to make a couple, very important phenomena and processes occur, whose significance goes beyond the fate of the members of the couple. As a result of the amalgamation, that is a merger of cultural groups following a marriage and the creation of hybrid forms of kinship, a new cultural order emerges". (Sowa-Behtane, 2016, p. 394)

Bi-national couples seem to be successful, the divorce rate in the European context is relatively low (Nahikari, 2016). However in the studies that have included the bi-national couples with a partner from their country of residence, you could observe the possible negative effects that it has on the majority partners and the minority ones. In the Netherlands, research showed that Dutch partners of bi-national couples are not as satisfied by the couple's life as the partners of other nationalities. The researchers have explained this phenomenon as being possible in the sense that "Dutch nationals in mixed partnerships receive more negative feedback on their relationship from 'third parties' such as family, friends and community members, altering their levels of relationship satisfaction" (van Mol and de Valk, 2014, p. 13). On the other hand, it seems that in Belgium the minority partners suffer mostly from social loneliness than the majority ones (Koelet and de Valk, 2016).

The three couples we discuss who live in the country of origin of one of the partners, two of them living in Belgium, confirm these results, two of the majority partners (Alexander and Edin) have mentioned a disproportion between the level of attachment towards their own family and the Romanian partner's family, being closer to the Romanians. Moreover, in the case of Romanian partners in Belgian couples, they can confirm not to have special relations with the Belgians, but fortunately a lot of their Romanian family members live very close in Belgium and they are closely tied to one another.

The practices of bi-national couples: the language of the families

If, in general, the language a family uses has no fundamental role, through the mixed/bi-national couples the language becomes a defining practice of the couple even in the way of doing the family (Morgan, 2011a, b) or presenting themselves as a family (Finch, 2007, 2008, 2011).

Sofia Gaspar (2009, 2010) mentions three types of life strategy of these families, depending on the selection of language/s used in the family: assimilation (when only one language is used), a bi-national strategy (when both) and a peripatetic strategy (that means the use of more languages in the family).

Closely connected to the context in which the couples emerged, as well as to the country they live in, we get the language or languages through which these couples unfold their life together. As we could expect, the couples formed and/ or staying in the country of origin of one of the partners end up assimilating the minority (Romanian) partner: Gabi and Cristina speak exclusively Flemish with their husbands.

On the other hand, even if they speak to their husbands in the language of the country they live in, Virginia in English and Mila in Serbian, they both taught their mixed children Romanian, too. In this case we have some sort of a bi-national strategy because the children use both languages, even if the majoritarian partner hadn't learned the minority partner's language.

Lilia represents a special case, being an ethnic Slovak from Romania, could speak her native language – Slovak – to her husband. But – quite amazingly – she decided to teach her children Romanian, and her husband learned it as well, even though they live in Belgium and there are few ethnic Romanians even in their larger family. We witness a peripatetic case here.

I speak Romanian wth the boys... Because I want them to learn the language, I insist, because they travel a lot to Romania, even if in Nadlac they speak Slovak in the store of wherever you go, but we go a lot to Romania and travel a lot so I want them to know it. Also, the wife of my brother is fully Romanian and doesn't speak Slovak so... for me it is very important they speak Romanian, so they speak it. But what's very interesting is that with Oliver, my third child, I don't know why (she laughs) I've started to speak Slovak, I mean ever since they were babies I used to speak it to them. Once when he was six or eight months, when he said his first words, I said to myself: I'm gonna change, because for me it's like.... It's the same, I mean it comes naturally for me to speak, and even if you study a language... I didn't have time and it's more difficult because for the previous two weeks I spoke with him in Romanian, I answered in Slovak, but I told my husband that he understood everything. Listening to me all day long around the house speaking Romanian with my brothers, for him it's this thing just to let go, so... Romanian. My husband speaks Slovak to them and in the house when we're all together we speak Slovak... He knows it. He tries. Even from the beginning, we didn't even have children and he wanted so much to learn and now that we have children and he hears me speak Romanian to the children, he understands it....he doesn't speak it fluently, but he can speak it. Yes, he speaks and he understands, he understands a lot. (Lilia, Belgium)

The other five couples of our analysis, the members of which do not live in their country of origin, speak English among them, whether they live in the UK or not. It is the language that they met in, it is the language of the couple.

T: Yes, mostly. She understands Romanian very well, because she's very good with languages. And she knows Spanish, so it's easy to learn Romanian. And she speaks a little bit as well, but she doesn't want to speak it because I'm very lazy to learn Bulgarian and she doesn't want to speak Romanian because I don't speak Bulgarian.

S: But the English that we speak... we put in a lot of words that are similar in the two languages. We already discovered like... 50 words that are the same. So we just substitute those. (Tudor and Stanka, Belgium)

Even if Agora speaks Spanish and Alonzo learned Romanian while staying in Romania, they communicate in English, while speaking Spanish or Romanian only with the members of the extended family, since Agora is Aromanian and at home she speaks Aromanian with her family, and Alonzo speaks to his family in Catalan, hence Romanian, respectively Spanish are already umbrella languages for each of them.

For English as a language of the couple, the way Cristi and Petra communicated at the beginning of their relationship is quite edifying. They have met on the Internet on a dating site and used to communicate in English, but after a few months of discussion, when Petra finally came to meet Cristi personally to the UK, they hit a huge barrier: Cristi couldn't speak Czech, but Petra couldn't speak Romanian or English either, since she uses Google Translate for online communication. Salvation came from the same application, namely in the iPhone version of it, capable to translate in real time – hence they used English end Czech, and communicated with help from the phone for the first few months. Slowly Petra, having moved to the UK, learned English.

This means of communication in a neutral language becomes even more interesting when one of the partners tries to communicate with the family of the other partner, neither of them knowing the language of the other. The practice of the transnational communication contributes to "doing family" (Nedelcu and Wyss, 2016), but in the case of those transnational families they become complicated and create a uniqueness in the communication:

K: Now I am talking with his mom on Facebook and how are we talking? I write in English and she is translating in Google everything and then, when she's writing me back, she's writing in English, but also using Google Translate. (Katarina, UK)

When children appear in a family and the family starts using multiple languages, we can say that this is a peripatetic strategy, but as long as in the bi-national couple the communication language is a neutral one, not even the language of the country they live in (for example Stanka and Tudor, Otho and Dana – they speak English even though they live in Belgium), we need to identify a fourth practice of language use: the neutrality strategy.

In mixed families, the language of the majority partner is the one predominantly used (Gaspar, 2010, Ducu, 2016), but not in our results where we have almost half of the cases in which they speak the language of the majority partner, a case in which even if the couple is bi-national the language is the same (Lilia being a Romanian of Slovak ethnicity) and 5 cases in which the bi-national couples speak a neutral language for the couple's members. This practice of using the language is very relevant in establishing equality in the couples on one hand, and on the other in constituting and defining them as a couple, as something new and hybrid, further than any of the partners. These practices of using a neutral language in the bi-national couples deserves to be researched with more attention because they transmit a new way of constituting the family in a neutral environment, they present some sort of emancipation of the new family.

Situations when displaying "bi-nationalities" of couples becomes important

Name and citizenship of the children

Choosing the names in a mixed family has been proven through much research as a turning point (Edwards and Caballero, 2008, Finch, 2008, Ducu, 2016), still it seems that this is not the case for bi-national couples; the children often receive names in function of the country in which they are born and not the country of origin of their parents, probably to avoid putting the child in delicate situations in the future (Moriizumi, 2011). In turn, the more delicate situation in bi-national couples has proven to be the choice of the child's citizenship.

> I don't know... I have a Romanian name, she has a Latvian name, so let's pick an English name for her. (Adi, UK)

We encounter more interesting situations when these children are born in a third country, hence they will be able to access multiple citizenships. Cristi told us of her daughter Petronela's situation, born in the UK to Romanian and Czech parents.

> Yes, she is born in the U.K., she doesn't have a U.K. passport, she can't get one until she's eighteen. She is a resident of the U.K., she has a U.K. birth certificate and if we wanted British citizenship for her, first of all, one of us has to earn it. So, we can't get it (for her, a.n.) until one at least has it and you have to be in this country for longer than five years, I believe... I am not going to bother with that. I am not very interested in British citizenship, not for me, not for her, not for my daughter. (Q: Is she Romanian then?) She is nothing yet! ...We applied for Czech citizenship, just because it lasts a few weeks shorter than our Romanian paperwork. There was the only choice. We are waiting for the papers. (...) Until she gets her passport, we can't go anywhere with her. I mean, we can, but we can't come back until

everything is sorted out (...). We are going to apply for Romanian citizenship as well, both of these countries do allow dual citizenship, so why not? (Cristi, UK)

But regardless of the administrative aspects of citizenship, the children of these families chose a country for themselves, such as in the case of the five children of Lilia (two born in Slovakia having double Slovak/Romanian citizenship and three born in Belgium with triple Belgian/Slovak/Romanian citizenship).

"My mother is from Romania, my father is from Slovakia", if somebody asks them. And they are from Belgium. "But we speak both Slovak and Romanian!", that is what they say. (Lilia, Belgium)

Raising and education of children is a medium for display of diversity. The way in which bi-national couples use language to communicate within the couple and with their children is a key part of the configuration of mixed families' functioning. Beyond the usual situation in which either the minority partner is completely assimilated and the child doesn't learn the minority language or the majority partner's language is spoken in the household while the child also learns the language of the minority partner (Lester Murad, 2006), lately one can meet bi-national couples in which the partners do not speak each other's language at all, speaking to each other in a third language.

In Cristina's case, who married Gabyn very young, at 19, the dominant language of the partner has extended over the child: her 23-year-old daughter has never learned Romanian, although she has travelled very often to Romania and was surrounded since a very young age by Romanian relatives, even if they live in the same town in Belgium and they meet often

Flemish. Yes! They manage, but no…No, unfortunately, now I'm sorry. But I cannot speak to her in Romanian. Nor G. (the aunt)…, nor C (the brother), nor I. (the wife of the brother)! We speak Flemish with the child. All of us (…) Ever since the beginning. I couldn't, I don't know why. I couldn't speak Romanian to her. (Cristina, Belgium)

The children of bi-national couples, irrespective of the country they are brought up in, receive the education to maintain their multiple ethnic identities. For example, Virginia's child born from the marriage with Alexander considers himself more Romanian than the child Virginia had born in Romania and with whom she migrated together, who, although raised throughout multiple countries, even if married to a Romanian woman, still considers himself rather English. Cristi, Adi and Mila speak Romanian to their children, even if Cristi and Adi speak English to their partners – the children of the latter being simultaneously exposed to three languages: Romanian – English – Czech; respectively Romanian – English – Latvian. We can see below the conversation plans drawn by two bi-national couples living in the UK: Cristi and Petra (Romania, Czech Republic), as well as Adi and Katarina (Romania, Latvia).

K: When I'm alone, I'm talking to her in Latvian. When we are together, we are speaking English and...

A: I am going to speak Romanian to her.

K: So, the main language for her, we want it to be English, but still, we are going to teach her Latvian and Romanian as well.

A: Is going to be good, you know, at least the basics to know in Latvian and Romanian

(Katarina and Adi, UK)

I'll speak Romanian to her, but in different situations. Our plan is like this: I'll speak Romanian to her only when I am alone with her. She (the wife) will speak Czech to her only when she's alone with her and we'll speak English when we are together, cause the trick to it is not to teach her the actual languages, cause that's easy enough, but the trick is to get her to talk to you in the language you are requesting. (Cristi, UK)

For these children, who grow with a minimum of three different languages, we need to offer diverse educational solutions. In the US, they speak about bilingual children and even developed a market of bilingual books for them (Barabs-Rhoden, 2011). These trilingual children of European families still do not get the attention they need in their forming and education. They have the right to be raised in all of the three cultures they belong to, through heritage, through birth and though family, and these families need to be helped to raise these children in all of the three cultures. This could be a research direction that is worth developing.

The role of religion in displaying differences

Choosing the religious ritual for the baptism of the children (Arweck and Nesbitt, 2010) or of the religious rite for getting married (Ducu, 2016) is a key moment in underlining difference.

For the Romanian partners or their families, the emphasis on the Orthodox rite is especially important. For Mila, for example, it was simple, since in the village in Serbia where she lives there are two Orthodox churches that hold mass in Romanian, respectively Serbian. Since there are many bi-national families, at important holidays such as Easter and Christmas the churches hold mass at different times so that bi-national families can attend both.

The choice of religion (or rite), especially in the case of children is another key part of bi-national couples' life choices, especially under the pressure of the extended family. Adi and Katarina chose to baptize their daughter in the Orthodox rite, even if they are not married, under the pressure of Adi's parents.

> *I am Orthodox, she (the wife) is Lutheran. (Q: And R. – their daughter?) She is Orthodox. Anyway, we're not into that religious stuff, but ...You know, I had some arguments with people, like: 'you said you're not religious, but why you baptize your kid?' 'Why you, when you're married, you go to the church?' Because I have parents and they are like: 'Tititititiiti, do it! Do it!' You know, it's annoying, but you have to listen to them sometimes. (Adi, UK)*

However, religion is not only decisive in the case of children, it can also be extended over the partner. Cristi even baptized Petra, his unbaptized partner, in the Orthodox rite when they baptized their daughter, even if Cristi and Petra are themselves not married.

> *Oh, religious parts. Ok. That was an interesting one. I am Orthodox, she wasn't baptized in any religion. ...However, I insisted she should look into something and I think she should look into Orthodoxy as well. I explained to her the whole situation. She read about it, she contemplated on it and... Orthodox and Orthodox. So, one plus two now. (...) We went to church and everything, so... (Cristi, UK)*

Unfortunately Otho, although a Protestant, was baptized a second time in the Orthodox rite by an overzealous priest before marrying Dana and him. More fortunately, Gabyn and Edin, both Catholic, have met a wiser Orthodox priest who only married them in the Orthodox rite to Cristina and Gabi. Gary, the mixed child of Virginia and Alexander who wasn't baptized in the UK came back baptized in the Orthodox rite from Romania after a vacation spent at the grandparents – Virginia's mother and sister having baptized the child without the consent of the parents

> *The boy is Orthodox, we've baptized him after three years. At the beginning it was very hard, but after three years we said let's baptize him and we did. I mean I don't want to lie, my mother baptized him when we've sent him on vacation (...) Aurica did it without permission, and my sister was the godmother. And he was three years old. Since then he's very religious, he loves the Bible, at Easter and Christmas he goes to Church, he knows "Our Heavenly Father" in both Romanian and English, he knows both Bibles but...no, he's Orthodox! (Virginia, UK)*

In contrast to imposing the Orthodox rite, we can see the respect for traditions from both cultures coming to the fore in Dana and Otho's wedding story, held in the Oltenia region of Romania, with the goal of showing the international invitees (colleagues of the multinational they both work with) the wedding ritual in Craiova, Romania, the German relatives didn't leave it like that and came with some specific elements they enriched the wedding's place and insisted in introducing the gathering of glass shards by the newlywed, a tradition to their area.

In the Romanian – ethnic Hungarian mixed marriages within Romania, the subject of religion is a delicate one (Brubaker, 2006, Haynes and Dermott, 2011, Ducu, 2016); it seems that in the bi-national marriages this subject is not so delicate for the Romanian partner who insists to impose his own rite whereas the foreign partner gives up rather easily. For us it was a surprising fact that all of the bi-national couples that chose to get married in the church chose the Orthodox religion, especially since in the case of Romanian-Hungarian mixed couples the most used version was that of both rites. This would be worth researching in more detail, as the explanations we have are oversimplifying – like Romanians are more religious or that being from another country they feel the need to keep their relations with the past.

Conclusions

The intersection of partners' countries of origin and the countries they live in as a couple molds the life modes of bi-national couples, with a direct influence on the language they use in the couple. We can see a growth in numbers in the case of bi-national couples that live in a third country, different from their country of origin, a phenomenon which is not, as previously considered, reserved for the elites. In what concerns the practices of the use of language in a couple, beside the three strategies used by Gaspar (2009, 2010) – assimilation, bi-nationality and peripatetic – we propose a fourth strategy, that of neutrality, represented by the couples who use a language different from the one of either of the partners.

Depending on the moment the couple was formed, bi-national couples with one Romanian partner faced different degrees of acceptance by the members of the extended family: more recent couples are indirectly affected by the negative perception of Romanian migrants in certain Western-European countries.

The key moments that strongly display bi-national couples are: children's raising and education; the role of religion in their family life; maintaining tradition within family life.

But the meaning of living in a bi-national family can be observed best when one can choose one's country of residence. When they speak of returning "home", they have at least two possible countries. When they decide which members of the community to meet, they also have several possibilities. With possibilities, the capacity for support is also open. Mila's case is edifying, who is married to a Serbian, and who initially lived in the Serbian community in the UK, and then reestablished Romanians as friends, whom she had almost completely been separated from.

With the Serbians in Serbian, so I had nothing to do with Romanians. Over the last three years I had... I found out about the group „Romanians in London", and the idea was to add myself... I added myself and they've accepted me (laughs)... to aaahhmmm... practice a little Romanian, both reading and writing. (Mila, UK)

She (illegally) possesses both Romanian and Serbian IDs. Depending on the need, she uses them alternatively. Moreover, since she is fed up with being looked down upon in the UK when identifying herself as Serbian or Romanian, she obtained a British temporary driving license, with a UK address, although she does not drive. Thus she can access any of her three identities when she finds it useful.

References

Arweck, Elisabeth / Nesbitt, Eleanor: "Religious education in the experience of young people from mixed-faith family". *British Journal of Religious Education*, Vol. 33 (No. 1), 2011, pp. 31–45.

Barabs-Rhoden, Laura: "Toward an Inclusive Eco-Cosmopolitanism: Bilingual Children's Literature in the United States". *Interdisciplinary Studies in Literature & Environment*; Vol. 18 Issue 2, 2011, pp. 359–383.

Brahic, Bénédicte: "The Politics of Bi-nationality in Couple Relationships: A Case Study of European Bi-national Couples in Manchester", *Journal of Comparative Family Studies*, Volume XLIV Number 6, 2013, pp. 699–714.

Brubaker, Rogers / Feischmidt, Margit / Fox, Jon / Grancea, Liana: *Nationalist Politics and Everyday Ethnicity in a Transylvanian Town*, Princeton, NJ: Princeton University Press, 2006.

Caballero, Chamion / Edwards, Rosalind: "What's in a name? An exploration of the significance of personal naming of 'mixed' children for parents from different racial, ethnic and faith backgrounds". *The Sociological Review*, 56 (1), 2008, pp. 39–60.

Dermott, Esther, E. / Seymour, Julie: "Developing 'Displaying Families': A Possibility for the Future of the Sociology of Personal Life". In Seymour, Julie / Dermott, Esther, (eds.) *Displaying Families: A New Concept for the Sociology of Family Life*, London: Palgrave Macmillan, 2011, pp. 3–19.

Ducu, Viorela: "Displaying Ethnically Mixed Families in Transylvania". *Transylvanian Review*, supplement Cosmopolitanism and Difference: Politics and Critique, section edited by Telegdi-Csetri Áron, 2016, under press.

Favell, Adrian: "The Changing Face of 'Integration' in a Mobile Europe", 2013. Retrieved 01.09.2016 http://www.adrianfavell.com/CESweb.pdf

Finch, Janet: "Displaying Families". *Sociology* 41 (1), 2007, pp. 65–81.

Finch, Janet: "Naming Names: Kinship, Individuality and Personal Names". *Sociology*, 42 (4), 2008, pp. 709–725.

Finch, Janet: "Exploring the Concept of Display in Family Relationships". In Seymour, Julie / Dermott, Esther, (eds.) *Displaying Families: A New Concept for the Sociology of Family Life*, London: Palgrave Macmillan, 2011, pp. 197–206.

Gaspar, Sofia: "Towards a definition of European intra-marriages a new social phenomenon". CIES e-Working Paper, 46, 2008. Retrieved 01.09.2016 http://www.cies.iscte-iul.pt/destaques/documents/CIES-WP46_Gaspar__000.pdf

Gaspar, Sofia: "Mixed marriages between European free movers". CIES e-Working Paper, 65, 2009. Retrieved 01.09.2016 http://cies.iscte-iul.pt/destaques/documents/CIES-WP65_Gaspar.pdf

Gaspar, Sofia: "Family and social dynamics among European mixed couples". *Portuguese Journal of Social Science*, 9, (2), 2010, pp. 109–125.

Haynes, Jo / Dermott, Esther: "Displaying Mixedness: Differences and Family Relationships". In Seymour, Julie / Dermott, Esther, (eds.) *Displaying Families: A New Concept for the Sociology of Family Life*, London: Palgrave Macmillan, 2011, pp. 145–160.

Huijnk, Willem / Verkuyten, Maykel / Coenders Marcel: "Family relations and the attitude towards ethnic minorities as close kin by marriage". *Ethnic and Racial Studies*, 36 (11), 2012, pp. 1890–1909.

Koelet, Suzana / A.G. de Valk, Helga: "European Liaisons? A Study on European bi-national Marriages in Belgium", *Population, Space and Place*, 20, 2013, pp. 110–125.

Koelet, Suzana / de Valk, Helga AG: "Social networks and feelings of social loneliness after migration: The case of European migrants with a native partner in Belgium", *Ethnicities*, 16 (4), 2016, pp. 610–630.

Lester Murad, Nora: "The Politics of Mothering in a "Mixed" family: an auoethnographic exploration". *Identities: Global Studies in Culture and Power*, 12 (4), 2006 pp. 479–503.

Morgan, David: "Locating 'Family Practices'". *Sociological Research Online*, 16 (4) 14, 2011a.

Morgan, David: Rethinking Family Practices, London: Palgrave Macmillan, 2011b.

Moriizumi, Satoshi: "Exploring Identity Negotiations: An Analysis of Intercultural Japanese-U.S. American Families Living in the United States", *Journal of Family Communication*, 11 (2), Special Issue: Family Communication and Culture, 2011, pp. 85–104.

Nahikari, Irastorza: "Sustainable marriages? Divorce patterns of binational couples in Europe versus North America". *Ethnicities*, 16 (4), 2016, pp. 649–683.

148   V. Ducu, I. Hossu

Nedelcu, Mihaela / Malika, Wyss: "'Doing family' through ICT-mediated ordinary co-presence: transnational communication practices of Romanian migrants in Switzerland". *Global Networks* 16, 2, 2016, pp. 202–218.

Robila, Mihaela: *Eastern European immigrant families*, New York: Routledge, 2010.

Sowa-Behtane, Ewa: "Binational Marriages and Multicultural Educational Environment", *Society. Integration. Education. Proceedings of the International Scientific Conference*. Vol. III, May 27th–28th, 2016, pp. 393–401.

van Mol, Christof / de Valk, Helga: "Relationship satisfaction of European binational couples in the Netherlands", Working Paper no. 13, 2014, Retrieved 01.09.2016 http://www.nidi.nl/shared/content/output/papers/nidi-wp-2014-13.pdf

Challenges of Transnationalism
towards Childhood

Georgiana-Cristina Rentea, Laura-Elena Rotărescu

Yesterday's Children, Today's Youth: The Experiences of Children Left behind by Romanian Migrant Parents

Abstract *This paper focuses on exploring the experiences of children from some Romanian villages concerning the effects of parental migration and highlighting the challenges and strategies of adaption lacking one or both parents' support, the evolution of family relationship, individual and family life plans.*

The migration process nowadays generates tremendous debates for developed countries concerning its consequences no matter what units of analysis we are referring to. Consequently, the transnational family as a result of emigration became a central issue to be analyzed in terms of its reconfiguration and arrangements that continue to exist even though its members are geographical separated but "holding together and creating something that can be seen as a feeling of collective welfare and unity, i.e. 'familyhood', even across national borders" (Bryceson and Vuorela, 2002). Schmalzbauer (2008, p. 331), analyzing the term of „frontiering" introduced by Bryceson and Vuorela (2002), argues that „transnational family members commonly negotiate in both friendly and confrontational ways to create identities, organize familial space, and sort out familial roles and expectations". In this line the process of negotiation is affected not only by the geographical distance and its communication obstacles but also by changing in values or lifestyles brought by contact with another society, by expectations across generations or by decision to migrate.

Despite the research interest dedicated to it, there are still shortcomings encompassing the social complexity of transnational families especially regarding "the evolution of norms regarding fatherhood, motherhood and parenting during the migration process" (Kraler et al. 2011, p. 35) or "the dominant focus on research on the family living in one location" (Mazzucato and Schans, 2011, p. 706).

Starting from the "fluidity, diversity, multi-facetedness" of the contemporary family, Finch (2007, p. 80) stresses that "families are constituted by "doing family things" (not by "being" a family), social practices specifically get constituted as "family" practices"; thus, the author is introducing the concept of "dislaying families" which enables us to better understand the family relationships and its practices.

In this analysis of transnational family, the situation of children left behind is of concern, taking into consideration the fact that the lack of direct parental support, more acute in the case where both parents are migrants, can produce severe transformation in their process of evolution as individuals.

Current literature on children left behind stresses the "emergent meanings of motherhood and alternative child-rearing arrangements" (Hondagneu-Sotelo and Avila, 1997, p. 548), the constitution of gender in the formation of migrant transnational households and its impact on children development (Parreñas, 2005), and also the effects of the migrant parent gender on children's well-being (Whitehead and Hashim, 2005). While Parreñas (2005) argues that lack of mothers in the households is taken over by other female figures and not the fathers, Asis (2006, p. 57) stresses that in case of migrant mother "half of the children left behind identified their fathers as the primary care-givers, a situation that suggests a reversal of roles and a new role for fathers, at least during the time of migration." Even though both cases refer to the Philippines families, the results seem to be in contradiction. From a micro and mezzo perspective, in terms of perception of parents' migration, Ducu (2014, p. 139) emphasizes the fact that "it is easier to accept that a father leaves in order to provide for his family, but if the migration of a mother is at issue, tolerance decreases"; this perspective envisages the role of the cultural norms regarding the families' functions in different nations, migrant women facing greater challenges in terms of roles and attitudes due to cultural and gender ideologies.

Marchetti-Mercer (2012) is pointing out that those members of the families left behind experience various emotions, ranging from emotional ambivalence to anger and distress; emigration is perceived as a vast loss, producing significant changes in social networks and relationships. Communication within transnational families is a key element in keeping its unity. The use of Internet and new technologies eases the process of communication, helping the members of these families to maintain ties across time and space.

In this paper we are aiming to explore the experiences of children from some Romanian villages regarding the effects of parental emigration, highlighting the challenges and strategies of adaptation when lacking one or both parents' support, the evolution of family relationship, individual and family life plans. Through the qualitative study conducted we contributed to the better understanding of the implications of parental emigration and the status of children left behind.

Consequences of emigration from Romania: children left behind

The migration of the Romanians to EU Member States started to increase from 2007, the year of accession, although the labor market was restricted from 2007 until 2013. Among the Member States, Romanian citizens occupied the first place in terms of intra-EU mobility exceeding 2.3 million in 2011 (over 75% settling in Italy or Spain). However, the economic crisis has led to an accentuated reduction of Romanian migrants settling for the first time in an EU Member State (compared with 2008, in 2011 was recorded a decrease of 36% according to DG Employment 2012). Most Romanian emigrants are from the active population (aged 20–44 years old), having economic reasons behind their choice of mobility within EU. The females outnumbered the males in 2012 (58.77%) and in 2013 (59.63%) (National Statistics Institute of Romania, 2016).

The Romanian Child protection law (Law no. 272/2004 on the protection and promotion of the rights of the child) stipulates that parents or the single parents intending to migrate abroad for work purposes have the obligation to declare the migration decision to the local department for social security and child protection 40 days in advance, specifying the person undertaking the responsibilities of child caring.

According to the National Authority for Child Protection Rights and Adoption (NACPRA) on the 31.03.2016, a total number of 70375 migrant families left behind 91400 children, registering an increase compared to the same period in 2015 (81725 children). Most of the children have one migrant parent (60.45%), 26.73% of children have both parents' migrants and 12.82% of children from single-parent families have the single parent abroad. In most of the cases where none of the parents can ensure child protection, the role is undertaken by the children's relatives up to the 4th grade. The current number of children left behind could be even higher, if we are taking into consideration the fact that, in practice, a significant number of parents avoid the obligation to declare their migration decision.

Figure 1: *The evolution of migrant families and children left behind in Romania, 2008–2015*

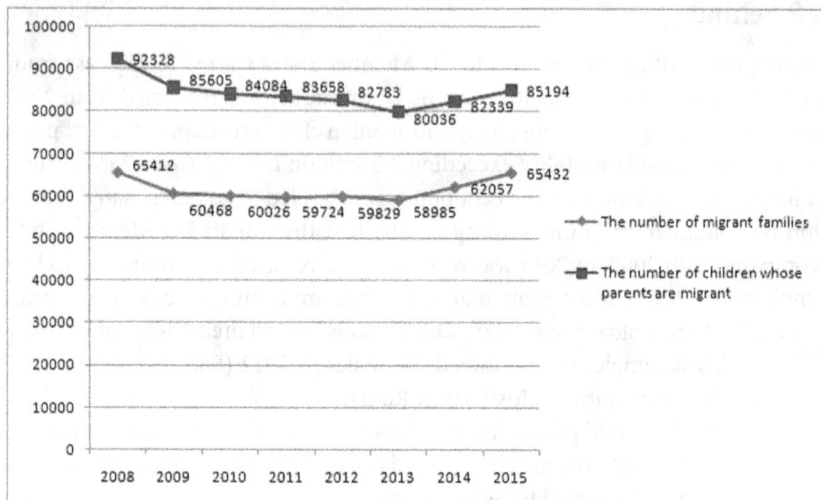

Source: National Authority for Child Protection Rights and Adoption, http://www.copii.ro/statistici/

Figure 2: *The evolution of children left behind in Romania based on family types, 2008–2015*

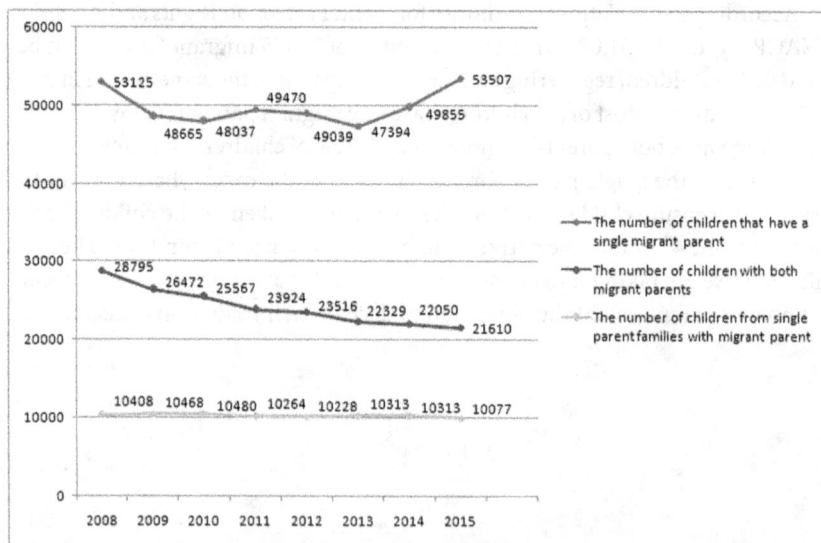

Source: National Authority for Child Protection Rights and Adoption, http://www.copii.ro/statistici/

Due to demographic impact, the Romanian government will have to reexamine their policies on migration, encouraging return migration. So far "initiatives targeting return migrants or Romanian citizens settled temporarily abroad are still rather limited in scope and effects, and that they should be expanded to address a larger variety of needs" (Rentea, 2015a, p. 135).

The way of which transnational families reconfigure in order to respond to challenges brought by the migration process has to transcend the private sphere. Both countries, of destination and origin, have to support the unity of these families through legislation, policies and institutions sustaining their unity and thus avoiding negative consequences hard to handle by families themselves (i.e. irregular status, child neglecting etc.). The situation of children left behind requires special attention in terms of developing policies in accordance to the children's needs. For instance, children left behind could not be only a result of family maximizing revenues due to the higher wages in the destination countries but also a consequence of the family reunification restrictive legislation, access to social protection system or attitudes of the host society concerning immigrants.

In the context of intra-European Union right to mobility, terms such as "welfare tourism" or "benefit tourism" have become increasingly present in the European public space (Rentea, 2015b); as a result, migrant families are becoming controversial for the host population concerning their right on social benefits in the destination country targeting children left behind (see for example the children allowance entitled to those who continue to live in the country of origin entailed to migrant parents in the destination countries). At present in Romania there is some information regarding the impact of migration on children (Irimescu and Lupu 2006; Toth et al. 2007; Alexandrescu/ Salvati Copiii România 2007; Toth, Munteanu and Bleahu, 2008; Stănculescu and Marin, 2012; Stănculescu, Marin and Popp, 2012; Ducu 2014; Tomşa and Jenaro, 2015). There are also some NGOs being very active in providing different forms of support to children left behind (see for example Save the Children Romania, Alternative Sociale Iasi/ Social Alternatives Iasi) or projects developed in partnership by associations like those of Romanian migrant women in order to facilitate the communication between migrant women and their children left behind. One of these projects is "Te iubeşte mama!"/ "Mama loves you!" implemented by Association of Romanian Women from Italy (ADRI) in partnership with National Association of Librarians and Public Libraries from Romania (ANBPR), IREX Foundation Romania, with support from Embassy of Italy in Bucharest, Romanian General Consulate in Milano, Libraries Association from Italy (http://www.anbpr.org.ro/index.php/programe-proiecte/parteneriate, accessed at 04.08.2016).

The findings of qualitative study

The young people taking part in our research come from Romanian villages, a part of them continuing to live there in order to complete their education, while another part already moved to the capital city, Bucharest, to continue their studies. In our qualitative study, we focused on analyzing the effects of parental emigration highlighting the challenges given the adaption to the lack of one or both parents' support, the evolution of family relationship, individual and family life plans. Thus in the first part of 2015 we conducted seven semi-structured interviews with young people between 19–22 years old with migrant mothers (3), with migrant fathers (2) and with both migrant parents (2). The children's age when the parent or parents left home to migrate are ranged between 10 and 18 years old. In many cases the year of the parent/parents' departure was 2006–2007. As expected, the main countries of destination were Italy (3) and Spain (2) completed with France (1) and Cyprus (1). All of them were young adults (over 18 years old) thus avoiding the power relations between children and adult researchers underlined in the literature on conducting research with children (see for example Punch, 2002), and were enrolled in different stages of their education in order to understand their experiences, emotions and needs as children left behind. Names are fictional and not the real ones of the research participants. We have changed the names of all research participants to protect their privacy.

We would like to underline that we conducted a small-scale qualitative study with an opportunity sample and our aim was to reveal the experiences of children people left behind, storied years after as young adults. From the position of a former child left behind for almost 16 years by both parents who emigrated to Italy, one of the authors of this study inevitably empathized with the research participants during the data collection and analysis, while the other author tried to be more reflexive, reducing thus the subjectivity during the research process.

Experiences as children left behind

The perception about their parents' emigration decision

All the young people presented their parents' emigration decision as a consequence of the financial problems they faced at that time i.e. lack of sufficient revenue as a result of unemployment or low wages. In many cases, the year of the parent/parents' departure was 2007, thus coinciding with the Romania's European Union accession and easing of the conditions to travel and in some countries to work abroad. Besides, the social networks facilitated the process of labor migration within EU. As a consequence, the number of transnational families has been significantly increased bringing to the fore the situation of the family members left behind, especially those of children.

They had to make the decision together to go abroad, because we had money problems... In 2007 when the financial crisis came, the wages decreased, money wasn't enough anymore and thus they were forced to leave. They got an offer from abroad, from some acquaintances and decided to go there to work. (Bogdan, male, 20 years old, with two migrant parents in Cyprus)

Their parents' migration decision has been perceived as a sacrifice to achieve the family's well-being. None of the interviewed children blamed their parents for their emigration decision bringing to the fore the advantages for their families, always comparing their situation before the migration took place. Thus in their perception the resources generated from migration, compensated the absence of direct parental support and the children are not feeling abandoned nor neglected. Parreñas (2005, p. 42) also observed this perception at some of her research participants although they experienced "an incalculable loss when their parents disappeared overseas".

Children's perception about the separation from a transnational mother and/or father

The *coping process* after the departure abroad of one parent could involve in some cases emotional distress. Ana experienced depression after her mother's departure, difficulty to adapt to a new educational environment, or tendency to drop out of school in order to accompany her mother. But in her case it seems that her mother succeeded to encourage and sustain her to complete her education in her home country and soon after that to join the family abroad. This migration plan is giving Ana for the moment the emotional security to understand the importance of education but with no other plan to continue it.

It was very hard for me at first. I had a period of depression. It was very hard for me to integrate in high school, with my schoolmates. I had moments when I wanted to go to her, to drop out of school. But I tried to encourage myself to graduate from high school at least, and after that to get a job there, to seek for some work. At that age it was a dramatic change, because before that everything was done by my mother and after she left I had to do it alone. (Eva, female, 19 years old, with migrant mother in Spain)

Gabriel, although is presenting both his parents' migration in terms of sacrifice and advantages, also confesses that it has been hard for him to accept the distance, didn't revealed feelings of abandonment.

"I reluctantly accepted the idea that we have to stay so long away from each other." (Gabriel, male, 19 years old, with two migrant parents in Italy)

When talking about their needs as children left behind, today's youth is bringing to the fore the different forms of transnational household arrangements in order to assure the well-being, to keep the unity of the family, to dare to plan a better future for them in many cases through education achievement.

> "At the beginning it was hard for me, because I missed them and now I also miss them, but there is nothing I can do. In order to live better, we have to make sacrifices...now we have more money, we can afford more things, I could come to college to study, to build a future for myself." (Bogdan, male, 20 years old, with two migrant parents in Cyprus)

Feelings of abandonment and neglect came from comparison with colleagues at school at periodically parents' meetings. Mirela felt different having only her mother present at these meetings. In a certain way her teacher was bulling her, knowing her father was abroad, giving her the feeling of abandonment. As a child she experienced tragically these situations and later on, as young adult, understood better the decision of her father to migrate for the well-being of her and her family.

> "It was very difficult because always, at the parents' meetings, both my colleagues' parents would come and I was under the impression that I was neglected, because only my mother would come. I was looked at differently by the other kids. All the time, my homeroom teacher would ask me where is my father, although he knew what our situation was, he knew that my father was not in Romania. He always "took care", so to speak, to make me feel bad. Now, as I am older, I figured out that he left for our well-being and he sacrifices himself in order to support me to finish my studies" (Mirela, female, 22 years old, with father migrant in Italy)

Grandparents represented also substitute for undertaking parents' responsibilities, but we encountered cases of women neighbors helping at completing tasks such as cooking or the payment of utility bills. Both cases were perceived very positively by young people describing their experience in a way of thinking to other children not being as lucky as they were at that time.

> "During my primary and middle school, I lived in the countryside and my grandparents raised me. I was younger then and I could not handle it alone, so at that time my parents decided for me to live with my grandparents... I got used to it. It was good that I was in my grandparents' care and they took care of me and my brother". (Gabriel, male, 19 years old, with two migrant parents in Italy)

> "I was thirteen years old when they left and all the house work I did it together with my brother. We were lucky that one of our neighbors helped us by paying the utility bills and cooking for us." (Bogdan, male, 20 years old, with two migrant parents in Cyprus)

Findings from other research (Stănculescu, Marin and Popp 2012; Ducu, 2014) suggest that children left behind remain mainly in care of their grandparents (usually the grandmother takes over the tasks of the mother, even when the father is present). *Assuming the adults' role within the family*, mostly by older siblings, was revealed in cases when both parents emigrated and no other persons from the extended family undertook their roles.

In case of the emigration of one of the parents, *the absence of the mother* was more often mentioned as bringing changes concerning support, offered both emotionally and instrumentally. In the same line, for Eva the absence of the mother was associated with the lack of surveillance described both in terms of a series of fears and of the possibility to spending leisure time as she wished.

> *I really miss her and I feel lonely here in Romania. I am exposed to more danger without my mother around... I have more leisure time ... Now I have more spending money, but I feel alone here. The fact that neither my brothers are with me, nor my father being like a mother to understand me and to be close to me, it's hard.* (Eva, female, 19 years old, with migrant mother in Spain)

> *You can figure out that I felt her absence especially when I went home, because I had to do all the housework. When my mother was home, I wasn't doing anything, I was spoiled by the family, and after she left, it was very hard for me.* (Ioana, female, 22 years old, with migrant mother in Italy)

Alexandrescu (2007) brings to the fore the problems of children left behind, stating that the absence of the mother creates more acute problems, for children the communication with grandparents becomes more difficult during the adolescence, and also stresses on the importance of communication with migrant parents in order to avoid deviant behaviors. Stănculescu and Marin (2012, p. 47) stress that a child left behind can be seen as one accumulating multiple vulnerabilities, for instance "depression associated with mother's migration for work abroad, together with poverty, neglect or abuse by an alcoholic father". Another study (Battistella and Conaco, 1998, apud Asis 2000, p. 265) showed that for elementary school children "the mothers' migration seems to have more adverse consequences — specifically lower academic performance and social adjustment — than when it is the fathers who migrate."

For those whose parent emigrated in their late adolescence, the departure was perceived less dramatic. Moreover, the anticipated move to another city to follow university studies also implied a process of adaptation, which decreased their concentration on the parent leaving and all the potential negative consequences of it.

Fatherhood in the context of family migration is brought to the fore by young people underlying facts such as limitation of fathers to undertake all the household tasks once done by mothers or incapacity to fully understand the feelings of their daughters in absence of their mother's presence. The absence at home of the migrant father is presented less dramatically especially when mothers are non-migrant. In this cases of mothers remained with children at home, the childcare time in allocated in a similar manner as do mothers from complete families (Stănculescu, Marin and Popp, 2012). Thus the mothers are struggling to compensate the absence of the father at home providing to their children quality time in order to protect them from potential social and emotional negative consequences.

In one case when the father emigrated temporarily, when the child was of an early age, and continued to do it repeatedly, the perception of him leaving wasn't felt so dramatically, even though sometimes the return was described more in terms of a meeting with a stranger.

> *My father has been gone for a long time, ever since we were little he used to leave to other countries and taking into consideration the fact that he left when we were little, practically that's how we grew up, without him... We were very little and we weren't used to him, actually we didn't know who he was...and when he came back for the first time, after such a long time, he had a beard, we couldn't recognize him anymore... You can imagine, we were afraid of him, and mommy was telling us to go to him, she told us "go, it's daddy" and we told her "who is daddy?"...we weren't aware of that. For us he was a stranger, a weird person, especially with that beard.* (Ina, female, 22 years old, with father migrant in France)

Lacking direct support from one or both parents was more deeply perceived in *key moments of their life-cycle stages* (e.g. birthdays, graduation) or at annual holidays (e.g. Easter, Christmas) when children are supposed to celebrate with the whole family members. None of the interviewed children missed to reveal it emotionally.

In case of Ana, she reveals that the departure of her mother didn't affect her so deeply due to her early age but this was only a form to justify her mother decision to migrate. The absence of the mother and the acceptance from her daughter are seen as a compromise for the sake of the daughter well-being. Eventually Ana is confessing that she felt strongly her mother absence, being aware of the impossibility to recover all these life events where only her father was close to her.

> *... didn't affect me, I was pretty small when she left. But it was difficult because in all the phases I went through, mothers are usually close to you. Because she had to leave, she wasn't close to me, it was my father... It was hard. When it was March 1, March 8, Mother's Day, my birthdays, my father's birthdays, her birthdays, all these are in one way or another moment that you cannot recover, but you have to make compromises.... She is doing all this for me.* (Ana, female, 21 years old, with migrant mother in Spain)

In terms of negative consequences, the absence of parents at home produces serious effects with respect to the quality of nutrition, i.e. unhealthy diets containing excess dietary energy, fats and refined carbohydrates (Stănculescu, Marin and Popp 2012). Another study (Toth et al., 2007) draws attention to the negative effects of parents' migrations on children which lead to deterioration of relationship with parents at home (more acute in case of father at home), lack of support for child's school work and depression especially when mother or both parents are abroad. Tomsa and Jenaro (2015) identified higher anxiety and depression as psychological effects of emigration among children left behind.

Although many children talked very emotionally about the absence of their parent/parents, in some cases they concluded the discussion with *"That's it!"* or *"… there is nothing I can do! To live better implies to do sacrifices"* (Bogdan, male, 20 years old, with two migrant parents in Cyprus), putting their emotional needs apart.

Children's thoughts on the costs of their parents' emigration process

Young people are presenting, as *advantages* of the migration process, the higher incomes, better living conditions and possibility to assure the family welfare comparing with their past situation in Romania.

Education is frequently brought into discussion by many young people when talking about the reasons for emigration in case of their parent/parents, besides their well-being. They are underlying that without financial support from their migrant parents, there was no possibility to continue with their studies, especially in the case of them attending universities.

> *"She left especially for me, to offer me financial aid during my studies and for my family..."* (Ana, female, 21 years old, with migrant mother in Spain)

Ducu (2014) argues, for instance, that in terms of main argument for migration, women participating in her research emphasized the material support of children's education as a mean to ensure a better future for the children comparing with their own.

School performance in all our cases was described in positive results after parents' emigration. Other studies (Stănculescu, Marin and Popp 2012) underline that the most at risk of dropping out school are those from rural areas and Roma. However from rural areas, a significant part of the young people we interviewed were attending the university at the time of the interview, this status is explaining somehow their positive school performance.

> *"On the contrary, her departure and the fact that she makes sacrifices to support me at the faculty, it motivates me to have better results".* (Ioana, female, 22 years old, with migrant mother in Italy)

For many of the interviewed children, the education is perceived as a mean to have better job perspectives, which offers them both financial independence (not continuing to rely on their parents' support) and possibility to choose, avoiding the same pattern as their parents i.e. working abroad as the best possible alternative to ensure the financial support for their families. On the other hand, Ducu

(2014) emphasized through her study a finding at odds with that of our research that migrant parent's children wished not to continue their studies and to launch in money-earning activities as soon as possible following their parents' model; in some cases, this life project is contrasting with that expected by their parents who are wishing their children to become educated in order to have an easier life than theirs, while children's wish is to earn quick material benefits.

> "(The parents' emigration)..motivated me to study hard, to come out as an engineer, to find a very good job and to not be forced to leave abroad, for work. I want to have a career in Romania... I hope that my brother will attend college, that we will handle things financially and we won't depend on out parents anymore." (Bogdan, male, 20 years old, with two migrant parents in Cyprus)

The perception of their parents' decision to be "forced" to migrate encourages the young people to find alternatives for a better life in their country of origin and education is a key to success. In the study of Schmalzbauer (2008) conducted with young people left behind in Honduras, the education was also seen as the key component to get a good job, facilitated through family migration, wishing to remain in their country of origin.

The lack of future educational perspectives due to the plan of migration that aims for the family reintegration doesn't motivate young people to achieve better results in school or to struggle to continue their studies after the high school graduation.

> "The fact that I don't want to go to college, doesn't motivate me to study harder. Finishing high school, that's what matters to me." (Eva, female, 19 years old, with migrant mother in Spain)

Some young people are also indirectly depicting the living and working conditions of their migrant parents, underlining the integration obstacles they are facing in the destination countries. But not all of our interviewees are aware of the stress their parents are under in the destination countries. Most of them are insisting on the family social and economic consequences of their parents' migration but not on their parents' status while living and working abroad.

> "She is away from us, we are away from her, the people from there are mean, her coworkers are also mean and she is suffering, but we have to move on one way or another. "(Ana, female, 21 years old, with migrant mother in Spain)

This perception of their parents' lives abroad is in accordance of Schmalzbauer's study (2008), young people imagining that their parents are paid well abroad, performing relatively good jobs in which they are hardly working but enjoying high standards of living.

The evolution of family relationship

Geographic distances require a well-defined strategy in order to maintain healthy relationship within transnational family.

Communication within transnational families is a key element in keeping its unity but this also requires a good strategy to respond to all family functions and needs considering its limits. The use of Internet and new technologies ease the process of communication, helping the members of these families to maintain ties across borders "as long as family members work hard at "staying in touch" by making use of all the technologies available to them, they can maintain mutually supportive relationships across time and space" (Baldassar, 2007, p. 406).

The *distance* was thoroughly mentioned as the primary disadvantage when talking about the parents' emigration process, but in almost all of the cases the access to Internet gives the opportunity to easily stay in touch. Instant messages via Facebook, voice calls via Skype together with phone calls were the most common means of parent–child communication for young people of our research. Just in one case the migrant father working in construction area weren't able to access Internet due to his accommodation in the same place as job; instead they were using phone calls.

Ioana is recognizing the role of the internet, including visual contact, in facilitating her communication with her mother, declaring:

> We are communicating daily by phone or Internet. I can say that in this respect the Internet is very important in the relationship between parent and child because you can see each other and not just hear. On the phone we are talking in the evening, and on the internet about anytime. (Ioana, female, 22 years old, with migrant mother in Italy)

The communication *frequency* is daily or at least weekly in most of the cases, at certain hours depending on the working hours of their parents or the school schedule of the youth. In one case where the migrant father employed labor migration as a way of life since his daughters were very young, the communication was weekly during the weekend by phone. Summing up, none of the young people complained about the impossibility of getting easily in touch with their parents abroad no matter what means of communication they are using. Although Romanian rural areas are not well-connected to the internet, access to the phones thanks to economic remittances from their parents, together with access to the internet using affordable mobile companies offers make communication across borders easier. Moreover, most of the young people from our research are currently studying in capital or other cities from urban area with better infrastructure including access to internet.

Technological communication with migrant parents has an important impact on children, helping them to easily overcoming the emotional hardships of separation and to maintain close family relationships. At the same time, regularly technologi-cal communication is seen by migrant women as a mode of care (Ducu, 2014), a way of maintaining the family "intimacy virtually" (Wilding, 2006). Schmalz-bauer (2008, p. 334) uses the expression of 'family-by-phone' as a way of keeping transnational families connected. Gabriel is expressing very well the role of com-munication with his parents abroad:

> *"Because I had the opportunity to communicate daily with my parents, it was easier to accept their departure."* (Gabriel, male, 19 years old, with two migrant parents in Italy)

The main themes approached when talking to their parents are education, other family members at home, parents' job, friends, leisure time, life at home and abroad, children's needs. Thus families are struggle from distance to maintain strong family ties, providing their children with the best care they afford in the given conditions.

> *"About school, about what we did, them with their work, about our friends, where we've been, what is happening in the country, how they are doing there, how we are doing."* (Bogdan, male, 20 years old, with two migrant parents in Cyprus)

The face to face interactions are very rare, usually one or two times per year with the occasion of the most important holidays (Easter, Christmas) or annual leave. A few young people revealed that they visited periodically their parents abroad although there are frequent flights between Romania and main destination coun-tries of Romanian emigrants. Some of them couldn't point out with certainty when they will meet their parents again.

> *"At most twice a year. On holidays, on Christmas and in the summer, sometimes. They haven't been in the country for 6 months. Now I don't even know, I hope we'll see each other soon."* (Bogdan, male, 20 years old, with two migrant parents in Cyprus)

In terms of family ties most of the young people described positively being aware of the negative consequences that the migration process could imply in some cases (e.g. jealousy, losing their trust).

> *My parents have a very good family situation, despite the fact that my mother left, there has been no fighting. There are some cases in which if one spouse leaves, the jealousy appears, the suspicion, it's nothing like that. My grandparents, from my mother's side as well as my father's side, are alive and I get along very well with them.* (Ana, female, 21 years old, with migrant mother in Spain)

Ana is looking forward, and is afraid of future financial shortages due to work-ing abroad without a legal contract. She is the only one being aware, among the interviewed youngsters, of the involvement of the current employment status of her mother at the age of retirement.

"... given the fact that she was gone, she has no seniority on the employment contract. I think that only my father will benefit of the pension when he retires." (Ana, female, 21 years old, with migrant mother in Spain)

Ina is describing positively her family relationship although this family functioned for many years as transnational. She coped to live without her father but the feelings of estrangement are present using words as "guest" when referring to him.

Now it doesn't affect us anymore, we got used to him coming more on vacations, as a guest." (Ina, female, 22 years old, with father migrant in France)

Going further Ina is also talking about the migration plans of his father (e.g. buying a house) when describing the family relationship. She seems to be satisfied with the family living conditions and her father's plans even though that means more time spent abroad. She is easily accepting commodities rather than affection that could be provided by her father being at home. On the other hand, Ina said that her father plans to live abroad until the retirement age and his frequent departure for work became a way of living for all the members of this family. Her father migration plan is becoming her family expectation especially when this comprises better life conditions.

"This was his dream...first to buy an apartment, and now after he bought it, his dream is to move in a house. Besides that, we are a united family, we talk, we understand each other, we don't fight...My parents get along very well, although my father has been gone for a long time." (Ina, female, 22 years old, with father migrant in France)

Individual and family life plans

The *goals and expectations of young people* in our research are rooted in their country of origin, being optimistic about their future at home and distancing themselves from the migration strategy employed by their parents. Most of their plans are related to education (graduation from high school and university) and seeking for well-paid jobs according to their level of education. They asserted that remittances gave them access to university studies and consequently to more opportunities to have better jobs prospective.

Despite the accepted sacrifice of their migrant parents for the sake of the family, only one interviewed is planning to join the family abroad. Most of the young people are planning to find a decent job in Romania in order to gain their financial independence (especially those attending university).

I want to find a part-time job so I won't neglect college and to get an extra income, in order to support myself, to have better conditions, to buy what I want, to go out with my friends when I want, not to depend on anyone ...not to be forced to leave abroad as well. (Bogdan, male, 20 years old, with two migrant parents in Cyprus)

I would like to go there faster, to be closer to my mother and my brothers. (Eva, female, 19 years old, with migrant mother in Spain)

Mirela is depicting her father's labor migration in terms of "forced migration" for the sake of the family's well-being. She is struggling to find a decent job which would not lead her to the same decision as her parents.

"I hope I won't find myself in my parents' situation. I hope to find a job, which will ensure me the necessary money for a decent living, not to be forced to leave abroad, like my father did in order to sustain me financially." (Mirela, female, 22 years old, with father migrant in Italy)

The financial situation of the family reconfigured the educational plans of Ana. In her case the mother is not functioning anymore as the financial provider, therefore can't ensure access to her daughter's continuation of studies. She is postponing her educational plan until she will financially afford it to run it. She is going to seek for a job in her country of origin and it seems that she is not worry about the result in order to save enough money to continue her studies.

"Until a couple of months ago I had other plans. I was supposed to finish college, to enroll in a master, but now, considering that the financial situation has dropped considerably, I think I will get a job for a while, at least a year, in order to gather some money to be able to do a master." (Ana, female, 21 years old, with migrant mother in Spain)

Ana is aware of her parents' sacrifice and is planning to repay them by finding a well-paid job. She is empathizing with her mother's past and is somehow considering her mother a martyr, making consistent efforts to help her daughter achieve the best education as she couldn't afford for herself due to the lack financial means.

To find a job in an area, pretty well paid in order to sustain myself, and then to be able to help them. Simply by sustaining myself, I could help them. Regarding my mother, I would like her to be at home, to work in a different environment, except as a tailor. Although she studied, she finished high school and started the post-secondary school, she didn't manage to finish it because her parents didn't have enough money to support her. That's why she does everything she can so that I have what she didn't. It means a lot for me the fact that I am her child and she wants the best for me. (Ana, female, 21 years old, with migrant mother in Spain)

While Gabriel is planning to attend post-secondary medical school in order to ensure enough money and his parents return, Ina is complying in the situation of spending less time with her father as the opposite situation will cause financial problems to the family.

I would like to enroll in the post-secondary medical school and to do all I can so that my parents will be able to come back in the country... I would like to change my future through what

I'm aiming for: to follow the post-secondary school, in order to find a decent job and to bring my parents back in the country, to be able to help them and to offer them a better life. I would like us to be together again... (Gabriel, male, 19 years old, with two migrant parents in Italy)

I would like to spend more free time (with dad), for him to be in the country, but considering the fact that this could affect the financial situation, we learn to live with it. (Ina, female, 22 years old, with father migrant in France)

Nothing was said about a certain timeline of the return of their parents at home. Some of the young people are bearing in their minds some life events as retirement age as a possible moment of their parents' return but none of them pointed out a certain date when they will certainly return. Their future plans in the country of origin are revealing their optimism using the advantages from their parents' migration. It appears that as long as family members are still keeping bonds although at distance, using especially new technology communication tools, they can maintain its unity across time and space.

Conclusions

Romania, the State with the highest number of migrants in EU Member States, registered a significantly number of children left behind by migrant parents. In terms of consequences, the family migration affects these children both positively (e.g. better living conditions) and negatively (e.g. drop-out school, delinquency, emotional stress) during the children's development. Through the lenses of the young adults we interviewed, their parents' migration decision has been perceived as a sacrifice to achieve the family's well-being. Consequently, the young people succeeded not to blame their parents for their emigration decision, bringing to the fore the advantages for their families, always comparing their situation before the migration took place.

Besides the increased level of the family revenues as a main advantage of the migration process, as a way to properly respond to the children's needs, better living conditions and possibility to ensure the family welfare comparing with their past situation in Romania, the disadvantages were also emphasized in terms of lacking direct support in key moments of their life cycle or sometimes assuming the adults' role within the family.

The absence of the mother was more often mentioned as bringing changes concerning support, offered both emotionally and instrumentally. The coping process after leaving abroad of one parent could involve in some cases emotional distress, such as depression, difficulty to adapt to a new educational environment, or tendency to drop out of school in order to accompany the migrant parent.

The communication process is eased by Internet and new communication technologies, none of young people complained about the impossibility of getting in touch with their parents abroad. Thus families are easily maintaining close bonds despite the physical distance between its members.

The realities presented by these young people reveal a family world where the fulfillment of the financial needs appear to be the most important goal. The resources generated from migration compensate the absence of direct parental support and most of the children are feeling neither abandoned nor neglected.

For many of the young people we interviewed, the individual life plan is to invest in education as a mean to achieve a good income in the country of origin through access to a well-paid job, income that can decrease their dependence on the parental financial aid or ensure their parents return.

References

Alexandrescu, Gabriela: *Impactul migrației părinților asupra copiilor rămași acasă*. Salvați Copiii/Save the Children Romania: București 2007.

Asis, Maruja M.B.: "Living with migration: experiences of children left-behind in the Philippines". *Asian Population Studies* 2 (1), 2006, pp. 45–67.

Asis, Maruja M.B.: "Imagining the Future of Migration and Families in Asia". *Asian and Pacific Migration Journal* 9(3), 2000, pp. 255–272.

Baldassar, Loretta: "Transnational families and the provision of moral and emotional support: The relationship between truth and distance". *Identities* 14(4), 2007, pp. 385–409.

Bryceson, Deborah / Vuorela, Ulla: *The Transnational Family: New European Frontiers and Global Networks*. Berg Publishers: Oxford/New York 2002.

DG Employment: *EU Employment and Social Situation Quarterly Review 2012*, retrieved 7.25.2016, from http://ec.europa.eu/social/BlobServlet?docId=7830 &langId=en. 2012.

Ducu, Viorela: "Transnational Mothers from Romania". *Romanian Journal of Population Studies* 1, 2014, pp. 117–142.

Finch, Janet: *Displaying Families. Sociology* 41 (1), 2007, pp. 65–81.

Hondagneu-Sotelo, Pierrette / Avila, Ernestine: "'I'm here, but I'm there': The meaning of Latina transnational motherhood". *Gender and Society* 11 (5), 1997, pp. 548–571.

Irimescu, Gabriela / Lupu, Adrian Lucia: *Singur acasă! Studiu efectuat în zona Iași asupra copiilor separați de unul sau ambii părinți prin plecarea acestora la muncă în străinătate*. Asociația Alternative Sociale: Iași 2006.

Kraler, Albert: *Gender, Generations and the Family in International Migration*. Amsterdam University Press: Amsterdam. et al. 2011.

Marchetti-Mercer, Maria: "Those Easily Forgotten: the Impact of Emigration on Those Left Behind". *Family Process* 51 (3), 2012, pp. 376–390.

Mazzucato, Valentina / Schans, Djamila: "Transnational Families and the Well-Being of Children: Conceptual and Methodological Challenges". *Journal of Marriage and Family* 73, 2011, pp. 704–712.

Parreñas, Rhacel: *"Children of global migration: Transnational families and gendered woes"*. Stanford University Press: Stanford 2005.

Punch, Samantha: "Research with children: The same or different with adults?". *Childhood* 9 (3), 2002, pp. 321–341.

Rentea, Georgiana-Cristina: *"Governmental Measures supporting Return and Reintegration of Romanian Migrants"*. Revista de Asistență Socială 3, 2015a, pp. 99–107.

Rentea, Georgiana-Cristina: "Mobility within the European Union and the access to social benefits: challenges of social policies". *Revista de Asistență Socială* 2, 2015b, pp. 127–137.

Schmalzbauer, Leah: *"Family divided: the class formation of Honduran Transnational Families"*. *Global Networks* 8(3), 2008, pp. 329–346.

Stănculescu, Manuela Sofia / Marin, Monica / Popp, Alina: *Being a child in Romania. A Multidimensional Diagnosis*. Vanemonde: Buzău 2012.

Stănculescu, Manuela Sofia / Marin, Monica: *Helping the invisible children. Evaluation report 2011*. UNICEF: București 2012.

Tomșa, Radu / Jenaro, Cristina: "Children left behind in Romania: anxiety and predictor variables". *Psychol Rep.* 2015, pp. 485–512.

Toth, Alexandru / Munteanu, Daniela / Bleahu, Ana: *Analiză la nivel național asupra fenomenului copiilor rămași acasă prin plecarea părinților la muncă în străinătate*. Alpha MDN: Buzău 2008.

Toth, Georgiana: *Efectele migrației: copiii rămași acasă*. Fundația Soros România: București. et al. 2007.

Wilding, Richard: "Virtual" intimacies? Families communicating across transnational context". *Global Networks*. 6 (2), 2006, pp. 125–142.

Whitehead, Ann / Hashim, Iman: *Children and Migration-Background Paper for DFID Migration Team*. Department for International Development: London 2005. Retrieved 7.25.2016, http://www.childtrafficking.com/Docs/dfid_05_child_mig_bac_0408.pdf

*** Information about the project "Te iubeste mama!"/" Mama loves you!", Retrieved 7.25.2016, <http://www.anbpr.org.ro/index.php/programe-proiecte/parteneriate

*** Authority for Child Protection Rights and Adoption (NACPRA), Retrieved 7.15.2016, http://www.copii.ro/statistici/

*** Law no. 272/2004 on the protection and promotion of the rights of the child

*** National Institute of Statistics, Romania, retrieved 7.5.2016, from TEMPO-Online https://statistici.insse.ro/

*** National Census 2011, Retrieved 7.20.2016, http://www.recensamantromania.ro/rezultate-2/

Bojan Perovic

Intercountry Adoption: a Human Rights Perspective

Abstract *Intercountry adoption has grown significantly over the last few decades but it polarized scholars and decision-makers. There is no consensus on how the best interests of the child are to be decided. This paper deconstructs the path which led to lack of trust in this institution and points out convergent trends in comparative law and practice.*

Introduction

Throughout its history adoption experienced various transformations but with no doubt has always been a difficult and sensitive subject. Intercountry adoption has always been the subject of various legal, sociological and psychological debates because this topic has not been able to reach a consensus primarily in academic circles as this institute has always been marginal theme filled with numerous controversies. In most modern legal systems in recent decades reforms of regulations on adoption were carried on, with the main goal, on the one hand, to achieve a greater integration of the adopted child in the adoptive family, and on the other hand, to achieve a cessation of all links between child and his natural family.

Intercountry adoption should not be viewed in isolation and out of context from the phenomena of the modern world such as depopulation, urbanization, huge variabilities in terms of development of the state, the crisis of marriage and so on. We are witnessing frequent criticism concerning the difficulties and inertia when it comes to adoption, and therefore when this matter is transferred to the field of international law and human rights, it is gaining even greater complexity. Intercountry adoption is an institute which includes transfer of children to the geographically distant places from their countries of origin, and "removal" to the social and cultural environment that is completely different from that in the country of origin (Bartholet, 2006, p. 107).

Development of the intercountry adoption

Intercountry adoption, as understood today, could be analyzed firstly after the Second World War, when the European orphans mostly from Germany and Greece were adopted by the American families. The result of the first legislative provisions in this area is contained in the so-called Displaced Persons Act (1948), when this type of adoption was provided. International adoptions were not common until the end of World War II. Then the individuals and families from rich countries have started what is now called humanitarian response in order to help children who have become victims of war. Although the Second World War left a huge number of orphans, true awareness of intercountry adoption became a global phenomenon slightly later, with the second wave (Katz, 1995, p. 286).

The second wave appeared after the Korean War in the 1950s. In the late 1960s, adoptive parents have turned to new decolonized and impoverished countries, mostly in Africa. After that, any emergency situation, such as earthquakes, armed conflicts, floods or other natural disasters, was accompanied by the appearance of a large number of orphans. During the 1970s, however, an intercountry adoption began to receive elements of classical "trade" where problems were easily solved by "intermediaries" and thus international adoption received criminal elements and caused scandals.

A well-known example is Romania, where after the fall of Ceausescu in 1989, the world was faced with photos and recordings showing disastrous conditions of the institutions in which children are housed. Only in 1990 the number of children internationally adopted from Romania was 3000 and during 1991 solely in the United States, 1300 Romanian children were adopted. Meanwhile, the world learned of the corruption of the Romanian authorities that was responsible for the adoption as well as illegal activities of intermediaries who exploited both biological and future parents (Vučković-Šahović, 2011, p. 137).

However, as intercountry adoption had not been widespread, many countries did not have the necessary legal framework that would protect the best interests of children. For example, in the UK, before making Adoption of Children Act of 1949, the courts did not have the authority to approve the adoption of a child who was not a British citizen resident.

Open questions and closure towards intercountry adoption

As the number of intercountry adoptions grew during the 1960s and 1970s, multilateral initiatives for the regulation of this institution appeared. The increased concern of the international community concerning the trafficking of children has led to the creation of a multilateral legal instrument governing intercountry adoption, the Hague Convention on Protection of Children and Cooperation in Respect of Intercountry Adoption, which entered into force on May 1, 1995. This Convention was adopted under the influence of previously adopted regional and multilateral legal instruments which include the European Convention on the Adoption of Children of 1967, the Inter-American Convention on conflict of laws relating to minors, the United Nations Declaration on Social and Legal Principles relating to the protection and well-being of children of 1986 and finally the Convention on the rights of the child adopted in 1989 under the auspices of the United Nations.

However, the evolution of modern adoption laws did not move only in favor of intercountry adoption. Many countries of origin limited the scope of the possibilities of this type of adoption. Adoption of children from Korea, after the war ended in 1954, is a unique phenomenon. A huge number of children who have been adopted in the United States were actually children of US troops stationed in Korea, who were perceived to face discrimination and difficulties to assimilate into Korean society (King, 2008, p. 420). The Republic of Korea was considered the largest "exporter of children" and at one point received a huge negative publicity that escalated during the Olympic Games in Seoul in 1988. Therefore, the Republic of Korea adopted a plan for the gradual reduction of this type of adoption. Since these steps did not show significant progress, the Republic of Korea went one step further when in 2006 the Government has sponsored a number of different projects which all aimed at the promotion of "domestic" adoptions. Potential Korean adopters were given the opportunity to be fully free of costs that accompany the procedure of adoption, then much easier conditions for adoption that are meant to older couples and individuals and even the implementation of the "adoption absence" which is equivalent to maternity leave (Kim, 2010).

Sporadic scandals that have occurred in this area brought to the fact that some countries have proposed a ban on adoptions of its children by nationals of certain countries. Thus, in China six civil servants were punished after three children were taken from their families, who were not able to pay a fine for violating regulations on family planning. The children were taken to orphanages, which were then sent abroad. In India, the 1999 scandal broke in which the leaders of an orphanage and social workers were involved in the "purchase" of babies from tribal group Lambada, whose members believed that the third, sixth and ninth female child brought a bad luck, so these little girls were therefore sold at very low prices. The action started by punishing the two women who were social workers and intermediaries in the purchase of children. After buying children (for 15 to 45 US dollars) they would sell them to orphanages (for 220–440 US dollars). These children were then, in the process of intercountry adoption, sold for two to three thousand dollars (Smolin, 2005). For these reasons, there is a tendency of the states to even fully prohibit intercountry adoption. Thus, United Arab Emirates expressly prohibit intercountry adoptions, so does Romania in which an exception is allowed only if the adoptive parents are close relatives (Cović, 2012, p. 316).

Two recent laws deserve additional attention. The above mentioned Romania in the early 90s of the last century was the first country in the world from which children were adopted by foreign nationals. British politician Baroness Nicholson, who was a Special European Parliament Rapporteur for Romania's accession to the European Union, is considered one of the greatest advocates against inter-country adoption, saying that such adoption "is taken by child traffickers and that the adoptive parents unconsciously accomplice in this crime." Opposing the idea of intercountry adoption, along with the supporters of her idea that this institute serves child prostitution, pedophilia, and slavery, Baroness was able to attract a lot of attention mainly in Romania but also in the European and world community (Carlson, 2011). After several unsuccessful attempts, in 2004 Romania passed a law which completely prohibits intercountry adoption (Selman, 2002). There is wide agreement that Romania has taken this step under pressure from the European Union. Paradoxically, each EU member state including Romania, has signed and ratified the Hague Convention, which in Article 4 enthusiastically approved the practice of intercountry adoption banned by Romania (Yemm, 2010, p. 566).

The latest case has caused great attention in international relations at the global level as it refers to two major world powers, Russia and the United States. This case includes a Russian boy adopted by an American citizen. An adopted boy died in a car of his adoptive father from heat stroke after nine hours being in a car because his adoptive father had forgotten to drive him to the kindergarten. This case triggered turbulence in Russia and led to the adoption of the so-called Dima Yakovlev Law named after the deceased boy. This law contains a list of people banned from entering Russia and the ban on the work of non-governmental organizations that receive money from US citizens or organizations. Additionally, the law prohibits the adoption of Russian children by American citizens. The Law entered into force on 1st January 2013. The law was signed by Russian President Vladimir Putin who received the support of the Russian Orthodox Church, but suffered a critique of the world's largest human rights organizations such as Amnesty International and Human Rights Watch, who claim that such a ban will not bring any good to either side and that actually damages only children who become hostages of politics. Much of the scientific community that deals with this subject stood on the view that in this case the intention was not to protect the interests of children but actually represents Putin's answer to US President Barack Obama's so-called Magnitsky Act (a US law that imposes visa and banking sanctions against the Russian officials who are considered to be accomplices in the death of Sergei Magnitsky, a Russian lawyer who was investigating tax frauds by Russian tax officials, and who died under suspicious circumstances in a Russian prison). By drawing attention to the sensitive subject as the adoption, the scientific community, which condemned this move by Russia, believes that this law is aimed at diverting attention from the corruption affairs. At the moment, Italy is the only country which is allowed to adopt Russian children. Russian Ombudsman for children's rights Astakhov explained that only Italy managed to meet two key criteria that Russia requires and that is a bilateral agreement with Russia and the ban on same-sex marriage. Bilateral agreements have been signed with the United States, France and Italy but the first two were suspended, the first for the elaborated reasons and the other because France recognized the right to same-sex marriages (Sean, 2013).

On the other hand, conservative Turkey in which the institution of adoption is regulated by the Turkish Civil Code, several years ago allowed the adoption of Turkish children to foreigners. This law was met with great approval of experts, social workers and psychologists in this country who believe that the new law only does good for children who are awaiting adoption because Turkey has retained a provision that adoptive parents should primarily be found among Turkish citizens and if this is not possible then the adoption may be granted to foreign nationals who meet the conditions laid down in Turkish law (Balkan, 2016).

Pro et contra arguments

Interconutry adoption is a complex situation and there are a fair number of those who simply describe this concept as child's separation from his true identity. Critics of intercountry adoption see it as exploiting the poor and vulnerable, considering that intercountry adoption in itself generates a commodification of children and the incentives for trafficking and serves the interests and wishes of rich Westerners to form families. United States is undoubtedly the most influential nation in the system of intercountry adoption, taking into account only the statistics that 50% of children of foreign nationality are adopted by Americans. However, scandals, corruption, abuse, human rights violations and countless examples of bad practices have shown that this country for the last two decades in fact gave a negative example in support for this institute (Smolin, 2013). Not a small number of human rights activists believe that this practice comes as a violation of individual human rights of the child and a violation of the rights of the community in which the child was born. The first argument is that a violation of children's rights occurs because there is a right to be brought up in a community with which a child shares the same cultural, ethnic, linguistic and religious traditions. Another argument implies that there is a collective right of the community to transmit all of these values to a child born in the community and that intercountry adoption makes this transmission impossible (Ward, 2008, p. 746). Also, critics argue that this institute is one imperialistic form of the receiving countries which take the best resources from the country of origin, and that such a practice can only have negative effects on the country of origin because it reflects a negative image that these countries are essentially incapable to provide conditions for the proper development of children without parental care.

Opponents believe that intercountry adoption is counterproductive and that usually leads to drastic measures taken by the country of origin because they feel the pressure of the international community to reform their practices in this regard, which usually leads to a reduction in the number of orphans which can be adopted by foreign nationals (Marx, 2007).

The energetic advocates of intercountry adoption claim that human rights are at the core of the debate about intercountry adoption. Proponents argue that this institute should serve for the realization of one of the basic human rights of the most vulnerable: children's rights to a family that will provide love and care and thus the chance to live a healthy and fulfilling life. What proponents see as a problem is the silence of human rights activists on these issues and the roots of this silence is that they see strong support against this institute by the organizations which are so powerful, such as UNICEF and the UN Committee on the Rights of the Child, although for example UNICEF insists that it holds a neutral position (Bartholet, 2007).

In support of intercountry adoption, main proponents always underscore the undeniable facts- number of children in institutions (public or private) in the long term, how and why they are there, how many children live on the streets or how many of them are working hazardous and dangerous jobs (Dillon, 2003, p. 182). One of the main ideas that the advocates challenge is that children are perceived incorrectly as a property of the country of origin and the biological parents who have custody of them (Bartholet, 2007 b). Proponents also state that the alleged concern about taking significant resources is a fairytale that illustrates the inability of the respective countries to make a radical change and that actually the last thing they need is a huge numbers of children they cannot take care of (Barthole, 1996).

Proponents stress that the central problem should be viewed through the prism of misery and poverty that characterizes the lives of a huge number of children who die every day because of malnutrition and disease and they love to make their point in one sentence: adoption literally and figuratively saves lives (Hubing, 2001, p. 664). There are five arguments commonly used in favor of intercountry adoption. The first is that intercountry adoption makes the child's right not to be institutionalized possible. Secondly, adults who want to be parents should have the opportunity to even consider adopting a child of another nationality. The third argument underlines that through intercountry adoptions orphans may be provided with parents. Fourthly, it leads to mitigation of the world's problems by reducing the number of children without parental care. The fifth argument is based on the promotion of tolerance and diversity at the international level so as to create a family with different national and cultural characteristics (Martin, 2007, p. 181).

From Eastern European perspective, Serbia may serve as an excellent example. Intercountry adoption is often negatively perceived, especially from the right wing and nationalist initiatives and political parties, critics are based on the above mentioned arguments but often the skipped fact is that the problem is internal. Alternative ways of taking care of children without parental care in Serbia are not properly developed and the results of the researches show that the placement in orphanages and other social protection institutions should be the last step taken and that adoption is the best way of taking care of children without parental care. Research from the Institute for Psychology and Save the Children UK in 2007 showed a striking fact that only 2.6% of respondents in the six institutions for children without parental care have not experienced some form of violence. The situation is even more complicated by the fact that only 10% of children from the Infirmary of the Mother and Child Zvecanska in Belgrade are suitable for adoption because only this number of children have regulated domestic legal status. Adoption of Serbian children by foreign nationals is not a common occurrence, but taking into account the reluctance of Serbian citizens to adopt Roma children or children with disabilities, it is possible to see that intercountry adoption, if properly used, could be an effective way to help children (Vučković-Šahović 2011, p. 145).

So, not only that the problem is not intercountry adoption but rather the protection of children without parental care itself, the statistics obtained from the competent Ministry show that hysteria about intercountry adoption is not justified. Serbian Adoption Registry shows that the number of children adopted by citizens of foreign nationality never exceeded number of 18 in the last 10 years. (2006-9, 2007-12, 2008-12, 2009-15, 2010-14, 2011-12, 2012-8, 2013-13, 2014-18).[1]

International legal framework

Although compared to other methods of child protection, intercountry adoption is a phenomenon of much smaller scale, this institute managed to attract a lot of attention in international legal circles. With numerous conventions and agreements that exist at the regional level, particularly in Europe and Latin America,

---

1 Informations obtained by the author (requested from the Ministry of Work and Social Issues). Sweden and the US are the first on the list of the Recieving States.

a number of international declarations and conventions established the principles and standards in this area (UNICEF). The most important documents were
originally adopted under the auspices of the Hague Conference on Private International Law and under the auspices of the Council of Europe.

In the first place the European Convention on the Adoption of Children (1967)
should be mentioned, which was revised in 2008 in order to comply with the new
changes that accompanied this area because the very preamble of the Convention
stresses that many provisions of the old convention are outdated and in contrary
to the European Court of Human Rights (Council of Europe). The European Convention on Human Rights does not contain explicit provisions on intercountry
adoption but the European Court of Human Rights has created a rich jurispru-
dence on the basis of Article 8 of ECHR- right to respect for private and family
life. The Court essentially dealt with issues relating to Article 8 of the European
Convention and especially with the right of the adopted child to know its origins
and with the legitimate interests of the anonymity, the rights of the father of an
illegitimate child who was not sufficiently involved or completely turned off in
terms of decisions on adoption, discrimination on the basis of sexual orientation
of potential adoptive parents and so on (Van Bueren, 2007, p. 126).

An important step forward was the adoption of the Convention on the Rights of
the Child (1989), where article 21 is dedicated to intercountry adoption by marking
it as an alternative mean of child's care. Before 1989 there were only regional agreements that dealt with intercountry adoption. In the late 1980s the United Nations
has begun to make efforts to establish an international base for the regulation of
intercountry adoption. The Convention on the Rights of the Child was adopted
under the auspices of the United Nations in 1989 and it is the first instrument of
such importance that explicitly recognizes the intercountry adoption (Eschelbah
Hansen and Pollack, 2006, pp. 109–110). During the negotiations on the draft
Convention, adoption was actually a most controversial area. This controversy was
based on complaints of Islamic delegations that were based on unknowingness of
adoption in the Islamic religion. The fact that the Convention on the Rights of the
Child provides intercountry adoption as an alternative mean of child care should
not be surprising, considering that this is the single most ratified convention in the
world and that it had to make compromises in order to be widely accepted in the
international community. It is also interesting that the creators of the Convention,
instructed by the negative experiences of the past in this area, require the Member
States to take all appropriate measures to eliminate any improper financial gain of
participants in the intercountry adoption process. Although the Convention regu-
lates intercountry adoption, the advocates of this institute consider that provisions

are automatically marked as negative, as a "last resort" in particular in the context of the Article 20, paragraph 3, which provides that in considering solutions, due regard shall be paid to the desirability of continuity in a child's upraising and to the child's ethnic, religious, cultural and linguistic background (Wechsler, 2010, p. 22). Article 21 of the Convention refers to States Parties which recognize the system of adoption that the standard of the best interests of the child should be of crucial importance. The same article provides that intercountry adoption may be considered as an alternative mean of child's care only if the child cannot be placed in a foster or an adoptive family or cannot in any suitable manner be cared for in the child's country of origin. The Convention itself is a practical platform for the creation of the Hague Convention. The importance of the provisions of the Convention on the Rights of the Child has been confirmed in the preamble of the Hague Convention. Therefore, it is often said that the Convention on the Rights of the Child sets the goals, while the Hague Convention provides ways to achieve these goals (Maravel, 1996). Besides, the two basic principles of the Convention on the Rights of the Child, the standard of the best interests of the child and the obligation of the state to take action against child trafficking are also incorporated directly to the Hague Convention (Kimball, 2004, p. 568).

Undoubtedly the most important document in this field is the Hague Convention on Protection of Children and Co-operation in Respect of Intercountry Adoption of 1993 (entered into force in 1995) under the auspices of the Hague Conference on Private International Law. The adoption of the Convention is a response to a worldwide phenomenon involving migration of children to distant geographical distance and their relocation from one society and culture in a completely different environment. Previous Hague Convention that dealt with adoption had its focus on traditional issues of conflict of laws such as jurisdiction, choice of law and recognition of the decision (Hague Conference on Private International Law). However it was clear that intercountry adoption is a serious problem that must be addressed through a structured co-operation between State of origin and the receiving State (Estin Laquer, 2010, p. 55). The Hague Convention relies on principles established in the Convention on the Rights of the Child but it is an instrument of private international law, which has a different legal status and scope in relation to the Convention on the Rights of the Child. The Convention is considered to be a compromise that tried to reconcile the two clearly polarized sides on this issue but failed to calm passions since the ratification of the Convention by the United States in 2008 (Hayes, 2011, p. 288). The Hague Convention already in its preamble recalls that each country in the first place must take appropriate measures to enable the child to remain accommodated in their country of origin but also that international adoption has its advantages and that it is therefore crucial that the international adoptions are to be based on the best interests of the child and with respect for their fundamental human rights, as well as to prevent the abduction, sale or trafficking of children. This Convention introduces security for all participants in the process of adoption and establishes a system of cooperation between authorities in the country of origin and the receiving country while possible abuses in the process of intercountry adoption are reduced to a minimum by prescribing clear procedures. The application is activated when the adopted child and the adoptive parents are not domiciled in the same country, if their respective countries are State Parties to the Convention. It is used to protect children without parental care under the age of 18 and full adoption is the form that the Convention recognizes. The greatest significance of the Convention is reflected in the automatic recognition of the adoption and its effects in all Contracting States.

Although the Hague Convention establishes protection and a certain level of uniformity, it does have its drawbacks. Experts put their remarks above all on the need to define or clarify the terminology of terms because the language of the Convention in certain places is too general and imprecise. As the Convention relies on the principles established in Article 21 of the Convention on the Rights of the Child and as its primary goal is the standard of the best interests of the child, the subject of some controversy could be a question of what is in the specific situation the best interests of the child when it comes to the case of a little child in a Ukrainian orphanage (Freeman, 2007, p. 22). Furthermore, the lack of penalties or sanctions for violations of the provisions of the Convention is another criticism and experts also suggest that the Hague Convention, despite good protection mechanisms it has, should contain a provision on DNA testing that could further secure preventing child abduction (Briscoe, 2009).

Good practice examples

In Ireland, the adopted children are predominantly of foreign nationality and Ireland is considered an example of good practice in assessing the general ability of adoptive parents. Therefore, at this point we will give a brief summary of this process. Together with the ratification of the Hague Convention, Ireland brought Adoption Act of 2010, which gives details on the conditions for eligibility of potential adopters. This Act established the main body, which is composed of doctors, social workers, lawyers, psychologists and scientists in the field of children's rights to make the final decision whether the parents are eligible to be adoptive parents regardless of whether a child is Irish or of foreign nationality. Prospective Irish adoptive parents must first apply to the local social work center, which employs its representative to provide necessary information and advices as well as to collect the necessary information for the preparation of the report that the local center for social work, in the form of recommendations (explaining the reasons for or against eligibility of potential adoptive parents) sends to the above mentioned main body. Prospective adoptive parents may appeal the recommendation and ask to be heard by the main body before a final decision on their eligibility is made. This assessment process is considered good because it not only reduces the risk of arbitrariness but also, during evaluation of eligibility, takes into account the capacity of potential adoptive parents to affect in the best possible way the physical, emotional, social, health, educational, cultural and spiritual development of the child (Lengsfelder, 2011).

At this point, a summary of the process of adoption in the case of Sweden and India will show that a good practice and monitoring is very much doable. In Sweden, the Government established the Committee for Social Welfare, which initially confirms that potential adoptive parents are Swedish citizens. After that, a social worker who is a Swedish civil servant performs the so called *home study* - including interviews, visits to homes of potential adopters, and the most important, screening the suitability to adopt a child of foreign nationality. Later on, the family is registered for adoption of a child from India through a licensed adoption agency in Sweden. This agency must be recognized and on the list approved by the Government of India. The duty of this agency is to firstly forward all documentation to Indian centers for social work, but most importantly it is responsible for monitoring the transfer of the child and it is obliged after the arrival of the child in Sweden to make reports, which is the requirement from the Indian's courts. In addition, under Swedish law there is an established body (NIA) whose main task is to monitor and supervise such a closed adoption. In case that any problem occurs, it has the authority to immediately react. In this way the adoption in Sweden is monitored in profound and proper manner (Narain, 2012).

Conclusion

The way in which countries form its own rules concerning this subject will heavily define the future role of intercountry adoption as an alternative solution for children without parental care. This is primarily because in this area there is a division in the world between the countries with low birth rates and therefore a small number of children who are eligible for adoption and those countries with a high birth rate and the large number of children without parental care. In the rich, especially Western countries, the number of the children left by their biological parents is drastically reduced in recent decades due to the increased tendency of single parents keeping their children as well as by the use of contraceptives and widespread abortion. In poorer countries, wars, political upheavals and economic conditions have led to a situation where a small number of potential adoptive parents exist compared to a huge number of children eligible for adoption (Bartholet, 1993).

By approaching the subject when taking into account the arguments of the opponents of this institute, which first report on the cultural concerns, interests of countries of origin, and possible unethical practices and exploitation that may accompany this process, we must be very careful. It is important to weigh the arguments properly and avoid by all means political connotations that are often reflected in the practice of political leaders and officials to oppose this type of adoption. Kidnapping, child trafficking, as well as financial malversations must be taken into account but as signals that will lead to better practices of the countries in the field of child protection, not as a complete closure of the state in the field of intercountry adoption.

Intercountry adoption should be partly solving the problem, along with other solutions that focus on providing an opportunity for children to grow up in a family. The international community has a positive obligation not be passive and wait for the adoptive parents, regardless of whether it is a domestic or international adoption, but to take steps to raise awareness in every state of the status and position of these children. Certainly we are of the view that the adoption is the best way for orphans in providing conditions for proper development. In such a constellation, institute of adoption should have the unconditional support, especially in the context of the country that would promote adoption as a way to protect children without parental care.

In international law, the adoption of some of the most important conventions gives the signal which legitimizes this institute while these initiatives still do not produce clear enough principles that would enable proper application of this institute. The Hague Convention is encouraging but not enough. Abuses and scandals that have occurred in this area should not lead to the closure of intercountry adoption but to establishing a much better system. Of course tackling with the possible abuses is very challenging, but instead of dealing with the consequences, every effort should be made in order to lead to the removal of the causes that lead to bad practice of this institute.

Bibliography

Balkan, İlayda: "*Adoption of Children in Turkey*", Retrieved 22.7.2016, from: http://www.admdlaw.com/adoption-of-children-in-turkey/

Bartholet, Elizabeth: "International adoption: Current status and future prospects". *The future of children Journal*, 1993.

Bartholet, Ellizabeth: "What's Wrong with Adoption Law". *International Journal of Children's Rights,* 1996.

Bartholet, Elizabeth: "International Adoption". in: Asekland Lori (ed.), *Children and Youth in Adoption, Orphanages, and Foster Care.* Greenwood Publishing Group Inc. 2006.

Bartholet, Elizabeth: "International adoption: Thoughts on the human rights issues". *Buffalo Human Rights Law Review,* 2007.

Bartholet, Elizabeth: "International Adoption: The Child's Story". *Georgia State University Law Review,* 2007.

Briscoe, Erica: "Hague Convention on Protection of Children and Co-Operation in Respect of Intercountry Adoption: Are Its Benefits Overshadowed by Its Shortcomings". *Journal of the American Academy of Matrimonial Lawyers,* 2009.

Carlson, Richard: "Seeking the Better Interests of Children with a New International Law of Adoption". *New York Law School Law Review,* 2011.

Cović, Ana: "Međudržavna usvojenja između akta nasilja i čina ljubavi". *Strani pravni život,* 2012.

Council of Europe: *European Convention on the Adoption of Children (Revised),* Retrieved 5.7.2016, http://conventions.coe.int/Treaty/en/Treaties/Html/202. htm

Dillon, Sara: "Making Legal Regimes for Inter-country Adoption Reflect Human Rights Principles: Transforming the United Nations Convention on the Rights of the Child with the Hague Convention on Inter-country Adoption". *Boston University International Law Journal,* 2003.

Eschelbah Hansen, Mary/ Pollack, Daniel: "The Regulation of Intercountry Adoption". *Brandeis Law Journal,* 2006.

Estin Laquer, Ann: "Families Across Borders: The Hague Children's Conventions and the Case for International Family Law in the United States". *Florida Law Review,* 2010.

Freeman, Michael: *Article 3: the best interests of the child.* Martinus Nijhoff Publishers. 2007.

Hague Conference on Private International Law: Convention of 15 November 1965 on Jurisdiction, Applicable Law and Recognition of Decrees Relating to Adoptions, Retrieved 29.6.2016, http://www.hcch.net/index_en.php?act=conventions. text&cid=75

Hayes, Peter: "The legality and ethics of independent intercountry adoption under the Hague Convention". *International Journal of Law, Policy and the Family,* 2011.

184   B. Perovic

Hubing, Bridget: "International child adoptions: Who should decide what is in the best interests of the family". *Notre Dame Journal of Law, Ethics & Public Policy*, 2001.

Lengsfelder, Savannah: "Who is a Suitable Adoptive Parent". *Harvard Law & Policy Review*, 2011.

Katz Lisa: „Modest Proposal - The Convention on Protection of Children and Cooperation in Respect of Intercountry Adoption". *Emory International Law Review*, 1995.

Kimball Caeli, Elizabeth: "Barriers to the successful implementation of the Hague Convention on Protection of Children and Co-operation in Respect of Inter-country Adoption". *Denver Journal of International Law and Policy*, 2004.

Kim, Eleana: *Adopted territory: Transnational Korean adoptees and the politics of belonging*. Duke University Press. 2010.

King Shani: "Challenging Monohumanism: An Argument for Changing the Way We Think About Intercountry Adoption". *Michigan Journal of International Law*, 2008.

Maravel, Alexandra: "UN Convention on the Rights of the Child and the Hague Conference on Private International Law: The Dynamics of Children's Rights Through Legal Strata". *Transnational Law & Contemporary Problems*, 1996.

Martin, Jena: "Good, the Bad & the Ugly-A New Way of Looking at the Intercountry Adoption Debate". *UC Davis Journal of International Law & Policy*, 2007.

Marx, Molly: "Whose Best Interests Does It Really Serve-A Critical Examination of Romania's Recent Self-Serving International Adoption Policies". *Emory International Law Review*, 2007.

Narain, Sukanya: "Inter-Country Adoption: A Legal Perspective", Social Science Research Network, 2012. Retrieved 18.5.2016, http://ssrn.com/abstract=2072515

Roberts, Sean: "The Russian Adoption Ban Fits the Putin Agenda". *FIIA Comment*, 2013.

Selman, Peter: "Intercountry adoption in the new millennium; the "quiet migration" revisited", *Population research and policy review*, 2002.

Smolin, David: "Two Faces of Intercountry Adoption: The significance of the Indian Adoption Scandal". *Seton Hall Law Review*, 2005.

Smolin, David: "The Corrupting Influence of the United States on a Vulnerable Intercountry Adoption System: A Guide for Stakeholders, Hague and Non-Hague Nations, NGOs, and Concerned Parties". *Journal of Law & Family Studies & Utah Law Review*, 2013.

UNICEF Innocenti Research Center: *Innocenti Digest Intercountry Adoption*, Retrieved 23.7.2016, http://www.unicef-irc.org/publications/pdf/digest4e.pdf

Van Bueren, Geraldine: *Child rights in Europe*, Council of Europe: Strasbourg. 2007.

Vučković-Šahović, Nevena: „Međunarodno usvojenje i Srbija". *Pravni zapisi,* 2011, p. 137.

Ward, Elisabeth: "Utilizing Intercountry Adoption to Combat Human Rights Abuses of Children". *Michigan State Univeristy College of Law Journal of International Law,* 2008.

Wechsler, Rachel: "Every Child a Chance: The Need for Reform and Infrastructure in Intercountry Adoption Policy". *Pace International Law Review,* 2010.

Yemm, Lisa: "International Adoption and the Best Interests of the Child: Reality and Reactionism in Romania and Guatemala". *Washington University Global Studies Law Review,* 2010.

Index

A

abortion 49, 50, 182
abuse, 32, 52, 55, 57, 159, 175
acceptance 131, 136, 137, 145, 160
adoption 58, 171–179, 181, 182
Albania 77, 78, 80, 87, 88
Albanian 77, 78, 82, 85, 89
anxiety 84, 86, 87, 161
Argentina 134
assimilation 100, 118, 138, 145

B

Belgium 66, 71, 72, 133, 134, 136–140,
    142
bi-national couples 131, 133, 135,
    138, 141–143, 145
breadwinners 44, 56, 64
Bulgaria 133, 137

C

caregiving 66, 67, 79
children left behind 28, 32, 36, 37, 59,
    151–156, 158, 159, 161, 167
Chinese 113–115, 117, 118–128
citizenship 131, 141, 142
couples 97–101, 104, 108, 109,
    113–115, 119–122, 124, 127, 131,
    133–139, 141, 142, 145, 173
criminal networks 59
culture 54, 65, 74, 97, 100, 118, 135, 179
Czech Republic 51, 98, 133, 134, 143

D

depression 157, 159, 161, 167
discrimination 44, 67, 80, 82, 110,
    123, 173, 178
displaying 131, 141, 143

diversity 142, 151, 177
division of labor 85, 86, 88
domestic worker 64, 80, 83–85, 87, 88

E

economic independence 85, 89
education 31, 34, 52, 65, 102–104,
    107, 115, 117, 128, 131, 137, 142,
    143, 145, 156–158, 161, 162,
    164–166, 168
egalitarian capital 97, 99–102, 104,
    107, 109
emancipation 44, 63–65, 67, 70, 73,
    85, 99, 141
empowerment 63–67, 70, 80, 85, 86
equality 65, 67, 98, 99, 103, 108, 141

F

family members 28, 30, 50, 52, 55, 82,
    127, 133, 135, 138, 151, 157, 160,
    163, 164, 167
family roles 28
Fatherhood 159
freedom of movement 27, 78

G

gender equality 64, 74, 85, 97, 99,
    100, 109
gender roles 36, 64, 77, 78, 88, 101,
    104, 109, 123
Grandparents 158
Greece 51, 77–80, 83, 85–89, 98, 171
Greek 78, 85, 89

H

human rights 47, 171, 174, 175,
    176, 180

Hungarian 43, 113-121, 123-128,
   136, 145
Hungary 43, 44, 98, 114-121, 123-128

I
identity 27, 31, 34, 68, 89, 113, 117,
   135, 175
income 34, 64, 84, 165, 168
India 173, 181
inhuman treatment 47
intercountry adoption 171-179, 181,
   182
international law 171, 179, 182
isolation 46, 48, 52, 54, 171
Italy 29, 30, 34, 43-47, 50-56, 59, 79,
   87, 98, 153, 155-159, 161, 163, 164,
   166, 167, 175

K
Korea 173

L
labor market 65, 77-79, 85, 86, 89, 153
Latvia 143
Love 71

M
manipulation 53
migrant men 27-29, 31, 33, 34, 36,
   37, 44, 67
migrant women 31, 44, 45, 48, 59, 63,
   65, 66, 70, 74, 77, 79, 82, 84, 85, 86,
   118, 152, 155, 164
minorities 43
motherhood 55, 58, 59, 64, 83, 84,
   86-89, 109, 151, 152

N
nationality 131, 134, 145, 175-177,
   180, 181
neighbors 29, 158
Norway 97, 99, 100, 102-105, 107-109

O
Orphans 56

P
parenthood 78, 83, 97
pedophilia 174
personal autonomy 89
physical care 88
Poland 97-100, 103, 109
Police 53
Polish 97, 99-102, 105, 109
prostitution 50, 51, 53-55, 174

R
residence permit 45, 78
return migrants 80, 88, 155
Romania 43-45, 49-51, 53-59, 64,
   68, 69, 70-74, 132-136, 139, 140,
   142, 144, 145, 153-156, 158, 159,
   161, 162, 164, 165, 167, 172-174
Russia 32, 174

S
segregation 45, 65, 77, 78, 80
Serbia 68, 69, 133, 134, 136, 143, 177
servitude 45
sexual exploitation 46-51, 53-57
Slovakia 98, 133, 134, 136, 142
smuggling 45
social adjustment 159
social capital 99, 117
social protection 155, 177
Spain 44, 51, 98, 133, 137, 153, 156,
   157, 159-162, 164-166
stereotypes 34, 101, 120
stigmatization 56, 82
Sweden 118, 177, 181

T
trafficking 27, 43, 45, 49, 51, 52,
   54-57, 59, 172, 175, 179, 180, 182
transnational communication 140

transnational families 27, 28, 30, 31,
    34, 36, 66, 140, 151, 152, 155, 156,
    163, 164
transnational fatherhood 28
transnational motherhood 78, 88

U
UK 44, 51, 67, 68, 70, 98, 133, 134,
    137, 139–146, 172, 177

Ukrainian 27–32, 34, 36, 37, 180
US 43, 63, 118, 137, 143, 173, 174,
    177

V
vulnerability 32, 46, 48, 50, 52, 54, 56,
    57, 59

www.ingramcontent.com/pod-product-compliance
Lightning Source LLC
Chambersburg PA
CBHW050512280326
41932CB00014B/2295